ceac

No

North Korea in a Nutshell

A Contemporary Overview

Kongdan Oh and Ralph Hassig

ROWMAN & LITTLEFIELD
Lanham • Boulder • New York • London

Published by Rowman & Littlefield
An imprint of The Rowman & Littlefield Publishing Group, Inc.
4501 Forbes Boulevard, Suite 200, Lanham, Maryland 20706
https://rowman.com

6 Tinworth Street, London SE11 5AL, United Kingdom

British Library Cataloguing in Publication Information Available

Library of Congress Cataloging-in-Publication Data
Names: Oh, Kong Dan, author. | Hassig, Ralph C., author.
Title: North Korea in a nutshell : a contemporary overview / Kongdan Oh and Ralph Hassig.
Description: Lanham, Maryland : Rowman & Littlefield, [2021] | Includes bibliographical references and index.
Identifiers: LCCN 2020051583 (print) | LCCN 2020051584 (ebook) | ISBN9781538151389 (Hardcover : acid-free paper) | ISBN 9781538151396 (ePub)
Subjects: LCSH: Korea (North)—Politics and government—2011- | Korea (North)—Politics and government—1994-2011. | Kim, Chŏng-ŭn,1984—Influence. | Kim, Chŏng-il, 1942-2011—Influence. | Kim, Dae Jung, 1925-2009—Influence. | Korea (North)—Military policy. | Korea (North)—Economic conditions. | Korea (North)—Social life and customs.
Classification: LCC JQ1729.5.A58 O5 2021 (print) | LCC JQ1729.5.A58 (ebook) | DDC 951.9304—dc23
LC record available at https://lccn.loc.gov/2020051583
LC ebook record available at https://lccn.loc.gov/2020051584

♾ ™ The paper used in this publication meets the minimum requirements of American National Standard for Information Sciences Permanence of Paper for Printed Library Materials, ANSI/NISO Z39.48-1992.

Contents

Preface

The first author of this book, Kongdan Oh, has been studying North Korea for almost four decades. In 1981, while a graduate student at Berkeley, she was hired by one of her professors to read documents on North Korea. This was no stretch for her because she grew up in South Korea, and her parents had come down from North Korea when the communists took over in 1945. After graduate school, she joined a think tank, where she conducted research on East Asian security affairs, which prominently included North Korea, and she has been engaged in these think tank studies ever since. The second author, Ralph Hassig, is a social psychologist by training, and since he is married to the first author, he began to take an interest in her North Korea work. They both spent an academic year in Europe in the early 1990s, giving Dr. Oh a chance to observe the process of German unification as a possible model for eventual Korean unification. Upon returning to the States, Dr. Hassig became actively involved in North Korea research. And that is how the two of us came to be interested in this strange and exasperating country.

Initially, most of our work dealt in some way with North Korea as a security threat to the United States, especially focusing on North Korea's nuclear weapons program. After the failure of the 1994 Agreed Framework, which the United States fruitlessly hoped would end North Korea's pursuit of nuclear weapons, we started to lose interest in the nuclear issue, which seemed destined to be unresolved for many years to come. Instead, we increasingly turned our attention to the lives of ordinary North Korean people, which were becoming known thanks to the flood of defectors that began arriving in South Korea in the late 1990s. We conducted interviews with some of these defectors and have remained in touch with them, gaining insight about their former lives in North Korea and the lives of their family members who remained behind.

Over ten years ago we came up with the title for this volume, and we liked it so much that we decided we had to write a book to go along with it. After several chapters, we set it aside to write another book, *The Hidden People of North Korea: Everyday Life in the Hermit Kingdom*. Only recently did we return to *Nutshell* and begin writing in earnest.

In some respects, this book encapsulates all the subjects we have studied in the course of our long careers, with a few topics added to make it complete. As such, it includes the traditional military-related concerns that have weighed on foreign governments for many years, along with issues relating to how ordinary North Koreans have adapted to life in a relatively harsh physical and social environment. Fifty short topical sections have been collected into nine chapters, which may be read in any order, followed by a conclusion that summarizes the book's themes.

To be sure, these sections are but a brief introduction to North Korea; any one of them could easily be expanded to book length, as indeed some have by other authors. When we began our research into North Korea, only a few books on the subject were on the market. Today there are hundreds, written by foreign writers such as ourselves, by South Koreans, and by North Korean defectors. Some books have also been written by North Koreans still living in their country, including dozens of volumes about their leaders, but since these authors are working for their government, their works should be treated as propaganda tracts rather than factual accounts.

A few words about translating Korean into English. The Korean alphabet can be transliterated into Roman letters in several ways. Until 2000, the most common method was to use the McCune-Reischauer system, which is familiar to several generations of Korean scholars and is also used by North Koreans to translate their works into English. We have simplified the system by dispensing with apostrophes (used to indicate aspirated consonants) and diacritical marks above vowels. The resulting simplification will be admirably suited to the needs of most readers. In 2000, South Korea's Ministry of Culture and Tourism introduced Revised Romanization, which has met with some resistance but is now widely adopted in South Korea. However, because it looks somewhat strange to many foreigners, ourselves included, we have chosen to stay closer to the older system.

In Korean, the family name usually comes first, followed by one or two given names. Some Koreans hyphenate their two given names, others write them separately, and some combine the two (for example, the book's first author). The official North Korean approach is to write them separately. Thus, in North Korea the names of the three men who have led the country would be written as Kim Il Sung, Kim Jong Il, and Kim Jong Un. However, to make it clear to foreign readers which are the family names and which are the given names, we have decided to use an equally popular approach and hyphenate the given names: Kim Il-sung, Kim Jong-il, and Kim Jong-un. Throughout the book, Korean names are presented in this manner except where Koreans outside of North Korea specifically use another form.

As for pronunciation, especially of the leaders' names, "Kim" (the most popular name in either half of Korea) is pronounced just as it would be in English. "Il" is pronounced like *eel*, and "sung" is pronounced much like the English word. "Jong" rhymes with *sung*, and "Un" rhymes with *soon*. In general, the vowels in the romanized spelling of Korean names are pronounced more as they would be in Romance languages than in English. For example, the letter *a* in Pyongyang, the capital city, is pronounced like the *a* in *almond*, not the *a* in *salmon*.

Chapter One

Geography and History

A Troubled Land

PHYSICAL GEOGRAPHY: A LAND OF GREAT POTENTIAL

Before North Korea, and for that matter before Korea, the peninsula where it is now located had existed in its present geological form for some twenty million years, making it possible, in the last few thousand years, for the people of Korea to remain separate from the inhabitants of China, at least most of the time.[1] The northern half is colder and more mountainous; the southern half warmer and somewhat flatter. In 1945, for the purpose of accepting the surrender of occupying Japanese troops, the United States and the Soviet Union agreed to divide the peninsula at the 38th parallel, about the same latitude as Kansas City; Washington, DC; Madrid; and Beijing. And so it was that Kim Il-sung's North Korea found itself in possession of a mostly hilly and mountainous land of approximately 46,000 square miles—about the size of the state of Pennsylvania or the country of Greece. Although North Korea ended up with slightly more land than South Korea, at 38,000 square miles, it is considerably smaller than neighboring Japan, at 146,000 square miles, and is hardly a smudge on the map compared to its northern neighbors, China and Russia. The two Koreas combined are the size of one of the larger American states such as Utah or Idaho, or one of the medium-size European states such as Austria or the Czech Republic.

The country's northern border is demarcated by two rivers: in the west the Yalu (Amnok) and in the east the smaller Tumen (Tuman), which freezes over four months in winter, making it easy to cross—if it were not for the armed border guards along the river. On the northern side of its border with China live two million Chinese Koreans. The country's southern border is marked by a military no-man's land that few have ever been able to cross. To the west is the West Sea or Yellow Sea, so named because of its muddy color, and to the east is the deep blue East Sea or Sea of Japan. Neither coast is blessed with many ports or beaches. Across the middle of the country, the distance from the western port of Nampo to the eastern port of Wonsan is 120 miles (156 miles by highway). The most popular north–south route would go from the southern city of Kaesong to the border city of Sinuiju, 187 miles to the north (220 miles by highway). The mountain ranges in Korea tend to run north and south, making travel east to west particularly difficult. With ethnic Koreans to the north and to the south, North Korea would seem to be ideally situated for international commerce, serving as an Asian bridge to Japan. However, almost as soon as the Kim regime took control of the government, the country firmly closed its borders.

Topographically, North Korea has more of the peninsula's hills and mountains, while South Korea has more plains suitable for farming. Neither country has many lakes because the glaciers of the last ice age did not reach the peninsula. With its hills, mountains, and rushing rivers, the North is ideally suited for mining, hydroelectric generation, and forestry. All of the land is owned by the government or a government-controlled organization such as an agricultural collective, so the stewardship and use of these resources is largely in the hands of government officials, who take their orders from the ruling Kim family.

After a promising start in the 1950s and 1960s, the government proved to be inept at economic management, and the bulk of the North's considerable mineral resources and its hydroelectric potential remain untouched. Coal is abundant, and most of it is exported to China; hydroelectric dams always seem to be in need of repair, and the country's forests have been decimated by illegal logging to satisfy people's need for heating fuel (given the lack of coal and hydropower). Many hillsides have been carelessly terraced to compensate for the lack of level agricultural fields.

North Korea has a rather unfortunate climate. Ocean currents sweeping up from the south bring relatively short, humid summers with occasional heavy rainfall, although major typhoons rarely make it this far north. In the winter the ocean currents are reversed. The temperature in the western plains, where Pyongyang (Flat Land) lies is somewhat milder than in the mountainous eastern half of the country. High and low summertime temperatures in Pyongyang are 84 and 68 degrees Fahrenheit (29 and 20 degrees Celsius), similar to Philadelphia and other northeastern American cities. In the winter Pyongyang's climate is much like that of Minneapolis–St. Paul, with an average high of 27 and low of 9 Fahrenheit (−13 Celsius). It is as if, come wintertime, the inhabitants of the city of brotherly love, instead of vacationing in Florida, found themselves in Minnesota. Strong winds whip onto the peninsula from Siberia. In Pyongyang snowfall is somewhat scarce, with accumulations of only a few inches at a time, whereas the northeastern mountains receive considerably more snow. Since the Korean War, few westerners have experienced winters in North Korea because most of the country's limited tourism takes place in the summer.

The three major climatic regions of North Korea are the western plains, where most of the larger cities are situated, the less inhabited eastern hills, and the sparsely populated northeastern mountains. Six of the country's ten largest cities are in the western region, with two lying on or near the coastline: the port of Nampo and the city of Sinuiju on the river border with China. The four largest cities in the east are wedged in between the mountains and the coast. Travel to these east coast cities is hampered by the intervening hills and mountains.

In the impoverished northeast, mountain peaks reach heights of seven thousand feet, with the "sacred" volcanic Mount Paektu (Baekdu) reaching nine thousand feet. In the east and southeast, the mountains are closer to three thousand feet. This same eastern mountain range extends into South Korea, where peaks are generally lower. The Korean Peninsula is bookended north and south by two volcanic peaks. South Korea's Mount Halla is on the southern island of Jeju. North Korea's Mount Paektu is on the Chinese border. Neither volcano has erupted in over a thousand years.

With its mountains, rivers, and beaches, North Korea could be an attractive tourist destination for South Koreans and Chinese, and this idea has occurred to the Kim regime, which is always eager to earn foreign currency. In the last decade the regime has opened three ski resorts, and it is building an ambitious beach resort near Wonsan on the east coast. North Korea's ongoing disputes with South Korea have blocked tourists from that country, and international sanctions have discouraged tourists from China and other nations. Ironically, North Korea operated a thriving mountain and beach resort from 1998 to 2008 in the southeast corner of the country in the Mount Kumgang area. The infrastructure was built by the South Koreans, and most

Chunji (Heaven Lake) at the top of volcanic Mount Paektu, 2012. *Wikimedia Commons, by Laika ac, CC-BY-SA-2.0.*

of the tourists were South Korean as well. The closure of the resort is another indication that the Kim regime is unable to profitably manage its natural resources.

CITIES: FEW AND FAR BETWEEN

With approximately twenty-five million people (half as many as South Korea) and a slightly larger land area, North Korea is less urbanized than its southern neighbor. In fact, with only about 62 percent of its people living in cities, North Korea ranks ninety-second among nations on an urbanization scale, comparable to China but much more rural than South Korea (at 81 percent), Japan (at 91 percent), and the United States (at 82 percent). Pyongyang, with a population of three million, is the only North Korean city with more than a million people. Two cities have between half a million and a million, and six cities have about three hundred thousand. South Korea has ten cities with more than a million residents, and the capital, Seoul, has almost ten million. North Korea is politically divided into nine provinces and

Major cities in North Korea.

three municipal districts, all tightly controlled by the central government in Pyongyang.

Although almost 40 percent of North Koreans live in small towns and villages, the appeal of large cities is as great in North Korea as in most other countries. Recognizing that rural life is more difficult than urban life, the Kim regime has made many, albeit halfhearted, attempts to improve rural life. The people themselves can do little about their place of residence because it is assigned by the government, so they usually end up living in the same place that their parents and grandparents lived. It is not in the interests of the regime to allow people to move to cities because North Korea lacks the infrastructure, such as transportation, electricity, water, and sewage systems, to support large cities. If people were permitted to move into the cities whenever they wished, North Korean cities would become as chaotic as large cities in other third-world countries, and Pyongyang would no longer have the appearance of a model city.

Another reason the Kim regime wants to limit the size of cities is that they provide a haven for people who want to lose themselves among the multitudes. Dictatorships put a premium on keeping people under surveillance. Party and government officials in small towns and villages can easily keep track of local residents. In cities, appointed volunteers in each apartment building or on separate floors of large apartment buildings are responsible for monitoring the lives of building residents and reporting any anomalies to local party and police officials.

Every North Korean needs a residence permit to live in government-owned housing, which is the only kind of housing available. Changing one's place of residence is legally difficult. Moving to another county is even more difficult, and moving to or even visiting Pyongyang is almost impossible, although some people are able to sneak into the city and live there undetected. Country folk can move to a city if they are assigned a job there or if they pay a sufficient bribe to police officials. As of 2018, the going rate to bribe authorities to obtain a Pyongyang residence permit was reported to be $1,500, an astronomical figure considering that the average official state wage for a North Korean is only a few dollars a month, and including income from the unofficial capitalist market, most people earn only a few hundred dollars a month.[2] Even for those fortunate enough to gain legal residence in Pyongyang, the future is not secure because the government periodically expels political undesirables from the city to keep the population numbers under control.

North Korean cities differ from cities in most other countries in several respects. During the Korean War, all of the North's cities were heavily damaged by American bombing. Pyongyang, for example, was 75 percent destroyed, and several of the country's industrial cities, such as Hamhung and Wonsan, sustained even greater damage. As a consequence, few North Korean cities have any historic old buildings. Moreover, in the haste to rebuild, most cities ended up with Soviet-style buildings of uninteresting functional designs. The majority of big-city residents live in apartment houses. Cities have little incentive to beautify themselves to induce tourism because Pyongyang is almost the only city foreigners are allowed to visit. For the most part,

North Korean cities fulfill a purely utilitarian function, and they do not even do that very well.

Most of the larger cities are situated in the western plain or along the eastern coast, leaving the mountainous swath through the center of the peninsula sparsely populated. The capital city of Pyongyang lies in the western plain at the junction of the Taedong (Daedong) and Potong (Botong) Rivers, surrounded by gentle hills. The city has a long history, having served as the capital of several Korean kingdoms. As the capital in modern times, it was the scene of fierce battles during the Korean War. The city is home to all of the country's important government centers and to numerous major monuments to the Kim family. Everyone wants to live in Pyongyang, and its residents get first call on the country's resources. Foreign visitors are usually impressed by the sleek high-rise apartment buildings that have gone up in the last two decades. When they see Pyongyangites walking along the streets wearing fashionable clothing, they marvel that communism has come a long way in North Korea. Few visitors are given the opportunity to see how the other twenty-two million North Koreans live.

The port for the city of Pyongyang is Nampo, near the mouth of the Taedong River about thirty miles to the southwest and connected to the capital by one of only two decent highways in the entire country. Unlike Pyongyang, Nampo has a short history. It was originally a small fishing village that became a port in the late 1800s and was built up by the Japanese during the colonial period. With the founding of North Korea, it became the country's second-largest port after the east coast port of Wonsan and now boasts a population of over 350,000. In addition to serving as a port and a base for important fisheries, it is also a major industrial center with steelworks and shipbuilding.

A little over one hundred miles to the southeast of Pyongyang, along the country's other modern highway, lies the old city of Kaesong. Like Pyongyang, Kaesong has a long history, including being the capital city during two Korean kingdoms. It is centrally located on the Korean Peninsula just a few miles north of the current border with South Korea. In fact, from liberation to the Korean War, Kaesong was the northernmost city in South Korea, but it was captured by North Korean troops during the war and ceded to North Korea in the truce negotiations. The city itself is not large, having slightly over three hundred thousand people. Many historical relics are located in the Kaesong area, making it a popular destination for domestic and foreign tourists, and virtually the only city other than Pyongyang that most foreign tour-

High-rise apartments in Pyongyang and pictorial monument of first two Kims, 2014. *Wikimedia Commons, by Bjørn Christian Tørrissen, CC BY-SA-3.0.*

ists see. Kaesong also has a history of being a commercial center, and because of its proximity to South Korea, it was chosen to host the only inter-Korean industrial compound, the Kaesong Industrial Complex, which operated from 2002 to 2016 and employed North Korean laborers in South Korean–built factories.

Sinuiju, 135 miles to the northwest of Pyongyang along the Chinese border, is North Korea's economic gateway to the outside world. The city itself is not large, with fewer than four hundred thousand inhabitants, but it lies just across the river from China's city of Dandong, with two and a half million people. The two cities are connected by a rail bridge and a new vehicle bridge over the Yalu River. The North Korean government has tried to make the city into a major commercial center, including designating an adjacent area as a special economic zone. The fortunes of Sinuiju rest largely on the health of North Korea's economic relations with China, which wax and wane.

Tongdaewon Street, Pyongyang, 2012. *Wikimedia Commons, by Laika ac, CC-BY-SA-2.0.*

To reach North Korea's eastern coast one must travel on either a relatively primitive highway or a very slow railway through the mountains. Wonsan, just over one hundred miles directly east of Pyongyang, is the country's busiest port. Its history as a port dates to the late 1880s, the same time that the western port of Nampo was developed. During the Japanese colonial period, Wonsan was the major port of trade between Korea and Japan. Wonsan was heavily bombed during the Korean War, and with North Korea–Japanese trade relations frozen in recent years, it sits quietly on the coast awaiting better days. Like the secondary cities to the west, it has less than four hundred thousand inhabitants. Although it is connected to Pyongyang by an expressway, road conditions make travel somewhat difficult. The government has designated the Wonsan area, with its beaches and mountains, as a future tourist mecca. Being on the coast, Wonsan is famous for its fisheries and is home to numerous industries, including the country's largest railway factory. Wonsan also hosts a major naval base.

Working one's way up the eastern coast on primitive highways, one finds several other important port cities sandwiched between the mountains and the sea. Next up from Wonsan is Hamhung, seventy-five miles to the north,

Street in Kaesong, 2014. *Wikimedia Commons, by Yoni Rubin, CC-BY-3.0.*

with a population of almost eight hundred thousand, making it the second-largest city in the country. Heavily bombed during the Korean War, it was rebuilt with East German aid. The Japanese had built chemical plants in the city, and it is still known for this industry, although like most industries in North Korea, the chemical industry is only a shell of its former self. Also like the other cities and towns along the east coast, Hamhung was largely ignored by the government during the famine of the 1990s, forcing its inhabitants to rely on local sources of food, which were scarce in this mountainous region.

The next port city on the coast, 125 miles farther north, is Tanchon, with a population of 350,000. The Tanchon area is famous for its mineral resources, and the city hosts important mineral-processing industries as well as chemical and textile plants. Another 140 miles up the coast is the port of Chongjin, developed during the colonial period by the Japanese, who built a large iron and steel complex in the city, the forerunner of North Korea's famous Kimchaek Iron and Steel Complex. With almost seven hundred thousand inhabitants, it is the country's third-largest city. Like its fellow cities on the northeast coast, it went through hard times during the famine, and today its major industries are barely operating. The only other notable locations on the east coast are the ever-struggling foreign trade zone encompassing the small cities of Najin and Sonbong ("Nason"), just south of the border with Russia, and far down the coast to the south at the South Korean border, the now deserted tourist reservation in the Kumgang mountain region.

Cities in North Korea are almost an afterthought. Other than Pyongyang, the center of politics and society and a showcase to the outside world, North Korean cities are a mystery, closed to foreigners. Except for the products turned out by their factories—products that are not exported—they are faceless clusters of people. An interesting question is whether North Korea could ever be a developed country without becoming more urbanized. The lack of large cities is easy to understand in the North Korean context. Poor transportation isolates individual cities, and part of the transportation problem arises from the difficult North Korean terrain. Infrastructure problems linked directly to the poor economy prevent modern cities from developing. It is even possible that military considerations have prompted the regime to avoid building bigger cities that would be easy targets for wartime bombing, recalling the devastation of the Korean War. In short, in the twenty-first century, North Korea remains to a large degree a semirural society.

KOREAN HISTORY: A SHRIMP AMONG WHALES

History was hard on the Korean people even before Kim Il-sung came to power in 1945. Living in a small territory sandwiched between China and Japan, the Korean people had to fend off encroachments and attacks for centuries, not to mention fighting among themselves. The peninsula's history, even more than its physical geography, has shaped the political views of the Kim regime and the North Korean people. The almost constant conflict on the Korean Peninsula among kingdoms and against foreign powers is similar to the conflicts that raged for thousands of years in other parts of the world, including Europe. It seems that when a country became strong, it decided to attack neighboring countries. Without constant battle, the warrior class had little to do.

Humans have been living on the Korean Peninsula for thousands of years, originally coming down from what is today northern China. Korean pottery can be dated to around 8000 BCE, although credible evidence of an organized Korean state goes back to only about 100 BCE. What is known as the Old Chosun state (*Gojoseon* in the new South Korean government spelling), with its capital in Pyongyang, certainly existed at that time and may even have been founded hundreds of years earlier. In any case, by 100 BCE the people living in Old Chosun on the Korean Peninsula were being ruled by the Chinese emperor. As the Chinese state came under attack from northern tribes, Koreans gained independence and formed three kingdoms—Silla, established in 57 BCE in the southeast; Koguryo (Goguryeo) in 37 BCE in the north; and Paekche (Baekje) in 18 BCE in the southwest.

Koguryo had to fight to keep its independence from the neighboring Chinese. Paekche loosely allied itself with Japan. Silla eventually allied itself with the Chinese across the waters to the west. The three kingdoms fought each other for several hundred years until Silla finally got the upper hand and in the tenth century consolidated the Korean state and named it Koryo (Goryeo), imitating the previous Koguryo kingdom but now having its capital in the commercial city of Kaesong, south of Pyongyang. Thereafter, Koryo had to battle the Chinese to keep its independence, which was finally won by the eleventh century, and this kingdom remained in control of most of the Korean Peninsula until the middle of the thirteenth century.

In the thirteenth century the Mongols invaded Korea, along with most of central Asia all the way to the Black Sea in Europe. When Mongol power waned in the middle of the fourteenth century, the Chinese again invaded Korea. Amid political rivalry in Korea, a strong general, Yi Song-gye, instead of repulsing the Chinese as he had been instructed to do, changed sides and successfully attacked his own government. In 1392 Yi established a new Korean dynasty, the Yi or Chosun (Joseon) dynasty, with its capital in Seoul, even farther south than Kaesong, and this dynasty lasted until the beginning of the twentieth century. During the dynasty's five-hundred-year history, the Koreans repulsed two invasions from the Japanese in the late sixteenth century, followed by Manchu invasions from the north a quarter of a century later. The Chosun kingdom remained intact by paying tribute to the Ming and later the Manchu emperors in China.

Eventually the Chosun dynasty became weak, leaving the Korean people vulnerable to intrusions from their next-door neighbors and from the expanding Western powers. It was during the nineteenth century that Korea's resistance to foreigners earned it the name "the hermit kingdom," but the resistance was useless and the dynasty finally collapsed in 1897. The Japanese first began meddling in Korean affairs in the 1890s and then sent troops into the country in 1905 before finally incorporating Korea into the Japanese Empire in 1910. Japan used Korea as a source of material and people as it built up its empire in Asia. The Japanese not only took political control of Korea but also tried to eradicate Korean culture in order to make Koreans loyal (though second-class) citizens of the empire. Small Korean revolts were mounted, and some Koreans, like Kim Il-sung (who would become the first ruler of North Korea), left the country to fight the Japanese in China. Although the Japanese upgraded Korean infrastructure and industry, forcing modernity on the colony, the Koreans have never forgiven them for their harsh colonial rule. In 1965 South Korea normalized diplomatic relations with Japan and received indemnities. North Korea has never normalized relations with Japan, and the two states and peoples remain hostile toward each other three-quarters of a century after the end of Japanese occupation.

Korea's long history (compared to the history of many contemporary Western nations) has given the Korean people a sense of pride, while their periodic experiences as subject people—especially in the twentieth century—have left them with an enduring feeling of victimization. The Kim regime has used both of these sentiments to strengthen its position with the people. The regime accuses South Korea of being a political puppet and economic colony of the United States. The Kim regime has boasted of its *juche* economy of self-sufficiency, although throughout the Cold War era North Korea received large amounts of aid from the Soviet Union and its Eastern European neighbors, and after the decline of that aid, China stepped in, providing North Korea with vital economic support. These facts are usually ignored by the North Korean media.

Korea's history has also influenced North Korea's political language. The regime considers itself the direct descendant of Old Chosun—the dynasty that fought against the Chinese and did not align itself with other nations. North Koreans refer to themselves as *Choson saram* (i.e., "Choson people," using the North Korean spelling), and call their country *Choson Minjujuui Inmin Konghwaguk* (the Democratic People's Republic of Korea). The South Koreans call their country *Taehan Minguk*, not related to the name of the Chinese Han people, and they refer to themselves as *Hanguk saram*.

The Kim regime made a particularly bold attempt to advertise itself as the one, true, independent Korea when it announced in 1993 that the tomb of Tangun (Dangun), the mythical founder of Korea, had been discovered in North Korea (foreign researchers have not been given access to the alleged tomb). All Koreans know that Tangun was supposed to be the first Korean king, born of a bear mother who had mated with one of the gods. His reign is supposed to have begun in 2333 BCE, making Korea almost five thousand years old. The Kim regime's official account of this alleged tomb discovery is intended to burnish Kim Il-sung's image as well as North Korea's:

> The history of the Korean nation has been exalted by two most distinguished great men of the present era. . . . [T]he great leader President Kim Il-sung personally formed a research group with scientists and wisely led their work. Under his deep concern, the scholars deepened their research and at last excavated the Tomb of Tangun . . . in September last year [1993]. . . . [I]t was confirmed unanimously that they [the bones] dated back 5,011 years. [3]

Another article continues: "The sites and relics prove with added clarity that Tangun founded ancient Korea, the first ancient state of our country, 5,000 years ago and Pyongyang was the center of ancient culture and one of the cradles of human civilization." [4]

Just as the adult personality can be strongly influenced by childhood events, so North Korea's national "personality" seems to have roots in the distant past, at least as the past is interpreted today. Two lessons seem to have been learned and vigorously applied by the Kim regime. First, a strong defense is necessary to deter invasions from foreign powers. Second, a country that is internally divided will succumb to foreign aggressors. The "military-first" policies of the three Kim regimes and their obsessive concern with political unity thus seem to be direct consequences of the country's difficult history.

THE NORTH KOREAN STATE: COMMUNISM AND KIM COME TO KOREA

It is not unusual for the birth of a nation to be credited to a founding father. In North Korea's case that father is Kim Il-sung, whose cult of personality eventually elevated him to godlike status. Through the 1990s, the North Korean media routinely referred to their country as "Kim Il-sung's country," as if it was his personal possession. North Korea is not a "people's republic" by any stretch of the imagination. Nor is it a communist dictatorship. It is best viewed as a kingdom ruled by three generations of the Kim family.

Three questions present themselves in regard to the creation of a separate North Korea. First, how was Korea liberated from thirty-five years of Japanese occupation? Second, how did Korea become separated into two countries after five hundred years of being a unified nation? And third, how did one man so thoroughly take control of the northern half of the peninsula? The Kim regime has one set of answers to these questions, whereas the rest of the world has another.

North Korea's creation myth goes like this—according to the version recounted in the official English-language biography of Kim Il-sung published in 1973, the version that generations of North Korean schoolchildren have been taught.

> In the beginning of 1943, the Soviet Army demolished the massive forces of Germany in the hard-fought battle of Stalingrad. The Soviet Union took the initiative in the war and annihilated the German Army on its territory. . . . The U.S. and British imperialists were panic-stricken. . . . The same condition prevailed with regard to the war in the Pacific. . . . The situation at the time pointed to the fact that only the Soviet Army which had defeated fascist Germany could finally destroy Japanese imperialism in the East.[5]

> In view of these conditions, the General [Kim Il-sung] mapped out in minute detail a strategic plan for the final decisive battle of the Korean People's Revolutionary Army against Japanese imperialism. . . . On August 8, the Soviet Union finally declared war on Japan. . . . General Kim Il-sung . . . immediately ordered the mobilization of all units under the Korean People's Revolutionary Army. . . . Many sacrifices had to be paid during this final decisive battle for the liberation of the fatherland. . . . The Japanese imperialist aggressor army which was boasting of fighting "to the last soldier" was completely annihilated in a week, and on August 15, 1945, finally surrendered unconditionally.[6]

> General Kim Il-sung returned home in triumph, leading the anti-Japanese fighters. The Korean people, welcoming their Leader they had longed to see, gave themselves up to a tumult of joy and excitement. The whole land of 3,000 ri [about 1,000 kilometers or 620 miles], hills and vales, fields and rivers, from Mt. Paektu [along the northern border with China] to Mt. Halla on Jeju Island [south of the South Korean mainland], united their voices in cheering the triumphal return of General Kim Il-sung, the sun of the nation.[7]

This North Korean version of events has little in common with the historical record, except the dates. By 1945, as American and allied troops closed in on the Japanese mainland, it was clear that Japan was close to defeat. The only question was how the defeat would occur—whether by surrender or virtual annihilation. The unconditional surrender terms were set out in the Potsdam Declaration of July 26, 1945, signed by the major powers, but the Japanese resisted accepting those terms. On August 6 the United States dropped an atomic bomb on Hiroshima. On August 8 the Soviet Union declared war on Japan. On August 9 an atomic bomb was dropped on Nagasaki. On August 12 Soviet troops moved into Korea from the north. Debate continued to rage in Japan over whether to accept unconditional surrender. On August 14, over one thousand American bombers staged another air raid on Tokyo. At noon on August 15 the Japanese emperor announced Japan's surrender, and Japanese troops immediately made preparations to leave Korea. On September 8, American general John Hodge arrived in Korea to accept the surrender of Japanese troops. In the subsequent weeks the Americans and Russians secured Korea. Kim Il-sung was not in any way involved in the surrender of the Japanese.

In the early 1990s Russia, seized by a period of glasnost, opened its historical archives that told the Russian version of North Korea's founding. In this telling a young Korean guerrilla fighter (whose name was originally Kim Song-ju rather than Kim Il-sung) was living in a Soviet army camp near Khabarovsk after being chased out of China by the Japanese. One month after the Japanese surrendered to Russian troops, the Russians transported Captain Kim Il-sung of the Soviet army to his native land after an absence of twenty-six years. The Russians considered Kim a trustworthy figure to head up a new Korean communist government since he was beholden to them and had no ties to the local communists.

Kim had received little education, and his Korean was not as good as his Chinese, so the Russians wrote a speech for him that he presented to a small crowd on his arrival in Pyongyang. This is the speech depicted in a colorful mural that dominates Pyongyang's Triumph Return Square. By no means was Kim welcomed by the entire Korean nation. In fact, it has been reported that among the small crowd that gathered to listen to his homecoming speech, there were many who doubted that this young man was actually the legendary guerrilla fighter known as Kim Il-sung.

As to the second question, regarding the division of Korea, the facts of the case are almost shameful. The dividing line between the two Koreas was drawn arbitrarily by the United States, with Russia's subsequent agreement. According to the memory of former secretary of state Dean Rusk, when he was a colonel in the army, he and a Colonel Bonesteel on General MacArthur's staff were asked to find a way to divide the two Koreas for the purpose of accepting the Japanese surrender in the near future (as it turned out, five days later). They wanted to keep Seoul in the American sector, so they looked for a line somewhere above Seoul. Not finding any geographic lines such as rivers, they picked the 38th parallel, which the US command and, surprisingly perhaps, the Russians agreed to. The Koreans were not consulted.

The division was to be only temporary. The major victorious powers—the United States, the Soviet Union, the Republic of China, and Great Britain— agreed that Korea would be put under a trusteeship for up to five years while the Koreans decided how they wanted to govern themselves. The communists in the North and the noncommunists in the South were unable to agree on the formation of a unified government, so they organized two separate governments, with the Republic of Korea or South Korea announcing its formation on August 15, 1948, and the Democratic People's Republic of Korea or North Korea proclaiming its statehood on September 9, 1948. For what it was worth, on December 12 the United Nations (UN) General Assembly recognized South Korea as the sole legal government on the peninsula.

With the patronage and protection of the Soviet authorities, and by some adroit political maneuvering, Kim Il-sung succeeded in establishing himself at the head of the new North Korean government. In the beginning, the country was modeled on Stalin's Soviet Union with some characteristics of Mao Zedong's People's Republic of China. To the people of North Korea, who had never known anything but autocratic rulers, this form of government did not seem unusual. At least they were now ruled by a Korean rather than by a Japanese or Chinese emperor. In control of the Korean People's Army, Kim was gradually able to eliminate his political rivals, just as Stalin and other communist dictators weeded out their domestic competitors one by one.

For several years Kim could count on the Soviet troops to back up his authority, and even though the troops did not actively intervene in politics, Kim's political opponents knew they were there. Kim was also a skillful and ruthless politician. In a country where the leader gains power not by elections but by violence, a successful politician must be willing and able to exercise force. Foreigners who met Kim found him to be a jovial and reasonable fellow, but behind the mask he was a cold-blooded killer. His son and grandson would turn out to be the same kind of leader. But arguably the most important explanation of Kim's political success was that he followed a time-honored method of taking power. Like Stalin, he took over gradually. Stalin was famous for eventually purging virtually the entire top level of the political elite in the Soviet Union, including the top generals and even the head of the secret police. He did this by starting his purge at the bottom and slowly working his way up over the years.

Kim Il-sung did very much the same thing. A gradual purge such as this has two virtues. First, it does not alarm the public, although the North Korean public, never having experienced democracy, were not in a position to cause Kim any trouble. More important, a gradual purge does not alarm the political elite. Those closer to Kim would even help with the purges, believing that they would never be purged themselves. Kim began his purges (which usually meant sending people for a life sentence to a prison camp) against politicians who had some connection with South Korea. Many South Korean communists had fled to the North at the end of the war, and they were the first to be sent to the prison camps. Then Kim started eliminating politicians who had connections with the Russians and Chinese. He had to be careful here because both the Russian and Chinese governments were providing North Korea with substantial aid, and Chinese troops remained in the North as laborers until 1958. When the Russians objected to the purges, Kim simply bided his time and then resumed the purges a few years later. Finally, he even purged some of his former comrades who he suspected had untoward political ambitions. By the end of the 1950s the only people who remained in the government were those who were completely subservient to Kim.

A word might be said about political events in South Korea during the period that Kim was consolidating his power in the North. The major powers were well aware when they put Korea under a trusteeship that Koreans seemed to have a predilection for political factionalism, if not outright chaos. To take but one example, during the Japanese occupation, members of the Korean government in absentia had been fighting among themselves. The politician best known to Americans was Syngman Rhee, who had lived in the United States, with only the occasional trip abroad, from 1910 to 1945— even longer than Kim Il-sung had lived in China and Russia. As soon as Korea was liberated, the US military brought Rhee to South Korea and supported his bid to become president. After serving two terms, President Rhee had the constitution changed so that he could serve longer. Finally, in 1960, after his election to a fourth term provoked an uprising, the CIA flew him back to Hawaii, where he died five years later. After a year of an interim government in South Korea, General Park Chung-hee led a coup against the civilian government and eventually gained the presidency, later declaring martial law. He was assassinated by the head of the Korean CIA in 1979. In short, neither Korea was prepared to embrace democracy in 1945.

THE KOREAN WAR: A DISASTROUS ATTEMPT TO
UNIFY THE COUNTRY

The Korean War may be a distant memory to most Americans, and even to most South Koreans, but in North Korea the memory of what they call the Fatherland Liberation War is constantly refreshed. The period from June 25 (when the war began in 1950) to July 27 (when a truce was signed three years later), known as the Month of Anti-US Struggle, is filled with rhetoric and events intended to persuade people that the Americans are barbaric and the North Koreans are heroic. During this period, all North Koreans are required to attend special lectures, children are taken to the Sinchon Museum or to the Victorious Fatherland Liberation War Museum, newspapers carry special articles, and occasionally a military parade is held. In years when the Kim regime is trying to woo the United States, the anti-US rhetoric is muted. In other years it is as shrill as if the war had just ended. It is worth noting that today, when outside information has become more available to the North Korean people, many of them are no longer convinced by what their government tells them.

The facts of the Korean War are well known and are covered in many excellent books. After obtaining the grudging consent of Stalin, who was more interested in Eastern Europe, and Mao, who was more interested in claiming Taiwan, Kim Il-sung launched a surprise attack across the 38th parallel on June 25, 1950. Kim apparently convinced his two allies that if he invaded South Korea, its citizens would rise up and help his army overthrow the American-backed government. This turned out to be a tragically false assumption.

The North Koreans, with between 150,000 and 200,000 troops supported by tanks, routed the South Korean army, which had 100,000 troops and no tanks. Within weeks the North Koreans had captured all but the southeast corner of South Korea. Unfortunately for them, the South Korean people did not join them, and the North Korean army's supply lines were badly stretched. The United States, leading a twenty-one-member UN coalition that had been authorized at a time when the Soviet Union was boycotting UN sessions, began moving into Korea a month later and hit North Korean forces on their western flank, subsequently chasing them all the way up to the Chinese border.

Faced with 180,000 UN soldiers, "General" Kim Il-sung was at a loss. Then China sent in what would eventually number three million "volunteer

Korean War Victory Day parade, 2013, Pyongyang. *Wikimedia Commons, by Stefan Krasowski, CC-BY-2.0.*

soldiers," and with the support of Soviet airpower, they pushed the UN forces back to the 38th parallel. After a year of fighting up and down the peninsula, the bitter contest became a stalemate on the ground, although during this time American warplanes enjoyed complete air superiority and systematically bombed North Korea's infrastructure. On July 27, 1953, the UN forces, China, and North Korea signed a truce that left the border close to what it had been before the war. South Korea refused to sign because its leader, President Syngman Rhee, wanted the UN to continue the fight. This truce still exists today, with all parties technically remaining at war.

Approximately 90 percent of the UN troops were Americans, of whom 33,686 were killed in battle and 103,284 were wounded. South Korea is estimated to have lost almost 138,000 soldiers. It is difficult to determine accurately what the Chinese and North Korean losses were, but estimates are in the range of 400,000 Chinese soldiers and 215,000 North Korean soldiers killed. Since both armies overran enemy territory, and the United States bombed North Korea for much of the war, civilians on both sides sustained high casualties. Total North Korean deaths are estimated at 600,000, compared to 1 million South Koreans. When North Korean troops occupied South Korean territory, they sometimes abducted civilians and took them back to the North. At the same time, in the chaos of war some North Koreans took the opportunity to flee to the South.

Kim Il-sung's gamble had failed. After the first year of fighting, the Chinese took over command of the Chinese and remaining North Korean troops, leaving Kim to sit on the sidelines. Yet his political position was sufficiently strong that he survived the disaster and remained North Korea's supreme leader.

The version of events that the North Korean people are taught is quite different, beginning with the claim that it was South Korea, egged on by the Americans, that started the war by attacking North Korea. It is true that for a long time prior to June 25, both Koreas had staged cross-border raids against the other side, but the North Koreans were clearly the ones who planned and launched a broad offensive with the intention of starting a war. Every year the North Korean media publish abbreviated versions of the war in which Kim Il-sung's sagacious leadership defeats the United States. An official version of the war, published by North Korea in 1981, opens with this foreword, which prudently avoids explicit assertions of Kim Il-sung's wartime role, although he is elsewhere referred to as the "Iron-Willed Brilliant Commander Who Defeated U.S. Imperialism":

> The U.S. imperialists who are out for world conquest launched an armed invasion on the Democratic People's Republic of Korea on June 25, 1950. It was their dream to make the Korean people their slaves and turn Korea into their colony to set up a military base for conducting a war against the Soviet Union and the Chinese People's Republic.
>
> The war of aggression unleashed by the U.S. imperialists was a severe test to the Korean people and the people's democratic system. The Korean people, however, stood up to safeguard the country's freedom and independence in their just Fatherland Liberation War.
>
> Under the correct guidance of the Workers' Party of Korea, and enjoying support from the peoples of the Soviet Union and other socialist countries as well as the peace-loving peoples the world over, the Korean people and their armed forces, the Korean People's Army, overcoming every difficulty and hardship, fought in cooperation with the valiant Chinese People's Volunteers and won a great victory in the three-year long severe war by displaying mass heroism, patriotic devotion and unbending fighting spirit.

The Fatherland Liberation War which was a landmark in the national independence and social progress of the Korean people came to an end with the truce signed on July 27, 1953. The war was a military, political and moral defeat for the allied forces of imperialism with the U.S. as the ringleader and for the Syngman Rheeites, hirelings of the U.S. But it was a brilliant victory for the Korean people and the entire peace-loving peoples the world over. [8]

In North Korea one of the two prominent buildings dedicated to the Korean War is the Sinchon Museum of American War Atrocities, located fifty miles south of Pyongyang. In the Sinchon area, during the period from October 17 to December 7, 1950, when the UN forces were pushing up through North Korea, an unknown number of civilians were killed. The fog of war and the patent prejudice of the North Korean media make it impossible to determine what happened. How many civilians were killed (the North Koreans claim thirty-five thousand), and who killed them, will probably never be known. In North Korea's telling, which is graphically displayed on giant posters throughout the museum, large and ferocious American soldiers are depicted as torturing helpless Korean women and children.

In 2015 the North Korean media announced that the museum had moved to a new building "excellently built in line with the demands of the military-first era, thanks to the rock-hard faith and will and wise leadership of respected and beloved Kim Jong-un, who is determined to win the final victory in the anti-US war of confrontation which has persisted from one century to another."[9] The alleged virtue of the museum is that it "helps the younger generation of the DPRK have a towering hatred against the U.S. imperialists and renew their revengeful will to wipe out the enemy."[10]

The Victorious Fatherland Liberation War Museum in downtown Pyongyang has also recently been remodeled. On July 27, 2013 (the sixtieth anniversary of the truce signing), Kim Jong-un cut a red ribbon to open the new building, which uses exhibits including captured American weapons to hype the alleged wartime leadership achievements of Kim Il-sung. The museum's premier attraction is not in the building itself and has nothing directly to do with the Korean War. It is the USS *Pueblo*, a small American research-spy ship captured by the North Koreans in 1969, during a time when the North Koreans were staging provocations against South Korea and the US military's attention was directed toward the war in Vietnam. The virtually unarmed ship was captured in international waters but inside waters over which North Korea claimed jurisdiction. One of its eighty-three crew members was killed during the capture, and the others were held for eleven months until the United States offered an apology. The ship was later moved from the east coast to a dock on the Potong River just outside the museum, where it is a popular tourist attraction.

In the United States, the Korean War has appropriately been called "the forgotten war." Today in South Korea, left-leaning teachers and textbooks have given school students a revisionist version of Korean War history. In 2013 the (conservative) government cited a media survey of teenagers' history awareness showing that 69 percent of students believed that the war was triggered by a South Korean invasion of North Korea.[11] For many Americans, the war, however vague the memory of its causes and events may be, is grounds for condemning the current North Korean government, which unlike the Japanese and German governments, has never owned up to its historic aggression. The war also serves as a warning that the same regime that started the war continues to be capable of future aggression.

Chapter Two

Leadership

The Kim Dynasty

KIM IL-SUNG: THE STRONG KIM

Kim Il-sung did two things for North Korea. First, through his strong personality and ruthless political skills, he founded the country and kept it together in the face of a notable Korean tendency toward divisive and contentious politics. Second, building on Korea's Confucian tradition, he created a national cult that has consolidated his family's control over the country for over seventy years.

Kim was born on April 15, 1912, with the name Kim Song-ju. His father worked at various times as a schoolteacher, clerk, and herbal pharmacist, and he had briefly attended an American missionary school and become a Christian. To escape the Japanese occupation, which had begun in 1905, the Kim family fled to China, where the adventuresome young Kim joined a communist youth league that harassed occupying Japanese troops. His arrest and imprisonment for several months ended his formal schooling after the eighth grade. In 1932, in his early twenties, Kim joined and then led a guerrilla band of Koreans that North Korean propagandists would later call the Korean People's Revolutionary Army, and around this time he adopted the name of a famous Korean guerrilla fighter, Kim Il-sung, which means "Kim the sun" in Chinese characters. The Japanese pursued Kim's guerrilla group, killing many of its members, but Kim was able to elude them with the help of other guerrilla bands and small contingents of the Chinese army.

North Korean historians say that the young Kim's most famous battle occurred in 1937 when his band launched a hit-and-run attack on a small Japanese police force occupying the Korean border town of Pochonbo and then quickly withdrew back into China. Notwithstanding its insignificance, North Korean propagandists have played up this attack as a turning point in the war against the Japanese, and over the years millions of North Koreans have visited this so-called revolutionary site.

As the Japanese consolidated their hold over northern China, Kim and his comrades fled into Russia, where they settled in a Soviet army camp near Khabarovsk, and throughout the remainder of the war Kim received additional military training, attaining the rank of captain in the Soviet army. It was during his encampment that he married Kim Jong-suk, who in 1941 or 1942 gave birth to a son, Kim Jong-il, and then died in 1949 giving birth to a daughter. Kim Il-sung apparently took a second wife, Kim Song-ae, in 1952, although the secrecy that has always surrounded the Kim family makes it difficult to know how many wives and mistresses Kim actually had.

In September 1945, a month after Japanese forces in Korea surrendered to American and Soviet troops, the Russians brought Kim back to Korea and installed him as their favorite to govern the country. Over the next several years, with the backing of Russian soldiers and through the use of his own ruthless political skills, which sometimes involved assassinating political opponents, Kim took control of North Korea. Despite his failure to win the Korean War or save his country from wartime devastation, Kim was able to consolidate his hold on the country, and by the late 1950s his political position was unassailable.

Kim's thinking was more like that of a small-town mayor than the president of a country. Despite his fear of flying (he apparently flew only twice, once to Indonesia and once to Russia), Kim traveled abroad almost every year in his private train, mostly to Russia and China. He never visited a Western country. At home he ruled by his common sense, never losing sight of the importance of eliminating all political opposition. He was a tall, robust individual with a hearty manner that charmed foreign visitors. He enjoyed traveling around the country giving "on-the-spot guidance" and greeting his people, who called him *suryong* (great leader) or *oboi suryongnim* (fatherly great leader). People looked upon him as their protector, and he probably thought of himself that way. True, in order to stay firmly in power, he and his minions sent tens of thousands of mostly innocent people to political prison camps, where as "tailless animals" (to quote the description of a former prisoner) they and their families served out their days in misery.[1] Wherever he went and whatever he touched was treated like a shrine. Under his firm guidance and with generous foreign aid from the Soviet bloc, North Korea rebuilt itself and, through the 1960s, was more economically successful than South Korea.

Kim was not an educated man or, for that matter, a modern man. As global economies developed, North Korea was left behind. Under his 1950s-style guidance, the country's industries faltered, and national multiyear economic plans usually failed to achieve their goals. By the 1970s Kim was in his sixties and enjoying his life as a revered leader. To keep pace with South Korea and the rest of the world, what North Korea needed was a new leader with fresh ideas, but that was unthinkable in North Korea.

In the 1970s Kim had to give some thought to who would succeed him. The choice seemed to be between his younger brother, Kim Yong-ju, and Kim Il-sung's oldest son, Kim Jong-il, who was in his late thirties in 1980. It was necessary to keep the country's leadership in the family in order to maintain the illusion that the Kim family was special, and to ensure that Kim's successor would not criticize or turn against him as Nikita Khrushchev had turned against Stalin. Kim settled on his first son, who was anointed at the 1980 party congress. Until his father died, Kim Jong-il stayed in the background and devoted himself to developing the Kim Il-sung cult, which would ultimately confer legitimacy on him when he stepped into his father's shoes. The cult included songs, most famously the "Song of General Kim Il-sung," which is more popular than the national anthem. Monuments were erected throughout the country; pictures of Kim adorned every household, public building, and public conveyance; and Korean history was rewritten to glorify Kim as the world's greatest leader, the "eternal sun of mankind."

Beginning in the 1980s it appears that Kim Jong-il was handling many of the day-to-day affairs of government, leaving his father free to preside over official functions, oversee foreign policy, and travel around the country meeting his subjects. Kim Il-sung is reported to have collapsed and died of a heart attack on July 8, 1994, dying in his bed at the age of eighty-two. News of his death was not announced to the nation and the world until thirty-four hours later. His preserved body lies in state in the Kumsusan Palace of the Sun, which Kim Jong-il, at a cost of tens of millions of dollars, converted from the Kumsusan Assembly Hall, which had been his father's official residence. The palace is a required stop for all foreign tourists so they can pay their respects to the "great leader." For years after Kim's death, volumes

Well-organized student and adult groups paying their respects to the two Kims.
Wikimedia Commons, by calflier001, CC-BY-SA-2.0.

of his "collected works" continued to be released, an effort that must have kept Kim's ghostwriters busy.

Kim Il-sung was a legend from the time he first appeared to the North Korean public, and over the years his legendary status grew, despite the fact that, after the first two decades of his rule, he didn't really do that much for his people. In some sense he was like the gods of many religions, who don't seem to answer prayers but are worshipped nonetheless. Kim is still respected today by most North Koreans, who think of him as part of their national heritage, like Americans might think of George Washington. It could be argued that Kim's greatest accomplishment was to hold the new country of North Korea together simply by his presence and by the existence of the cult that was built around him. Like most dictators, Kim almost certainly believed that his firm and oftentimes cruel leadership was necessary to preserve the country. He did not seem to be a man of many doubts. In the end, he failed to deliver on two important promises he had often made to his people. First, he did not achieve the reunification of the Korean nation. Second, he did not deliver on his promise to make it possible for his people to "eat rice and meat soup, wear silk clothes, and live in a house with a tiled roof."

KIM JONG-IL: THE SECRETIVE KIM

It is almost a truism that dictators try to hold on to power until they die. They enjoy the exercise of power and believe they can do a better job of running the country than anyone else. In the case of North Korea, Kim Il-sung may also have considered the fact that so many lies adhered to his reign that it would be best to choose a successor within his own family, who would have a personal interest in perpetuating those lies.

Kim Jong-il took his first party position immediately after graduating from Kim Il-sung University in the mid-1960s, working under his uncle Kim Yong-ju and apparently showing promising signs of ambition and competence. By the early 1970s, when he was in his early thirties, which was the same age as his father at the time Kim Il-sung was brought back to Korea by the Russians, the young Kim seemed to have the inside track in the succession race.

However, one potential obstacle to his succession was the glaring fact that hereditary succession was not politically acceptable in a communist society, or for that matter in any society other than hereditary kingdoms. The 1970 edition of North Korea's *Dictionary of Political Terminologies* denounced hereditary succession as "a reactionary custom of exploitative societies" and "originally a product of slave societies . . . later adopted by feudal lords as a means to perpetuate dictatorial rule." In making this judgment the dictionary was, ironically, providing quite an accurate description of North Korea, but since this dictionary entry was manifestly inconvenient for Kim's succession, it was deleted in the dictionary's 1972 edition.

Another obstacle to the young Kim's succession was that in a dictatorship there is room for only one dictator, so it would be necessary for Kim Jong-il to stay in the background while his father was alive. Perhaps for this reason, during a period in the 1970s and sometimes even in later years, Kim was referred to in the press rather cryptically as the anonymous "party center." When he was mentioned by name, he was most often referred to as the Dear Leader, to distinguish him from his father, the Great Leader.

Kim Jong-il had to clear the political path to succession by banishing and purging potential political rivals, most especially his uncle Kim Yong-ju, who pretty much disappeared after Kim gained power. Jong-il's half-brother,

Kim Pyong-il, the handsome and popular son of Kim Il-sung's second wife, Kim Song-ae, was posted to ambassadorships in Eastern Europe, where he remained under close supervision of North Korea's security services for many years. These two were lucky. Over the years many other officials suspected of being less than enthusiastic about Kim Jong-il were imprisoned or murdered.

Kim was apparently not emotionally close to his busy father. Like his father, he was overweight—one of the few people in the country who was—but he stood only five feet five inches tall, several inches shorter than his father, and to make up for his short stature he wore platform heels and sported a bouffant hairdo. Unlike his father, he was uncomfortable around everyone except close friends. He gave only one public speech, whose entire content was, "Glory to the heroic KPA officers and men."[2] This was spoken from the reviewing stand at a military parade in 1992, and apparently it was not even supposed to be broadcast. Kim continued his father's tradition of closely guarding his personal life. The public did not know if he was married or had any children; the best guess is that he married twice and had numerous mistresses. Like his father, he avoided airplane flights, and the only countries he visited after becoming the supreme leader were China and Russia, which he traveled to on one of his luxurious armored trains.

After his public introduction in 1980, the young Kim needed to find a role for himself, so he decided to be the party's theoretician and the caretaker of the people. The theoretical work was done by others, most notably Professor Hwang Jang-yop, who elaborated on the idea of *juche* before becoming dissatisfied with the young Kim and defecting to South Korea. Kim's role as the "dear leader" who looks out for the North Korean people was carried out by adopting his father's on-the-spot guidance activities. In Kim Jong-il's case the entire process of this guidance encapsulated his approach to leadership: controlled, secretive, and remote from the people. His perfunctory visits were then given maximum play in the North Korean media to demonstrate how much Kim cared about the lives of the people. For example, a summary report of Kim's guidance during the famine of the mid-1990s, which was heroically dubbed the "Arduous March," read like this:

> Keeping in mind President Kim Il-sung's lifelong desire to have the people "eat rice and meat soup and live in tile-roofed houses," General Kim Jong-il has undergone all sorts of hardships for the people for the past three years [1995–1997] without taking care of his own health. With a pain in his heart about the fact that the people cannot afford to eat their fill, the general said that

"I do not care if I eat only soup," and that "Day and night, I always think about ways to have our people live more affluently." In fact, he often ate merely a bowl of corn soup or a rice ball as a meal while giving on-the-spot guidance to the Army and people. Who is really on the "arduous march"?[3]

Reports such as these added another lie to the Kim family myth. Foreigners obtained particularly accurate reports on the reclusive Kim's lifestyle from the writings of a Japanese chef that Kim hired to serve him in the early 1980s. The chef became a virtual family member, traveling around the country with Kim and visiting Kim's luxurious private estates. After returning to Japan and changing his name, the chef wrote several books about Kim's lifestyle.[4] He assures his readers that Kim did not, in fact, live on rice balls and soup. Rather, he was a true connoisseur of fine food. Special farms grew food only for Kim, and many of the ingredients for his meals were imported from Europe and Japan. Kim threw extravagant parties to entertain his top officials, and he himself loved a good party. Not a word of these pleasures ever reached the North Korean people.

Kim took over after his father's 1994 heart attack at a particularly bad time for North Korea. In the early 1990s the country's principal economic supporters, the Eastern bloc and China, were transitioning to capitalism and had little patience with the Kim regime's insistence on sticking with socialism. North Korea's foreign aid and trade income dropped dramatically, and severe weather triggered several years of famine during which as many as a million North Koreans (out of a population of twenty-three million) died of starvation. During this time Kim Jong-il did nothing for his people, and from that time on they ignored him as much as possible, comparing him unfavorably to his father.

The dissatisfaction of the North Korean people never posed a threat to the Kim regime, which was protected from the people by the police and military. Kim did, however, have to be sure that the top generals were on his side, especially because, unlike his father, Kim had never been a soldier. Thus, one of his greatest challenges was to convince the top generals and party cadres, as well as the North Korean public, that he was somehow a military man.

The official story of Kim's birth has him being born in a humble log cabin at a "secret camp" on the slopes of the semisacred Paektu Mountain on the Korea-China border. According to this version of history, his father was making raids on the Japanese from the camp, along with his wife and the rest of his guerrilla band, thus giving rise to the myth of the "Paektu line" of

Kims who are destined to rule Korea. The North Korean propaganda media frequently spoke of the "three generals of Mount Paektu," meaning Kim Il-sung, his wife, and his son, even though his wife was actually a housewife in a Russian army camp and his son was just a child with the Russian nickname "Yura." This myth became the foundation of the story that Kim Jong-il was a military genius.

Even before his father died, Kim had been appointed "supreme commander" of the military, and from 1994 until his death in 2011, the name given to his policy of governance was *songun* (military-first). By putting the military first, he hoped to please them and ensure that they sided with him and kept the people in check. People would say (in private), "Kim Il-sung took the people's train, but Kim Jong-il takes the military train." The military-first policy also made Kim look like a real general, even in the absence of any fighting. For example,

Ubiquitous image of the "three generals of Mount Paektu." *Wikimedia Commons, by Mark Fahey, CC-BY-2.0.*

In a showdown with an enemy, one can wait for the situation to develop in favor of one and then strike at it or outflank it rather than mount a frontal attack. However, such methods are definitely conservative and passive. The most aggressive method capable of inflicting an ignominious defeat on the enemy is an offensive, and such a bold strategy can be executed only by a great military commander [i.e., Kim]. The disposition of the respected and beloved general, the general of Mount Paektu, is such that he, unmoved in the face of a formidable enemy, boldly confronts the enemy and strikes at it mercilessly . . . overwhelming the enemy at one stroke. [5]

Moreover, adhering to a military-first policy provided Kim with a ready-made excuse for not improving economic conditions, because as the people were frequently told, money and material resources had to go to the military to protect the country from the United States, which he claimed was always on the point of invading North Korea. And so Kim Jong-il, whose tenure was marked by a serious economic downturn but no fighting, became known in North Korea as a military commander. What the North Korean people really needed after international socialist aid and trade ended was an economic leader who would help the country transition toward capitalism, as all the other socialist countries (except Cuba) were doing. The best that can be said for Kim is that, most of the time, he allowed the people to develop small private enterprises to support themselves, even while extolling the alleged superiority of socialism. He himself, of course, continued to lead the life of a capitalistic fat cat.

At a relatively early age, Kim's health began to decline. In August 2008, at the age of sixty-seven, he suffered a stroke and failed to appear in public for two months. In 2009, looking gaunt and unsteady, he resumed his on-the-spot guidance visits and apparently remained in control of the government. In October 2011 his visits included a turtle farm, a pig farm, a duck farm, and a net-weaving factory. He conducted his final guidance tour on December 15, 2011, ironically visiting a Chinese joint-venture supermarket in Pyongyang. The Korean Central News Agency (KCNA) announced that he had passed away "of a sudden illness" on December 17 "on his way to field guidance."[6]

His official epitaph, made up almost entirely of lies, read in part,

The grief-stricken people look up to the portraits of leader Kim Jong-il in his ordinary field jacket. His picture makes everyone feel pangs of compunction as he made the long journey of field guidance, going in his field jacket all his life. He had inconvenient naps and simple rice-balls in cars or on trains while making the journey of field guidance for the country's prosperity and people's happy life, not even taking a day off. Mourners cried in choking voices: "General, you have had pain only for people all your life. How can you, General, pass away so early leaving us behind? We have not fulfilled our obligation. Kim Jong-il found himself among the people and shared joys and sorrows with them all his life and the Korean people cannot live even a moment without him. People were always on his mind and he was always on their minds. That's why people weep so bitterly, crying, "General has not left us; he is always with us."[7]

KIM JONG-UN: THE YOUNG AND RUTHLESS KIM

In early 2009, Kim Jong-il's failing health signaled an urgent need to prepare a successor. According to the logic of the Kim cult, which sets the Kim family apart from all others, Kim had to choose one of his sons to succeed him, although if the succession after Kim Il-sung had been awkward, a third-generation dynastic succession might be even more so. The tradition of Confucianism on which the Kim cult is based favored the eldest son, Kim Jong-nam, a taller and fatter version of Kim Jong-il and the son of Kim's former mistress, the actress Song Hye-rim. Unfortunately for Jong-nam, in 2001 he had been detained by immigration authorities while entering Japan on a forged Dominican Republic passport, making him a laughing stock in Japan and bringing shame on the ruling Kim family. Since then, Jong-nam had been banished to Macau and other Asian locales, where he lived the life of a playboy.

As far back as 2002 the North Korean propaganda organs began to elevate Ko Yong-hui, another one of Kim Jong-il's wives or mistresses, to cult status, suggesting that one of her two sons, Kim Jong-chul or Kim Jong-un, might be in line for succession. Little was known about either of the young men, who, like Kim Jong-nam, had both spent years (in Kim Jong-un's case, almost ten years) enrolled in Swiss schools under assumed names. The North Korean public did not even know of their existence, and no adult photograph of them was available to the public. The younger of the two, Kim Jong-un, was probably born in 1982 or 1983 and was reportedly tougher in character than his older brother.

Kim Jong-un's public introduction was gradual, as one might expect given the sensitivity of the situation, but unlike the introduction of his father, which had played out over almost two decades (from the 1970s to the early 1990s), Kim Jong-un was established as the successor within two years. South Korean intelligence reported that in January 2009 Kim Jong-il issued a directive to top party members naming Kim Jong-un as his chosen successor.[8] In the first half of 2009 soldiers were given political instructions coming from a mysterious "Morning Star General." By June the North Korean people were beginning to hear about a "brilliant General Kim," and they were taught a new song titled "Footsteps" that mentioned a General Kim. In February 2010 the North Korean media broadcast "Footsteps," a song of three stanzas whose first stanza goes like this:

> Stomp stomp stomp stomp stomp footsteps
> Our General Kim's footsteps
> Sprinkling the soul of February
> One strong stomp of footstep after footstep
> The mountains and waters of the entire country rejoice with stomp stomp stomp.[9]

The popular assumption was that the "general" referred to Kim Jong-un (Kim Jong-il was by this time a "grand marshal"), and the month of February could indicate the month of his father's birth. Thus, the new general would be marching in the path of his father.

In September 2010 a conference of the Korean Workers' Party was convened—the first conference (not congress) in forty-four years. A number of top party posts were filled, and twenty-eight-year-old Kim Jong-un received his first public appointment, as a vice chairman of the party's Central Military Commission, one day after being appointed to the rank of four-star general. Throughout 2011, Kim Jong-un continued his preparations for succession, reportedly assisting his ill father with administrative affairs and publicly accompanying him on his travels, including a trip to China. When Kim Jong-il died in December 2011, the North Korean media assured the people that, "at the forefront of our revolution, there is our comrade Kim Jong-un standing as the great successor to our *juche* ideology and as the leader of our party, army, and people."[10] Within a few months Kim Jong-un had secured all the necessary trappings of power, being named supreme commander of the Korean People's Army (KPA), first secretary of the party (his late father became the "Eternal General Secretary"), chairman of the Central Military Commission, and first chairman of the National Defense Commission (his late father became the "Permanent Chairman"). In July 2012 the Morningstar General received the title of marshal, second only to the grand marshal title that his late father and grandfather held.

As a public figure, Kim Jong-un was not his father's son but rather his grandfather's grandson. His speech marking Kim Il-sung's hundredth birthday on April 15, 2012, lasted twenty minutes and twenty-six seconds, surpassing his father's only public speech by a full twenty minutes and twenty seconds. Observers could hardly help noticing that the young Kim imitated some of the distinctive speaking mannerisms of his grandfather, sometimes dressed like him, and was much more assertive in public than his reclusive father. Beginning in 2013 the new leader resumed his grandfather's tradition of personally delivering the New Year's address.

Kim Jong-un was also more open about his personal life than his father had been. Whereas his father, and for that matter his grandfather, never appeared before the Korean people with any of their wives or mistresses, in July 2012 the North Korean media introduced the woman who had recently been accompanying Kim Jong-un as his wife, Ri Sol-ju, a former North Korean singer, and from then on she was frequently seen by his side. And although the North Korean media have never mentioned his children, foreign intelligence agencies believe the couple has two or three young girls and one young boy.

Kim Il-sung spent over a decade winnowing the North Korean political establishment until he had collected a small cadre of comrades he could trust. Kim Jong-il had two decades to replace many of these first-generation cadres with ones closer to his own age. Kim Jong-un had only a year or two to replace his father's people with his own. Because of Kim's young age and lack of experience, his father had already selected a handful of powerful officials to guide and protect him during his first years in power. At the very top, these were the people who accompanied Kim Jong-un as he walked beside his father's hearse. They included his uncle, Jang Song-taek; two other civilians; and four top military leaders. Within a few years all but one had been demoted, had been executed, or had died of natural causes. From the day he took office the young Kim showed that he was going to be his own man. In his first year he ran through four defense ministers, and he has continued to rotate and purge top military men, presumably for fear that they might plot against him. His uncle, who for years had been the second most powerful person in the country, was accused of disloyalty, publicly humiliated, and promptly executed. His stepbrother, Kim Jong-nam, was assassinated while traveling in Malaysia.

Already chubby, Kim Jong-un, like his father and grandfather, became obese, weighing in at about 260 pounds and standing five feet seven inches tall. Also like his father, he adopted a unique hairstyle, somewhat reminiscent of his grandfather's but more extreme. He promoted North Korea's nuclear and missile programs even more vigorously than his father had, and like his father, he tolerated corruption and the informal adoption of a capitalist economy, even while paying lip service to socialism. He replaced his father's military-first policy with a *byungjin* (dual-track) policy of simultaneously trying to pursue nuclear weapons and economic development. After North Korea had conducted several nuclear and missile tests, he announced that the country had completed its basic nuclear program and had become a bona fide nuclear state, thereupon replacing the *byungjin* policy with an economy-first program, despite the fact that, owing to his commitment to a nuclear program, North Korea was struggling under increasingly severe international economic sanctions.

In ruling style, Kim Jong-un worked hard to project the image of a strong leader, perhaps in part to compensate for his youthfulness. Foreigners often described his ruling style as a reign of terror, but whether the atmosphere was more fearsome than under his father and grandfather is debatable. The young Kim was quick to take advantage of opportunities. When South Koreans elected a president who was more concerned about détente with the North than with eliminating its nuclear weapons, and when Americans elected a president who had little knowledge of foreign affairs but was partial to dictators, Kim quickly took advantage of the situation and arranged summit meetings with both presidents, dramatically enhancing his reputation at home and abroad.

After almost ten years in office (at this writing), Kim Jong-un seems more politically secure than ever. Yet he still has not found a way to alleviate the widespread poverty of the masses, and as a grossly overweight male in his early thirties, with potential health problems and only a few very young children, he should be worried about the succession issue. If North Korea's "Paektu line" of leadership should end, it is difficult to imagine who else will have sufficient authority to rule the country. Some foreigners speculate that his sister, Kim Yo-jong, who has been given several important party posts and seems to be a confidante of her brother, might be in the running, but it is difficult to believe that North Korean political culture is ready for a female leader.

What the three Kims have shared in common and what has kept them in complete control of the country for the last three-quarters of a century is their ruthless use of power. They have differed in their personalities and in their life circumstances, but all three have adapted to prevailing circumstances. Some autocratic leaders stay in power by forming political coalitions or rewarding influential supporters, but these strategies are not for the Kims.

Any potential competitor who tries to gain political power is mercilessly crushed. Loyal followers are given rewards, but just as often are punished for the slightest sign of disloyalty. For the Kims, there is no room for error. The second and third Kims seem to have alienated almost everyone, from high to low, so if they show any sign of weakness, they have no one to call on for support.

Kim Jong-un is clearly the most modern of the three Kims. He seems to be comfortable with the latest technology and realizes the importance of international media, but rather than using this knowledge to change the basic characteristics of his country, he has employed technology to keep control of his people and to deter foreigners from interfering in North Korea's domestic affairs. When Kim Jong-il first came to power, and then Kim Jong-un, some foreigners speculated that North Korea might be in for important policy changes. This has not happened. Looking to the years ahead, there is no reason to believe that North Korea will be anything other than the kingdom of the Kim family.

GUIDANCE: AN EXERCISE IN PUBLIC RELATIONS

In bygone days, Korean kings would send out officials, sometimes in disguise, to report on conditions around the kingdom. Unlike ancient kings, Kim Il-sung liked to conduct inspections personally. According to the North Korean press, he made eight thousand "on-the-spot guidance" tours in his lifetime, and his son and grandson have continued the tradition, each reportedly making 100 to 150 visits a year.[11]

The Kim family rulers live at a remote distance from their people. They don't have to conduct election campaigns because they are appointed for life. They don't give press interviews. On the first day of the year, Kim Il-sung and Kim Jong-un broadcast a New Year's Day address, comparable to the American president's State of the Union speech, while the New Year's editorial addresses of the reclusive Kim Jong-il were read by a radio announcer. Thus, in North Korea the only direct contact between ruler and ruled is when the leader deigns to make an inspection visit. Only a few people are present on these occasions, but within a day or two the front page of the party newspaper is filled with reports of the visit. Inspections are made to every conceivable site: cooperative farms, state stores, military bases, and construction sites. The inspections keep people on their toes and serve an important public relations function by suggesting that the Kims care about their people.

"On-the-spot" inspections or guidance (*hyonji-chido*) are not supposed to be the sole responsibility of the leader. In remarks attributed to Kim Il-sung back in the late 1950s, he complains that party and government officials are not doing a proper job of going among the masses to investigate conditions and instruct them, and he insists that such inspections are an important part of socialist governance. [12] This type of guidance came to be associated exclusively with the leader because in the North Korean press the leader is almost the only person ever to be mentioned by name.

At least as reported in the press, these guidance visits depart from the ideal that Kim Il-sung advocated. Rather than being an in-depth investigation into conditions (Kim recommended a visit of several days), the visits gradually turned into a carefully orchestrated public relations appearance in which the leader demonstrates his wisdom and expertise in all fields of knowledge. A problem with this demonstration is that often the leader does not in fact understand what he is talking about, yet the advice he gives must be followed to the letter, even if it is completely wrong.

A special unit called the "Support for Inspection Unit" makes preparations for these "number 1" (presidential) visits by sprucing up the inspection sites so they will please the leader. [13] People who live in the vicinity undergo new background checks to confirm their political reliability. Those not deemed politically reliable are cleared from the area or told to stay inside their homes on inspection day. People who will come in contact with Kim are given health checkups to ensure they will not pass on any germs. If an adoring crowd is needed to welcome Kim, actors and the most attractive children and adults in the area are selected, trained, and provided with appropriate clothing and flags to wave. Old equipment at the inspection site is swapped for new equipment from other organizations. Food supplies are provided. If the farm to be inspected raises livestock, a full complement of healthy animals must be procured.

Shortly before the leader arrives, Kim's bodyguard unit thoroughly inspects the site and seals all entrances and exits. If Kim is inspecting a military base, small arms ammunition is locked up, and tanks and artillery pieces are secured with their gun barrels pointing away from where he will be standing. At a time of his choosing, Kim appears briefly, speaks to the top officials or commanding officers, walks around the site, has his photograph taken, and departs in his caravan of black Mercedes. A plaque will later be placed at the site commemorating Kim's visit, and if he sat in a chair or at a table, the furniture will be taken out of service and preserved as a historical relic.

A typical news report of guidance to a military base goes something like this: "Comrade Kim Jong-il, great leader of our party and our people, who is general secretary of the Workers' Party of Korea, chairman of the DPRK National Defense Commission, and supreme commander of the Korean People's Army, inspected KPA Unit Number 802, honored with the title of O Chung-hup-led Seventh Regiment."[14] Then follows a list of the generals who accompanied Kim on the visit. The news report will claim that Kim acquainted himself carefully with the unit's operation, especially emphasizing his interest in the soldiers' living conditions: "Comrade Kim Jong-il looked into every detail of the soldiers' living, ranging from entertainment means and room conditions to every photograph they had taken and their personal belongings."[15] The leader also inspects any agricultural operations run by the unit to support themselves, such as pig farms, catfish ponds, orchards, and cornfields. According to the press reports, he is almost always satisfied with what he finds and declares that the unit is highly prepared to protect the people and defeat any aggressors. Guidance photos of the leader usually show him smiling broadly or laughing. At the conclusion of his visit, he has his photograph taken standing in front of the assembled soldiers and then gives them a few commemorative presents, typically an engraved rifle and pair of binoculars. These "number 1 articles" will be displayed in the special room set aside at every military post and civilian workplace to study the works of the Kims.

News reports of Kim's military visits usually conclude by painting a word picture of the soldiers enthusiastically cheering the departing Kim: "All the officers and soldiers . . . were full of burning determination to death-defyingly protect the nerve center of the revolution, becoming guns and bombs like the members of the anti-Japanese Seventh Regiment did, and to defend the outpost of the fatherland as an impregnable fortress."[16] Follow-up news reports often explain how Kim's guidance benefited the people he visited. For example, in a television program titled *Legend of Love That Blossomed on the Path of On-the-Spot Guidance*, Kim Jong-il is credited with providing uniforms to soldiers, instructing that barracks be built with smaller windows to keep the cold winter air out, and instructing that soldiers be provided with heavy blankets (to be supplied by a "magnificent blanket-producing factory" commissioned by Kim). Kim is said to have supplied soldiers with toothpaste and toothbrushes (rare commodities in North Korea) and even taught the soldiers the correct way to brush their teeth.[17]

At least as reported in the press, the inspections can be used to launch important economic and political initiatives. For example, the so-called Chongsan-ri management method was named after the Chongsan-ri Cooperative Farm, which Kim Il-sung visited in 1960. The following year Kim visited the Taean Electrical Appliance Factory and formulated a similar management system for industry called the Taean work system. Another reform, this one under the guidance of Kim Jong-il, is the August 3 Consumer Goods Program. After conducting an on-the-spot inspection of an exhibition of light-industry products in Pyongyang on August 3, 1984, Kim urged workers to use locally available resources to make consumer goods for the local population.

The visits have even been used to introduce the chosen successor to the people. When Kim Jong-il began to accompany his father on inspections, his presence was mentioned in the press. Photographs showed him helpfully pointing out details to his father with outstretched arm. The elderly Kim was a smiling, authoritative presence, while his son played the role of earnest acolyte. After Kim succeeded his father, his visits to military installations became more frequent, and especially in later years, his facial expressions became rather grim. In 2009, foreign analysts scrutinized photos of Kim Jong-il's guidance visits in an attempt to identify his probable successor, for whom no adult photograph was available. By 2010 the North Korean press was mentioning Jong-un as part of the guidance delegations. Once he started doing his own guidance visits, Kim Jong-un reduced the number of visits to military sites, and he is generally shown smiling and laughing.

In addition to illustrating how wise and knowledgeable the leader is, these inspections also show the people that the leader is completely in charge. He is always accompanied by a group of high-ranking officials and military officers. Foreign analysts closely watch the order in which these followers are mentioned in the press to gauge what their current standing is with the leader. Photographs of the assemblage always show some of the officials, as well as the country's top generals, assiduously taking down notes of whatever the leader says, which reinforces the impression that they are subservient to him.

MANSIONS: LIVING LIKE KINGS

In perhaps no other country is the gap between the leader and people wider than in North Korea. During Kim Il-sung's lifetime, many North Koreans would not have objected to the wealth he enjoyed, even if they had been aware of it, because they absolutely worshipped him. The same cannot be said for his son and grandson. Over the years, especially during the Kim Jong-il era, the leader's wealth vastly increased, which is to be expected given that his supreme power gave him a claim on all the country's assets. Foreigners have sometimes speculated that the son and grandson may have as much as $5 billion stashed away in Swiss bank accounts, but whether this is true is beside the point. When you own a country, you can take whatever you want whenever you want it. This seems to be the principle on which the Kims operate.

The veil of secrecy hiding the supreme leader's wealth was parted in the early years of the twenty-first century by a curious circumstance. In 1982 a young Japanese sushi chef was recruited to work in a Pyongyang restaurant. This in itself was unremarkable. Foreigners are sometimes hired to work in North Korea, under very restrictive conditions. The chef, who took the pen name "Kenji Fujimoto" when he returned to Japan, worked in North Korea from 1982 to 1983, returned to Japan for several years, and then worked almost continuously in North Korea from 1989 to 2001.[18] He then returned for a brief visit with Kim Jong-un in 2012 and returned again in 2017 to run a Japanese restaurant in Pyongyang. Although he was always at the beck and call of his unpredictable boss, Kim Jong-il, life in North Korea was one long adventure for Fujimoto.

Fujimoto's first encounter with Kim, before he even knew who Kim was, reveals how the "Kim court" worked. One night the manager of the restaurant where he worked told him to prepare sushi materials for twenty to thirty people. Three Mercedes picked up Fujimoto and his assistants and drove them two and a half hours to a villa at Wonsan beach on the east coast. At two in the morning they were called into a banquet hall to serve Kim Jong-il and his guests.

After preparing sushi for Kim two or three times a month, Fujimoto was invited to join in card games and other entertainments and eventually became a member of Kim's personal secretariat, traveling around the country with him and taking on added responsibilities such as house-sitting with Kim's children. After Fujimoto became estranged from his wife and family back in

Japan, Kim Jong-il observed that his chef was attracted to one of the young entertainment women attending Kim's parties and arranged for them to be married. The marriage ceremony was attended by Kim but not by the girl's parents, who were not permitted to associate with the Kim court. The couple was given an eight-room apartment, complete with imported furniture and appliances. The girl's family, who lived in a one-room apartment, was eventually permitted to make a visit to the Fujimoto household, where they were amazed to discover that running water was available twenty-four hours a day and not just a couple of hours in the morning and evening as is the case in most Pyongyang apartments.

Fujimoto had a particular interest in Kim's cuisine and kept records of some of his dinners. Here, for example, is a menu for a family dinner: chilled flowering fern, radish dressed with vinegar, quail egg jelly, grilled pheasant, sautéed rice noodles, sautéed mushrooms, fried octopus with ginkgo nuts, Chinese cabbage stew, and dog meat soup, not to mention the usual selection of side dishes that accompany every Korean meal.[19] Kim also liked Western food and even hired two Italian chefs to come to Pyongyang and teach his staff how to make pizza.[20]

The domestic ingredients for Kim's meals came from special farms. For example, Kim's beef came from a cattle ranch staffed by former bodyguards who enjoyed a princely standard of living but were not permitted to leave the ranch to mix with ordinary people.[21] A defector who had a relative working on one of Kim's farms told how the organic apples were cultivated by adding sugar to the soil and severely pruning each tree to produce just a few sweet apples.[22] Foreign ingredients for Kim's table were procured by North Korean officials stationed in embassies around the world.

This culinary state of affairs contrasts with a description of Kim's travels provided by a writer for the party newspaper *Nodong Sinmun*: "the general was always on the move from front to front, having short and uncomfortable sleep in the car, instead of staying home and getting a comfortable sleep in his own bed, and . . . he ate rice balls and scorched rice gathered from the bottom of the pot on the road instead of eating proper meals prepared by the people."[23] Indeed, Fujimoto estimated that Kim traveled outside of Pyongyang about three hundred days a year, staying in his mansions rather than visiting "fronts." Kim's entourage was not informed about trips until the last minute—obviously for security reasons—and Kim usually traveled at night in an attempt to avoid surveillance from American satellites. For journeys lasting more than a few hours, Kim would take one of his personal trains, while shorter trips were made in a caravan of Mercedes, with Kim's car in the lead driving as fast as the roads would allow. Kim's destination would be one of a dozen or so villas situated in the country's scenic mountain and seaside locations.

Fujimoto and other sources have provided detailed descriptions and photographs of some of the Kim family country hideaways, which are not simply large homes but rather extensive estates.[24] Each estate has a resident staff, and Kim Jong-il traveled with a retinue of as many as one hundred security people, staff, and guests. All but one of the estates has a movie theater, a shooting range, and a basketball court. Three houses have indoor swimming pools. Most of the furnishings were imported from Japan and Europe. The Wonsan estate seemed to be Kim Jong-il's favorite. It faces the sea and features water sports in the summer and duck hunting in the winter. The estate also has a basketball court (the Kim boys loved to play basketball), a nine-hundred-meter horse race track, and numerous guesthouses. Guest House No. 72, near Hamhung, also on the East Sea, has a beautiful beach where Kim could enjoy jet-skiing. The building actually looked like a modern seven-story condominium, with three of the floors below ground. The Mount Myohyang guesthouse has two basketball courts. The Tanchon guesthouse is located at a hot springs, as is the nearby Sinchon guesthouse. The Changsong guesthouse, along the river border with China, is another place Kim enjoyed jet skiing. The Chindalle guesthouse, near Pyongyang, has a three-hole golf course. Guest House No. 22 has a three-thousand-meter horse track and a small amusement park. Excellent satellite photos of these estates can be found on various Internet sites. While some of the estates were built in Kim Il-sung's day, Kim Jong-il added to the network of estates, and satellite photos indicate that some have been renovated under Kim Jong-un.

Fujimoto had more freedom to travel than do most North Korean officials, although he always had to obtain Kim's permission. Once he was sent to Moscow, along with three cooks and three waiters, to prepare box lunches for a private Moscow–Pyongyang flight carrying members of the Kim family back to North Korea. Another time he joined a small group of officials sent to Macao to test a gambling system Kim had developed. He was sometimes sent to Japan to purchase fish and other ingredients for Kim's meals, and on one of those trips, in 2001, he decided to stay home. After returning to Japan, he wrote several books about his North Korean experiences, all in Japanese.

Few other foreigners had an opportunity to meet with Kim Jong-il on a daily basis. One who did was Konstantin Pulikovskiy (Pulikovsky), who accompanied Kim on a trans-Siberian rail journey to Moscow in the summer of 2001 as President Putin's personal envoy.[25] Kim Jong-il's railcars included his private car, a car for meetings, a dining car, and a car that carried two armored limousines. The North Korean staff lived in their own railcar. Among Kim's entourage was a "charming young woman" who acted as Kim's assistant and four attractive young women entertainers who danced and sang in Korean and Russian. The train had a satellite hookup so Kim could keep up with the news.

Dinners on the train consisted of fifteen to twenty dishes prepared by Kim's chefs, although like Fujimoto, Pulikovskiy reported that Kim ate only a small portion of each dish. Kim revealed his keen interest in food by discussing the next day's menu with his Russian host. Four times during the journey the North Koreans flew in a planeload of fresh food and flew back the garbage. Kim also had French Bordeaux and Burgundy wines flown in from Paris, thus belying the claim made by the North Korean press that "the whole world knows that his state visits to foreign countries are not as luxurious and comfortable as those made by foreign presidents, and that they are partisan style, field operation style."[26]

The wealth of information available about Kim Jong-il's lifestyle does not necessarily reveal how his son lives, but judging by Kim Jong-un's corpulence, he seems to be keeping up the same standard of living as his father.

Chapter Three

The Government

Of the Party, by the Party, for the Leader

GOVERNANCE: RIDDLED WITH CORRUPTION

North Koreans have never lived under a democratic government. In fact, the only time in their history that they have been without a king-like figure was during the Japanese colonial period, when they were considered to be subjects of the Japanese Empire and therefore owed their allegiance to the emperor. For two or three years after being liberated from the Japanese they lived under a communist government that had not yet fully organized around Kim Il-sung, but by the middle of the 1950s Kim Il-sung had become an absolute ruler and communism as a political system no longer existed in North Korea.

The role of the government is to implement the policies of the Workers' Party of Korea (WPK). These policies are formulated by the leader, who holds a variety of positions in the government and the party but rules simply as the "supreme leader," above the government and the party. It is relatively easy to describe the government structure of North Korea. Unlike Western democracies, with their separate government organizations that provide checks and balances on each other, their multiple political parties contending for power and influence, and their changing leadership, North Korea has a monolithic government that remains the same decade after decade. Calling North Korea the "Democratic People's Republic of Korea" means no more than calling China the "People's Republic of China." In neither case do the people play any meaningful role in governance.

One way to describe North Korea's political system is to liken it to a pyramid. At the very top is the leading member of the Kim family: from 1945 to 1994, this was Kim Il-sung; from 1994 to 2011, Kim Jong-il; and since then, and presumably until his death, Jong-il's son Kim Jong-un. The leader is above all organizations and all laws. He exercises life-and-death power over the other twenty-five million North Koreans. Kim Il-sung was considered by many North Koreans to be semidivine, which is not surprising considering that the neighboring Japanese believed that their emperor was divine as well. Kim's son and grandson are more simply viewed as men to be feared. Kim Jong-un is never referred to in the media simply by his name, but rather by his titles; for example, "Comrade Kim Jong Un, supreme leader of our party, state, and army; chairman of the Workers' Party of Korea; chairman of the State Affairs Commission of the Democratic People's Republic of Korea; and supreme commander of the Korean People's Army."[1] The North Korean constitution makes it very clear whose country this is, beginning with the first sentence of the preamble: "The Democratic People's Republic of Korea is the socialist State of Juche where the ideas of the great leader Comrade Kim Il-sung and the great leader Comrade Kim Jong-il on State building and their exploits in it are applied."[2]

Below the leader is the WPK, which advises him on policy and watches over all North Korean citizens and organizations (the party is sometimes called the "great mother" of the people, with the leading Kim playing the role of the father). Article 11 of the constitution states that "the Democratic People's Republic of Korea shall conduct all activities under the leadership of the Workers' Party of Korea." Below the party is the government, whose task is to implement the party's policies, or as the popular saying goes, "What the party decides, we do!" And below the government are the people, who do whatever they are told—at least when party or government officials are watching them.

In an examination of the party, government, and military structures of the country, it is not necessary to pay close attention to the people who head up various organizations, because the only power they have is what the leader grants them, although they can promote or hinder the implementation of policy, at their own risk. As one wag put it after Kim Jong-un took power, "North Korea has a government, but only three people really matter—and two of them are dead."[3]

Another way to look at the government is not as a structure but as a functioning organization. Koreans experienced Confucianism for half a millennium during the Chosun dynasty, and this philosophy has been translated into modern politics. In Confucian tradition the nation is like one big family, with the leader as the father and the people as obedient and grateful family members. The preamble to the 2019 constitution explicitly expresses this idea: "Regarding 'The people are my God' as their maxim, the great leader Comrade Kim Il-sung and the great leader Comrade Kim Jong-il always mixed with the people, devoted their whole lives to them and turned the whole of society into a large family which is united in one mind by taking care of the people and leading them through their noble benevolent politics." Kim Il-sung was frequently referred to as *oboi suryongnim* (fatherly great leader). The leader is even today sometimes described in the press as the "nerve center" of the country, with the people constituting the rest of the body. From an early age, North Koreans are taught to thank their leader for everything good that happens to them.

All organizations in North Korea, including social organizations and trade unions, fall under the purview of the party. All government officials must be party members, and top members of the government and military also hold leadership positions in the party. In actuality, the party's main function is to support the leader of the Kim family. The party charter defines the party as "the great Kimilsungism-Kimjongilism Party." As to its "nature," the 2016 party handbook puts it in these words:

> It is a party of the working class and other working masses, which embraces the progressive elements selected from among the working masses including the workers, farmers and intellectuals, who are ready to dedicate their lives to the struggle for the victory of the cause of socialism, and which has struck its root deep among them.
>
> It is the highest form of political organization among all political organizations of the working masses and the leading political organization of society, and is the General Staff of the revolution that guides the political, military, economic, cultural and all other fields in a unified manner.
>
> It is the core and vanguard detachment of the working class and other working masses that are solidly united in an organizational and ideological way with Kim Il-sung and Kim Jong-il as its eternal leaders and with Kim Jong-un at its center.[4]

In 1988 North Korea claimed that the party had three million members. A foreign estimate in 2015 was four million members out of a population of twenty-five million.[5] The relatively small size of the party suggests not so much that it is difficult to become a party member as that membership is not particularly valued in North Korea today.

The party's supreme governing body is the party congress, which is supposed to convene every five years but which only meets when it suits the leader. By 1970 the congress had been convened five times; the sixth congress met in 1980 to anoint Kim Jong-il as the future successor; and the seventh congress did not meet until May 2016. When the congress is not in session, its Central Committee makes policy, with Kim Jong-un as one of the five members of its Presidium. As the chairman of the separate Executive Policy Bureau, Kim formally leads the party. The party's Central Military Commission controls the army, with Kim the chairman of this commission as well. The party has offices throughout the military and all the way down to the local level of civilian society.

On the government side, the leading organization is the Supreme People's Assembly (SPA), with its 687 members "elected" (i.e., appointed by the party) every five years. According to Article 4 of the constitution, "the sovereignty of the Democratic People's Republic of Korea resides in the workers, peasants, soldiers, intellectuals and all other working people. The working people exercise State power through their representative organs—the Supreme People's Assembly and local People's Assemblies at all levels." Article 5 adds this important proviso: "All State organs in the Democratic People's Republic of Korea are formed and function on the principle of democratic centralism." And Article 6 is a complete lie: "The organs of State power at all levels, from the county People's Assembly to the Supreme People's Assembly, are elected on the principle of universal, equal and direct suffrage by secret ballot." It turns out there are no secret ballots, and party officials closely monitor voters to ensure that "democratic centralism" is achieved.

All the Assembly members are from the WPK except for a token number of "independents" and a handful of members from other parties, which like all organizations in North Korea are under the WPK's control. A former SPA member who defected to South Korea recalls that each delegate received a new suit of clothes a few weeks before the day of the Assembly and received free train tickets to Pyongyang. Delegates were assigned seats in the assembly hall based on their status, and they stayed in a double room at a Pyongyang hotel. At the beginning of the morning session, they all rose and yelled *"manse"* (long live) when Kim Jong-un entered the hall and did not sit down until he indicated. In the morning and afternoon sessions they all held up their registration cards to indicate a yes vote to whatever had been proposed. The next day they returned home. [6]

The Supreme People's Assembly usually meets for a few days in the spring and sometimes also in the summer or fall to rubber-stamp the latest party policies. The actual running of the government is in the hands of departments, including the State Affairs Commission (SAC), the Presidium, and the cabinet. Under Kim Jong-un, the SAC has been designated as the country's highest organization (replacing the National Defense Commission that his father chaired), with Kim as its chairman. Under the SAC is the Ministry of People's Armed Forces (Korean People's Army, or KPA) and the KPA General Staff, which take orders from the party's Central Military Commission (chaired by Kim). The Presidium is headed up by the president of the country, who handles formal diplomatic duties such as accepting credentials of ambassadors but does not exercise any political power. In April 2019, ninety-one-year-old Kim Yong-nam retired from the position after serving for almost twenty years and was succeeded by the relatively youthful (at sixty-nine) Vice Marshal Choe Ryong-hae.

Whereas North Korea's form of monolithic dictatorial bureaucracy would appear to be a simple form of government, official descriptions of the party and government hide a certain amount of bureaucratic complexity. First, as is the case in any gathering of two or more people, political undercurrents swirl around. Former North Koreans report that political infighting for power, influence, prestige, and spoils within and among organizations is rampant. Only when this conflict reaches the top does it become publicly known, as in the case of Jang Song-taek, the second most powerful man in North Korea, who apparently became too powerful for Kim Jong-un's liking and was executed in December 2013 for being a "counterrevolutionary." Thousands of his associates in the party and government were purged as well.

Another fly in the ointment of bureaucracy is corruption. Since the mid-1990s it has been impossible for any government employee to live on a government salary. Officials from top to bottom must engage in a bewildering array of corrupt practices to support themselves, and this corruption spreads throughout society.

SOCIAL CONTROL: DOMINATING THE PEOPLE

How is it that the head of the Kim family is able to govern the fate of the other twenty-five million people living in North Korea, especially when so many of them are suffering and unhappy? The Kims do not have supernatural powers, although many North Koreans believed that the founding Kim did, so the method of control must be ordinary, if severe.

In all societies, social control is predominantly exercised in the form of internalized norms that dictate or at least suggest to people how they should behave in order to benefit themselves and stay out of trouble. For example, police officers need not be posted at every traffic light to ensure that people stop on red—they stop without thinking twice. Going hand in hand with internalized norms is the human tendency toward inertia—that is, taking the habitual path—which requires less effort than calculating the best course of action in each and every situation. In Korea, Confucian norms imported during the Chosun dynasty taught that family members should unquestioningly obey the father and citizens should obey their ruler. Today that translates into North Koreans obeying Kim their leader and his appointed officials. The regime has spent a great deal of time and effort in cultivating a Kim family cult that gives the leader unquestioned authority.

Yet there must be more to social control than conformity to norms because during the Chosun dynasty, and especially in its final years, many people no longer respected or obeyed the ruler. Likewise, during the Japanese colonial period, when people were supposed to obey the Japanese emperor and his officials, occasional outbreaks of resistance kept Japanese officials on edge. By the time Kim Il-sung had consolidated his political position in the 1950s, no such resistance was possible apart from isolated instances of graffiti and vandalism.

A social control problem arises when many people become dissatisfied with the prevailing norms. A relatively unimportant example is the desire of many North Koreans to wear brighter and more interesting clothes than the revolutionary style authorized by the state. After the regime tried to hold the line by having police stop people who were wearing "antisocialist" clothing styles, restrictions were finally loosened, and almost anything is now allowed except immodest clothing and blue jeans, which are considered to be synonymous with Western culture. A far more serious conflict arose in the 1990s when the state was unable to provide food through its Public Distribution System (PDS). People who continued to go to their state-assigned workplaces and trusted that they would receive food rations as part of their payment simply starved. Those who skipped work and started small private businesses, even in the face of threats from their supervisors, survived. Twenty years later, most North Koreans engage in private enterprise at least some of the time.

The primary means of implanting and reinforcing norms are through education and propaganda. It has been estimated that as much as half of student class time during the elementary and middle school years is devoted to ideological education, including many classes devoted to praising the Kim family. For adults, there is continuing education in the form of weekly political study classes. Instead of commercial advertisements, throughout North Korea public propaganda displays in the form of banners, posters, murals, and monuments promoting socialism, the party, and the leader are everywhere present. In the home, school, and workplace, radio and television programs, films, songs, and plays try to instill the required norms and broader values. One of the party's most important departments, the Propaganda and Agitation Department, is in charge of all domestic information and entertainment venues.

The Kim regime cannot rely entirely on education and propaganda to keep people in line. Various police forces watch over the people, and ordinary citizens are recruited to spy on their neighbors. Most work and play activities in North Korea are undertaken in groups, which are easier to monitor than individual activities. People live together in apartments where their coming and going is monitored. They work under the surveillance of party cadres. Although North Koreans can find time to be alone, for example, by taking walks with friends, most of the time they are exposed to public scrutiny.

A particularly intimidating form of social control is the system whereby people who violate norms are punished along with their family members, friends, and work colleagues. This method of control has its roots in centuries of Confucian tradition and has been brutally developed and applied under the Kim regime. Those who are willing to break the rules and accept the consequences must consider the impact on the people they are connected with, who would be punished even though they are innocent. In high-profile cases, hundreds and even thousands of people have paid the price of being associated with an individual whom the regime purges.

And finally, North Koreans, like dissatisfied people everywhere, face the challenge of taking action. The Kim regime has banned all civic organizations, so unlike the case in Eastern Europe in the final years of the Cold War, potential North Korean revolutionaries cannot look to churches or trade unions for support, because these organizations are firmly under the control of the party. Unauthorized public gatherings are strictly prohibited. If an individual wants to protest, he or she must do it alone, which is virtual suicide.

Even with all the forms of social control it has mustered, the Kim regime has found that its grip on the people is slipping. Political indoctrination is largely ignored, except by children, because the official propaganda contradicts everyday reality. Hardly anyone believes that the party knows best or that the regime is looking out for the people's welfare or that socialism is the best economic model. The rise of markets to replace the bankrupt PDS has made the government economically irrelevant. Moreover, these markets, even though patrolled by police, provide citizens with a place to meet and exchange news and opinions.

It is easy to bribe police to overlook "antisocialist" acts because they need money as much as anyone else. Everyone knows that demonstrating loyalty toward the regime is just a game, yet it is still a serious enough game that people do not step far out of line. People do not like their leaders and they do not believe in socialism, but they dare not advocate something different. North Koreans have become experienced in using what has been called the "weapons of the weak" to protect their interests and protest against conditions.[7] These weapons include malingering at work, pilfering, absenteeism, lying to superiors, and pretending to be ignorant of their duties. None of these responses openly challenges the government or party, but the collective result constitutes a kind of silent rebellion that holds back the socialist economy and makes a mockery of the regime's politics. Government and party officials pretend that everything is working because to report shortcomings would make them look bad in the eyes of their superiors. The people at the top do not ask questions because they do not want to be held accountable for failures either. At the very top, Kim Jong-un must be aware of how rotten North Korean society has become, but there is little he can do about it short of instituting the kind of reforms that would threaten to disrupt decades of Kim family rule. In short, North Koreans are constructing their own reality— not a coherent ideology or worldview so much as a rough-and-ready guide to everyday survival.

CRIMES: ORDINARY AND POLITICAL

At first glance North Korea appears to be an exceptionally law-abiding society. The citizens of Pyongyang move around with a purpose. Road traffic is relatively light. Police officers and soldiers are everywhere. Thousands turn out to celebrate special events with mass orchestrations of the sort that Westerners would not dream of participating in. The media carry no reports of domestic crimes.

North Korea has plenty of laws, although many of them are not really laws but rather principles, guidelines, or simply statements of government policy. For example, there is the law on the national flag, the state funeral law, the fruit culture law, the library law, and the law on fish breeding. In 2013 the government even published a "law on consolidating [the] position of [a] nuclear weapons state," which reads in part, "The DPRK is a full-fledged nuclear weapons state capable of beating back any aggressor troops at one strike, firmly defending the socialist system and providing a sure guarantee for the happy life of the people."[8] In the 1990s the government published many of its commercial laws, not to enlighten its citizens, who were barred from engaging in commerce, but to attract foreign investors. However, few foreigners put any faith in the laws because they realized that the regime is above the law.

North Korea does have a criminal code, modeled on the criminal codes of many other states.[9] The ultimate purpose of the legal system is to keep people obedient to the Kim regime. Thus, there are many laws of a political nature as well as the usual criminal laws. All laws and legal institutions are under the control of the party. Kim Il-sung himself said, "Our judicial organs are a weapon for carrying out the functions of the dictatorship of the proletariat."[10] Common to all dictatorships, the law is a tool to protect the ruling party and maintain the authority of the ruling class, while at the same time providing a patina of legitimacy for the government. Another important characteristic of North Korean law is that it is socialist in nature, which means that the rights of the community take precedence over the rights of the individual. And since the community is represented by the party, and the party is a tool of the leader, the leader's interests take precedence over the interests of everyone else.

Ordinary crimes may be as common in North Korea as in most other societies. Foreigners have no exact knowledge about the crime rate because ordinary crimes are almost never reported in the (government-controlled) media. The official government position is that crimes are rare because North Korea is a paradise on earth. Defectors from the country report that the kinds of felonies and misdemeanors committed in other countries are common in North Korea and fall under the jurisdiction of the Ministry of People's Security (MPS), also known these days as the Ministry of Public Security and, most recently, the Ministry of Social Security. Occasionally an internal party document detailing a crime wave or a government campaign to stamp out a particular type of crime makes its way out of the country, but even government authorities do not have an accurate picture of the crime situation because local officials hesitate to report crimes to their superiors.

Murder, rape, robbery, and gang violence are the most serious crimes in North Korea, whereas bribery is the most common crime—almost nothing gets done without the payment of a bribe. Minor crimes such as pickpocketing, for example by youth gangs, are rampant in cities. Drug use is widespread. For years the North Korean government manufactured illicit drugs and smuggled them abroad.[11] These drugs are still manufactured, but in the new quasi-private economy it is not clear who is making the drugs. A growing middle and upper class of North Koreans can now afford to buy the drugs for themselves. Opiates are often used as a substitute for the prescription medicines that are rarely available from doctors and hospitals. The most popular drug group appears to be methamphetamines, especially in the crystalline form known in English as "speed" or "ice"; in North Korea it is called *pingdu* (from the Chinese language) or *orum* (Korean).[12] Crystal meth is a powerful stimulant used as a recreational drug and as a short-lived source of energy.

Political crimes are much more serious offenses and fall under the jurisdiction of the State Security Department (SSD, also known in English as the State Security Administration or Ministry of State Security). For example, Article 68 of the 2012 criminal code, concerning "Treason against the Nation," specifies that anyone "who suppresses our people's struggle for national liberation or the struggle for the reunification of the country or betrays the nation by selling national interests to imperialists, shall be punished by reform through labor for more than five years. In cases where the person commits a grave offense, he or she shall be punished by a life term of reform through labor or the death penalty, and confiscation of property." Since almost anyone could be considered guilty of such a crime, it is a handy tool for the regime to use to punish whomever it wants.

The political crimes listed in North Korea's criminal code are merely the official reflection of a more important political code, one that every North Korean learns from childhood. This code is a list of party principles rather than government laws and goes by the title of the "Ten-Point Principle (Ten Principles) for Solidifying the Party's Monolithic Ideological System." The principles first appeared in 1974 and were revised by Kim Jong-il during the days when he was making his reputation as the interpreter and enforcer of his father's ruling ideology. It appears that the principles were revised in 2013 after Kim Jong-un took power. [13] In the short form, each principle is a single easily memorized sentence. An elaborated version expands on each point. The first principle of the original list reads, "Fight, with all your strength, to make the whole society colored by the revolutionary ideas of the Great Leader, respected comrade Kim Il-sung." The entire list can be paraphrased in the following manner:

- Make the entire society influenced by the ideology of Kim Il-sung.
- Respect, revere, and be loyal to Kim.
- Make Kim's authority absolute.
- Believe in Kim's ideology.
- Carry out Kim's instructions with unconditional loyalty.
- Strengthen the party's unity and solidarity around Kim.
- Imitate Kim's personality and work methods.
- Repay Kim in loyalty for the political life he has given you.
- Establish strong discipline such that everyone uniformly follows Kim's lead.
- See to it that future generations inherit Kim's revolutionary task.

The 2013 revised principles are identical except that they include Kim Jong-il and the party as authorities to be respected.

Just before Kim Jong-il died in 2011, a South Korean survey of North Korean defectors asked what they had considered to be the law before they left the North. In descending order of importance, they mentioned Kim Jong-il's words and instructions, proclamations of the Ministry of People's Security, state laws based on the constitution, orders from the National Defense Commission, and party directives. [14]

People who commit what might be called "generic" crimes against the state, such as criticizing North Korean government policy or speaking well of South Korea, are usually sent to prison for a period of "reeducation." Anyone

whose words or actions pose a specific threat to the position of the leader—
that is, transgress one of the Ten Principles—is likely to be imprisoned for
life or executed. The most public example of such a case is that of Jang
Song-taek, who was a top member of the Kim Jong-il regime and the husband of Kim Jong-il's sister. Jang was intelligent and ambitious and initiated
many economic projects, including establishing business connections with
China. He presumably amassed a considerable amount of money and worked
with an extensive network of associates throughout the North Korean
government. In fact, next to Kim Jong-un, Jang was probably the most corrupt politician in the country. Within two years of Jong-un's taking power he
decided there was not room in North Korea for such a successful official.
Jang was secretly arrested in mid-November 2013 and detained for a couple
of weeks, during which time he was presumably tortured in an attempt to
reveal the identities of many of the people associated with him. Then he was
forced to attend a meeting of the party's Politburo, of which he was a member. During the meeting he was hauled out of his chair by soldiers—in front
of television cameras—and taken back to prison.

Jang was branded a "traitor for all ages" and "an anti-party, counterrevolutionary factional element and despicable careerist and trickster."[15] The
official criminal report accused Jang of "dreaming different dreams," "desperately working to form a faction within the party," leading a "dissolute and
depraved life," having "improper relations with several women," using drugs
and "squandering foreign currency at [foreign] casinos," and other crimes
"baffling imagination."[16] At the heart of the matter was that Jang ignored the
spirit of the Ten Principles. As the report said, "it is the immutable truth
proved by the nearly 70-year-long history of the WPK that the party can
preserve its revolutionary nature as the party of the leader and fulfill its
historic mission only when it firmly ensures its unity and cohesion based on
the monolithic idea and unitary center of leadership [i.e., Kim Jong-un]."
After the meeting Jang was given a brief military trial where he was photographed, and then he was sentenced to death. He was presumably executed
immediately. It is rumored that hundreds or thousands of people associated
with Jang were executed, imprisoned, banished, or demoted. Finally, all
mention of him was expunged from official records and the government-
controlled media.

In some political cases, the procedural steps leading up to imprisonment
or execution (i.e., arrest, trial, conviction, and sentencing) may be dispensed
with entirely. The victim and perhaps his immediate family are abducted by

SSD officers and taken to a prison camp where they can expect to spend the remainder of their days. SSD officers have even been reported to summarily execute individuals in public. Over the years numerous reports have emerged describing public trials and executions, which local people are required to attend. Usually the crime involves "antisocialist" activities such as selling drugs or foreign videos, and the presumed purpose of the public trial and execution is to frighten the public. [17]

Like all other North Korean institutions, the criminal justice system is riddled with corruption. Many crimes are never reported because payment of a suitable bribe settles the matter on the spot with the police, or if an arrest is made, the bribe convinces a judge not to try the case. In this sense crime is an absolute boon for the police, prosecutors, and judges because it enables them to supplement their salaries. Corruption in the police and courts actually increases the crime rate by making the officials guilty of accepting bribes, which is proscribed in Article 230 of the 2012 edition of the criminal code. [18] One defector has said that standard practice is for a police officer to investigate the financial standing of the accused (and family and friends) to determine how much money can reasonably be extorted. [19] Consequently, there is little chance that anyone with money will go to jail. On the other hand, if someone is accused of a serious political crime, money will not help, although it can make life in prison easier. If the crime is against the leader, nothing but the leader's mercy can save the person.

Individuals arrested by the police cannot consult with an independent attorney because all lawyers work for the state. Legal proceedings are often perfunctory because the accused is presumed to be guilty, which is to be expected since the prosecution is an arm of the party, and the party is supposed to be infallible.

Foreign visitors are subject to several vague laws, as a number of tourists have discovered to their misfortune. According to Article 69 of the 2012 criminal code, "a foreign national who suppresses the national liberation struggle of the Korean people or the struggle for the reunification of the country shall be punished by reform through labor for more than five years and less than ten years. In cases where the person commits a grave offense, he or she shall be punished by reform through labor for more than ten years." Usually this law seems to be applied to foreigners who speak ill of North Korea or bring in religious literature or try to engage in religious proselytizing, although the offense is not always clear. The foreigner is tried in a closed court, invariably admits to all charges, and is usually released in a matter of months as part of a quasi-political bargain with a foreign government.

PRISONS: CRUEL AND USUAL

Information about North Korea's prison system has been revealed by former prisoners and a few prison guards who have defected to South Korea. Numerous reports on North Korea's prison systems have been published in English, including excellent reports by the Committee for Human Rights in North Korea, which also publishes satellite images of the prisons. [20]

The Ministry of People's Security, similar to the local and state police in other countries, operates local jails (*kamok*) where prisoners are held for initial interrogation, which is frequently accompanied by beatings and torture. Arrestees convicted of minor offenses are sent on to local labor-training camps (*jipkyulso*) to perform up to six months of very hard labor. At both the local jails and the labor-training camps, prisoners are beaten, work for long hours, and receive so little food that they rapidly lose weight.

Those accused of more serious offenses are transferred to prisons. Criminals who have committed felonies, which may be as minor as stealing food, are sent to the MPS's "reeducation camps" (*kyohwaso*), some of which are prison buildings surrounded by walls, barbed wire, and guard towers. The larger prisons consist of one or more villages located in remote mountain valleys and surrounded by barbed wire. Prisoners captured trying to escape are beaten so badly that they cannot stand and then dragged into camp to be executed by hanging or firing squad in front of other inmates, who may be forced to kick or throw stones at the corpses.

Former prisoners comment that upon arriving at a prison camp they were shocked to see walking skeletons, many hunched over and limping, wearing dirty rags; very soon the new prisoners come to look like this. The daily prison diet consists of at most five hundred grams (two cups) of corn, potatoes, or cabbage. Resourceful prisoners supplement their diet with rats, snakes, insects, grass, and tree bark. Families of prisoners can often send in food, which must be shared with the prison guards. Prisoners work in mines and logging camps for ten hours or more a day, seven days a week, with half a dozen holidays a year. Prison factories make cement, bricks, glass, textiles, shoes, bicycles, and furniture. Prisons also operate farms to feed the inmates. Because safety measures are lacking, prison workers are frequently maimed or killed on the job, especially in the mines.

Prisoners have little access to medical facilities. Those who are injured or become seriously ill may be sent to the prison sanatorium to die or released back to their families in order to save the prison the burden of burying them. Ill prisoners who recover at home are then returned to prison. The "reeducation" that prisoners receive is the same education that is imposed on all North Koreans: evening study of the works of the Kims. Prisoners are told that although they are guilty of failing to repay the leader for his benevolence and are not worthy to live, they may redeem themselves through hard work. It is unlikely that prisoners believe this justification for their harsh imprisonment. A survey of North Korean defectors conducted in 2017 estimated that about 25 percent of prisoners die before they are released and that 80 percent are undernourished. Specific causes of death include infectious diseases and digestive and respiratory problems.[21]

Bad as conditions are in the reeducation camp prisons, they are better than in the political detention camps known as "control and management centers" (*kwanliso*) run by the SSD. No dictatorship can do without its political prisons to isolate those accused of being disloyal to or critical of the leader; in North Korea's case, political prisons are for those who violate the Ten Principles and can't buy their way out of trouble. In response to accusations of running political prison camps, the North Korean government has patiently explained that "there can be no 'concentration camp' in the DPRK as it is a man-centered society where man is valued most."[22]

The rule of thumb is that once a person is sent to a political prison camp, he or she is there for life. Occasionally, however, political prisoners are released, and a few have even managed to defect and tell their stories to the outside world. Prison camp guards have also defected and identified the camps they served in from satellite imagery. Sensitive to bad publicity, the North Korean government has closed some of the camps and presumably relocated their inmates.

Political *kwanliso* facilities are much like the village *kyohwaso* prisons, with each camp, of which there are about half a dozen, housing anywhere from five thousand to fifty thousand inmates deep in mountain valleys. Since agents of the SSD rather than the MPS run the political prison system, inmates and their families are often committed without formal arrest, trial, conviction, or sentencing. Security agents suddenly appear and abduct political suspects from their homes, often in the middle of the night. Neighbors, friends, colleagues, and relatives are never told what happened to the missing, and anyone foolish enough to ask risks investigation. The North Koreans have a saying: "They die without the birds [in the daytime] or the mice [at night] knowing." Almost the only way out of political prison camps is suicide, which is a serious crime: families of prisoners who commit suicide are treated even worse than families of other prisoners, and prisoners who fail in their suicide attempts are tortured. Occasionally a prisoner is released from a political camp, often for unknown reasons. And anyone who has sufficient money to bribe the right officials has a chance of at least being moved to a reeducation camp.

Because entire families are sometimes incarcerated, prison camps have schools where the young prisoners are taught their lessons, including the all-important political lesson of worshipping the Kim family. Prisoners have no rights. Many die from beatings, starvation, or illness. Surviving for longer than a few months in a political prison requires a strong constitution, a certain amount of luck, or a family able to send the prisoner food. Some inmates survive for many years; others, especially the young and the old, die within a year.

Prisoners live several to a room in unheated wooden barracks. If an entire family is incarcerated, they may be permitted to build a little hut from scraps of wood, with a straw roof and a dirt floor. In winter, prisoners keep warm by huddling together; frostbite is common, resulting in amputated fingers, toes, and limbs. Some camps supply enough electricity to light a single bulb for an hour or two a day, while at other camps wooden torches provide the only illumination. Prisoners get a chance to wash their faces only a few times a month. They go to the bathroom in a hole in the ground. They wear the same clothes they came into the camp with, and when these wear out, they appropriate the clothing of dead prisoners. When approached by a guard, political prisoners must bow down or, in some prisons, get down on their knees. Infractions of camp rules, failure to complete work quotas, and similar offenses are punished by a reduction of food rations, which is an immediate threat to life because most prisoners live on the edge of starvation. Prisoners are beaten by guards and by other inmates on the guards' orders. Every prison has its special detention cell where prisoners are beaten and starved more severely. Few survive the experience, which is used as a warning to others.

North Korean prison guards are taught to look upon prisoners as animals. A former prisoner has titled her autobiographical book *Eyes of the Tailless Animals*.[23] Prisoners are sometimes addressed by their first names, but male prisoners are more frequently addressed as "this son of a bitch" (*ee ssaekkee*) and "this bastard" (*ee nom*), and female prisoners as "this low-class bitch" (*ee jaabnyon*) and "this bastard" (*ee nyon*). It probably does not help that the gaunt, crippled, dirty prisoners come to look like wild animals. Guards who are too kind to prisoners are themselves punished.

One might ask why prisoners who recognize that they are slowly and painfully dying do not fight back. The brutal truth is that any resistance on the part of prisoners not only results in harsher punishment but brings down punishment on the rest of the family, whether they are already in prison or not. Consequently, most prisoners see no way out and simply work until they die. In their own small way, their imprisoned lives support the continued dictatorship of the Kim regime, and by the same token, their future testimonies or the memories of their friends and families will one day put the final nail in the Kim regime's coffin.

CORRUPTION: THE CURRENCY OF THE REALM

Every defector from North Korea has stories to tell about the pervasive corruption throughout society. Every foreigner who has tried to do business in North Korea has his or her own stories to tell. Transparency International, which publishes the most widely cited annual index of corruption, consistently ranks North Korea at or near the bottom on its list of the world's most corrupt countries, along with a handful of African states that hardly have a functioning government.

Corruption, which can be simply defined as the abuse of official power for private gain, is an unavoidable defect of large bureaucracies that enjoy a monopoly over scarce resources (especially daily necessities) and that have the discretion to allocate those resources without lawful oversight.[24] Examples of corruption include bribery, embezzlement, fraud, extortion, blackmail, influence peddling, favoritism, and nepotism—all of which are rife in North Korean society.

The former communist regimes provided fertile ground for corruption with their government monopolies on consumer goods and their party supremacy over legal institutions. Countries with weak governments are also prone to corruption in the absence of effective law enforcement. Countries without independent news media and investigative organizations allow corruption to be hidden. And any country run by a dictator will almost inevitably suffer from corruption, as the dictator and his family and friends help themselves to whatever they want.

In North Korea, corruption most commonly occurs when government officials provide goods, services, exemptions, and opportunities in return for bribes. In addition to the revenue stream officials can tap into when they demand bribes from those they provide services to, these officials must also bribe their supervisors to stay out of trouble, because soliciting and accepting bribes is illegal (Article 230 of the 2012 criminal code). The chain of bribery goes all the way to the top, with higher officials living off illegal proceeds of lower officials. At the very top, the leader openly receives what are called "loyalty funds" that go to finance his luxurious lifestyle.

Bribes are required for permits that allow people to travel outside their county of residence, and those who are able to obtain such permits still must pay to pass through the numerous checkpoints that are set up on highways and at train stations. People must bribe officials to gain admission to universities, to be promoted on the job, and to get exemptions from their workplace duties so they can make money in the private economy. In the local markets, vendors must bribe market managers and inspectors for permission to sell their goods. People must also pay bribes to get better government housing, to avoid mandatory state labor, to avoid the draft or receive better treatment in the army, to obtain medical care, and to avoid arrest or receive better treatment in prison. Traders pay bribes to cross into China and return with foreign goods. The list goes on and on.

The collapse of state-centered socialism and the rise of capitalism in North Korea (and elsewhere) in the 1990s has somewhat changed the nature of corruption.[25] Now that the government has few goods to distribute, people go into the markets to buy what they need. Likewise, since the government's bankruptcy, government officials no longer receive payment in daily necessities and must rely on their salaries to survive—salaries that are and always have been negligible. At the 2019 rate of exchange, a mid-level official's monthly salary comes out to be less than ten dollars a month, which is not enough to feed his family for a week. Consequently, instead of asking for bribes in the form of favors or small gifts, officials now often demand monetary payment for whatever services they provide, and with this money they purchase what they need in the markets. Upper-level officials in Pyongyang still receive state distributions of daily necessities to supplement their meager income, but they want bribes in order to buy the luxury goods that are becoming popular among the newly wealthy commercial class.

The most corrupt person in North Korea is the leader, who needs cash to finance his lifestyle—this being especially the case for the second and third generation of Kims. Even when the government distribution system was functioning under Kim Il-sung, it was not used to supply the leader, who had his own private sources of domestic goods. His son and grandson have preferred foreign imports, including French wine, Belgian chocolates, Japanese sushi, German automobiles, Japanese electronics, and Italian yachts. The leader must reward his closest associates in order to keep their support, and yet he must not permit subordinates to become too wealthy for fear that they could use their wealth to undermine his position. The difficulty of curbing society-wide corruption when the top person is corrupt is embodied in the old Korean expression, "For the downstream to be clear, the upstream needs to be clear."

When officials are arrested for corruption, the arrest is usually motivated by politics, as when one official launches an investigation of another in order to eliminate a political rival. The leader himself occasionally accuses officials of corruption as an excuse for purging them. This is always a safe tactic because virtually all officials are corrupt. Sometimes the campaign targets a top official, such as Jang Song-taek, who was the second most powerful official in the country before being executed for treason and corruption. More commonly the leader will order that an anticorruption campaign be mounted as a gesture of good government. Teams of inspectors are sent out from Pyongyang to try to clean up particular cities. For example, in 2018 and 2019, yet another anticorruption drive commenced, with the party newspaper *Nodong Sinmun* announcing an "uncompromising struggle" against corrupt officials "regardless of their rank."[26] In his 2019 New Year's address, Kim Jong-un duplicitously urged officials to "intensify the struggle to eradicate both serious and trivial instances of abuse of power, bureaucratism and corruption, which would wreak havoc on the harmonious whole of the Party and the masses and undermine the socialist system."[27] Millions of these officials hoped that the campaign would not touch them, and by and large their hopes were justified.

Raids conducted by inspectors sent out from Pyongyang temporarily reduce corruption but have no lasting effect. While the visiting inspectors are in town, merchants lie low and local officials suspend their usual bribery activities. If the inspectors stay for long, local officials and merchants become acquainted with them and buy them off, because the visitors need money as much as anyone else. A few unlucky people will be arrested to show that the inspectors are doing their job, but they can usually bribe their way out of serious trouble. It might not be inaccurate to say that, for inspectors, the goal of anticorruption efforts is not to eliminate corruption but to profit from new bribery opportunities.

The tentacles of North Korean corruption reach beyond the country's borders. Corruption affects foreign businesspeople who want to buy, sell, or manufacture in North Korea. Money must be paid by foreigners to arrange legitimate political meetings, the most famous case being the reported half billion dollars that South Korea had to pay in 2000 to get its first summit meeting with North Korea. Bribes are also required to accomplish humanitarian goals: North Korea demanded the reopening of the lucrative (for North Korea) South Korean concession in the Kumgang resort area in return for letting aging North and South Korean family members meet for a few days.

North Koreans who have defected to South Korea are not beyond the grasp of corrupt officials. Police extort money from the families of defectors in return for allowing them to communicate with their departed family members in South Korea, and the middlemen who arrange for these communications are taxed as well. Most defectors clandestinely send money back to their families, and as much as half of this money goes to the brokers who arrange the transfers and to the police who extort money from the brokers.[28]

The North Korean people's acceptance of corruption as a fact of life bodes ill for their future. How can they join the international marketplace with such a reputation? And what will happen when the North is finally reunited with the South, where corruption is not as widespread? Systemic corruption has robbed the North Korean government of its legitimacy in the eyes of its citizens and the foreign community. The former US special envoy for North Korean human rights may not have been far off the mark when he labeled North Korea a "corrupt mafia state."[29]

LIES: SECOND NATURE TO THE REGIME

All governments lie. Government officials lie to the news media, to their citizens, to other governments, to each other, and sometimes to themselves. That is, they say things they do not believe are true in order to mislead others. Government officials also utter falsehoods, saying things that are not true because they have not made an adequate effort to find the truth. It is not hard to find reasons to lie.[30] Those who tell lies gain a measure of informational power over those being lied to—liars have a superior knowledge of what's what in the world. Lies are also useful for impression management in that they make government officials look like they're doing a better job than they actually are.

Those who are lied to are rarely pleased. When they finally discover the truth, they typically become disillusioned, disappointed, or even angry. In the future, they will discount the truth value of whatever the liar says. If it is the government that is lying, they will lose trust in their government, and they may even come to distrust society in general. After all, if a government official is lying, maybe those who are in less responsible positions are also lying. Trust is a "social good"—something that is necessary to keep society functioning.[31]

The North Korean government probably lies more than any other government currently in power. It lies to the outside world and to its own people. Arguably the damage to its people is greater than to the outside world, because the world knows the truth and has long since ceased to believe much of what the North Korean government says. The North Korean people have much less information on which to judge whether they are being lied to. They are living in a fog. While they stay in their country, they can only grope for the truth. If they defect to another country, they find themselves at an informational disadvantage because the world they were told about is not the world they are now living in.

Why does the North Korean government so frequently resort to lies? First, because reality, especially economic reality, reflects so badly on the government that it quite naturally prefers fiction. Second, given that the government controls all the media, there are no independent news organizations to act as a watchdog over the government's communications or to provide alternative information that would enable people to determine the truth for themselves. As for the lies it tells to the international community, the government knows that its political reputation is so low that it can hardly do itself any further damage. And finally, government organizations are assigned the task of disseminating certain propaganda themes, which they continue to do regardless of the effect the messages have on audiences. The same fictional themes, such as the superiority of socialism, have continued to be mindlessly churned out for decades.

If one were to list the top ten lies the North Korean media have been telling over the years, the list might look something like this:

1. The Kim family is an irreplaceable family of heroes.
2. Socialism is the bedrock of the economy; world capitalism is doomed.

3. All the policies of the Workers' Party of Korea are absolutely correct.
4. *Juche*—that is, doing things our own way—is the correct guiding principle for all endeavors.
5. North Koreans are the only people who are truly free because they are guided by *juche*.
6. South Koreans, on the other hand, have always been slaves of the American imperialists.
7. The United States and South Korea started the Korean War, which was won by the North Koreans under the brilliant generalship of Kim Il-sung.
8. The North Korean military is the strongest in the world—and needs to be because the United States is always trying to start another war.
9. North Korea's nuclear weapons are a guarantee of future peace.
10. North Korea's prestige in the international community has always been high.

Who believes these lies? The international community largely ignores North Korean propaganda, although throughout the world there are a few people, usually virulently anti-American, who profess to believe North Korea. As for the North Korean people, only children believe most of the lies, although many people with responsible positions in the government and party are so wedded to its future that they appear to have convinced themselves that some of these lies are actually true.

For most North Koreans of sound mind, the lies are unconvincing. They can compare what they are told with the economically poor and politically controlled lives they actually lead. They also have access to increasing amounts of information from outside the government propaganda machine. And like people in all countries, they are frequently dissatisfied with and skeptical of their government. Publicly disputing government lies is suicidal in the North Korean police state. So they joke about them in private, but mostly they ignore whatever the government tells them.

How will the North Korean people react when, after the Kim regime finally falls, they are able to discover the truths that have always been known to the outside world? In Russia, the truth about Stalin temporarily dimmed his reputation, but he is now fondly remembered by many Russians, who miss the economic security the state formerly provided. The experience of Americans during the Donald Trump presidency has shown that a large segment of the population does not care whether the president lies or not. This indifference is not an indication that they have adopted a "postmodernist" relativistic view of truth, but rather that what is true or false is of no interest to them—except on a personal level. People don't want their friends or family members to lie to them, but getting at the truth about the national economy, global warming, or other seemingly remote topics is not considered to be part of their personal world. They don't realize that they are paying a price for their lack of interest in pursuing the truth and that their children will pay a price as well. For their part, the only safe response for North Koreans in the face of an avalanche of government lies is to put their nose to the grindstone and not ask any questions.

Chapter Four

Human Rights

An Alien Concept

POLITICAL CLASS: LOYALTY TO THE REGIME

All societies have classes of one sort or another. Because communists came to power in a revolution of the working class against the bourgeoisie, societies like North Korea that were originally based on the communist model have at least two classes. Even today the North Korean media speak of the "uncompromising and merciless struggle" that the working class must wage against class enemies that include "remnants of the overthrown exploiting class and reactionaries."[1]

Nevertheless, North Koreans are not classified according to their loyalty to communism or to a political class but rather according to their loyalty to the Kim regime. From the moment he took power, Kim Il-sung based his political purges on his assessment of loyalty rather than on political leanings or professional competence. A 1993 secret manual on political classification lists loyalty to the regime as the most important determinant of class membership: "Thoroughly ensuring the personal safety and health and longevity of the great leader [Kim Il-sung] and the respected and beloved comrade supreme commander [Kim Jong-il] and protecting their high authority and status in every way possible is the most important principle."[2] In 1958, the entire population was politically classified, with successive classifications culminating in a system of three classes and fifty subclasses, which were announced by Kim Il-sung at the 1970 party congress. It seems the three-class structure has generally been maintained since then, with some minor updates.

When North Koreans speak of a person's *songbun* (literally, personal or individual class membership), they are referring to a family's political history.[3] The Kim regime has classified people into approximately twenty-five *songbun* categories, with "revolutionaries" (who fought against the Japanese during the colonial period) at the top, "poor farmers" (during the same period) somewhat further down, small businessmen further down still, and Korean bureaucrats who worked for the Japanese at the very bottom of the list.

The regime then assigns people to three political classes and fifty subclasses based on their *songbun*. Foreigners have usually labeled these three classes the core class, the wavering class, and the hostile class, estimated by South Korean authorities to constitute 28 percent, 45 percent, and 27 percent of the North Korean population, respectively.[4] The secret document referred to above used slightly different terminology: the basic masses, the complex masses, and the residual elements of the hostile class.

The Kim regime considers members of the basic or core class, many of whom are party cadres, to be its loyal supporters. The regime counts on the wavering or complex class for nominal support but fears that enemies of socialism or the waverers' human frailties could lead some of them astray. Members of the hostile class are suspected of silently opposing socialism and, more important, being disloyal to the Kim family.

The fifty subclasses are quite detailed. For example, the basic masses include the revolutionaries, wounded war veterans, their family members, members of the Workers' Party of Korea, and farmers. Members of the complex masses, who are not considered to be outright enemies of the regime but do carry historical or contemporary political baggage, include those who have tried to evade conscription, those who have attempted to defect, and those accused of practicing religion. The residual elements of the hostile class include those who were wealthy landlords or businessmen; those who professed pro-Japanese, pro–South Korean, or pro-American sentiments; those who were "religious activists"; and those who were members of political factions opposed to the Kim regime. These classifications are largely based on people's activities many years ago, but class membership is extended to their descendants.

Under the Kim regime, those who held the highest social, political, and economic positions in precommunist Korean society became members of the lowest political class, whereas many members of the low class moved up to the new privileged class. This was certainly the case for Kim Il-sung and his military comrades, who became the leading figures in North Korea despite coming from working-class and middle-class backgrounds.

Like any caste system, *songbun* is based primarily on family membership. Core-class members pass their privileges on to their children. An individual's political mistakes can lead to a downgrading of *songbun*, but meritorious service can rarely move a person into a higher *songbun* category. The political system, based as it is on loyalty to the Kim family, bears a striking resemblance to political and economic systems in ancient kingdoms. There is also a resemblance to political hierarchies in the twentieth-century communist states, which were dominated by the communist *nomenklatura*. However, unlike in other Communist Party states, in North Korea a single family kept power generation after generation, and so the form of loyalty that counted most was personal rather than political.

A person's *songbun* has many ramifications. People with better *songbun* get better food rations (when any rations are available) and receive better medical care. *Songbun* largely determines what kind of job a person can aspire to. People with "bad" *songbun* cannot expect to be employed in any job that has decision-making powers or that is part of the communication infrastructure—positions that would enable them to have a negative impact on the stability of the regime. Instead, they are limited to jobs that are either menial or at best administrative. Such people are unlikely to be accepted as members in the Workers' Party of Korea or to become military officers or directors of state organizations. People with bad *songbun* aren't likely to be accepted to any of the top universities, even if they have an excellent academic record. They rarely receive permission to live in the capital city of Pyongyang or anywhere near the border with China, for fear they might defect. People with the worst *songbun* are forced to live in the countryside, especially in the least developed parts of the country such as the mountainous east. And lawbreakers with poor *songbun* can expect to receive harsher prison sentences than those with good *songbun*.

Not surprisingly, *songbun* also influences one's social life, including marriage prospects. Few parents of "good" families would approve of their sons or daughters marrying someone with bad *songbun*. Those who have been expelled from Pyongyang because of a downgrading of their political status may even be shunned by neighbors in the small communities to which they are sent.

Whenever someone applies for a job, school admission, or membership in an organization, officials investigate that person's *songbun*. Whenever the leader travels around the country making inspections, the people living nearby are investigated. And whenever a social or political problem is detected—a rash of crimes or defections, for example—officials are likely to review the *songbun* of local residents. Beyond this, it appears that periodic blanket inspections have been ordered in cities and even throughout the country when new identity cards are to be issued, although how thoroughly these investigations are conducted by police and party officials is difficult to say.

Inequality is obviously implicit in the *songbun* concept. Although Article 65 of the North Korean constitution asserts that "citizens shall have equal rights in all spheres of the state and social life," the constitution also emphasizes at numerous points that the working class, as represented by the leader and the party, is in the vanguard of North Korea's ongoing socialist revolution. For example, Article 8 boasts that "the social system of the DPRK is a man-centered social system whereby the working popular masses are the masters of everything, and everything in society serves the working popular masses. The state shall safeguard the interests of, and respect and protect the human rights of the working people, including workers, farmers, soldiers, and working intellectuals, who have been freed from exploitation and oppression and have become the masters of the state and society." Other people are apparently on their own.

Since the mid-1990s, when the government ran out of food to distribute, millions of North Koreans have gone into business for themselves, sometimes very successfully. Today, the economically disadvantaged segment of the population is not just those with bad *songbun* but also those who work for the party, state, and military and have not been able to get into a part-time moneymaking business. Millions of North Koreans who have gone into business have earned a substantial amount of money (by North Korean standards) and are using their newfound wealth to bribe officials for privileges that would otherwise be restricted to those with good *songbun*. With money, it is sometimes possible for a person with bad *songbun* to get into a decent university, receive permission to live in Pyongyang, or convince a judge to hand down a lighter sentence.

In short, the new economy has created a class of people with a different base of status and power. Being wealthy is not the same as having good *songbun* and can rarely buy it, but it provides a means of ameliorating the effects of bad *songbun*. People with new money must still rely on those with good *songbun* to intercede for them. They cannot even succeed in business without the cooperation of officials. But in North Korea money has become an important determinant of life chances, just as it is in capitalistic societies.

DEFECTORS: AN EXIT FOR PEOPLE WITHOUT VOICE

Unhappy people do not necessarily try to change their situation in life to make themselves happier. If they are prisoners, for example, they must make do with what they have. The people who seek change are those who believe they can find a practical alternative that will make them happier. For years the North Korean people, growing hungrier by the day, didn't realize they had a choice. The borders of their country were tightly sealed, and little information came in from the outside world. Their government told them that they were better off than people in other countries, especially in South Korea, and they believed it.

North Koreans today know better. Except for the one or two million elite supporters of the Kim regime, most North Koreans escape from the life that the Kims have fashioned for them in one of two ways. The majority escape psychologically by focusing on their personal lives and paying as little attention to the regime as possible. A relatively small number of other North Koreans have chosen to escape physically by fleeing the country. These people are referred to by a number of terms, the most popular being "defectors." The regime calls them "traitors" and punishes them accordingly if they are caught. Local officials, not wanting to take responsibility for lax supervision, often simply refer to them as "missing." In South Korea they have been given different names over the years. Before 1993 they were often called *gwuisunja* ("people who voluntarily came to South Korea"). For the next ten years, the favorite name was simply *talbukja* (literally, "defector"). For several years beginning in 2005, they became known as *saetomin* ("new settlers"), and since then, either *talbukja* or *Pukhan italjumin* ("citizens who defected from North Korea") seem to be the most popular terms.

North Koreans cannot legally leave the country except under special circumstances, because the regime does not want them to be exposed to foreign environments and ideas. Those who choose to leave anyway have three choices. They can try to cross into South Korea through the demilitarized zone (DMZ), which is blocked by soldiers and minefields; the few who have taken this route have been soldiers themselves. A second alternative is to go by fishing boat down the west or east coasts. A few people, mostly fishermen, have made this attempt, but North Korean fishing boats are not seaworthy and naval boats patrol the sea near the border. Almost all defectors choose instead to cross the northern border into China, which means they are traveling in exactly the opposite direction from their ultimate destination of South Korea.

Until the 1990s the Kim regime did not have to worry much about defections because economic life in North Korea was at least bearable. True, political freedoms were more restricted than in South Korea; but Koreans had never in their thousands of years of history experienced political freedom, so it was not something they missed. And in any case freedoms under South Korean governments until the 1980s were restricted as well. After liberation in 1945, many Koreans in the North did not want to live under communism, and an estimated 580,000 of them moved south across the open border between 1945 and the beginning of the Korean War, with another half million coming down during the chaos of the war. After that, the border was closed. Over the next forty years, only about six hundred North Koreans defected to South Korea. However, beginning in the mid-1990s a population that had been growing hungrier every year was faced with a famine caused by floods and droughts. Hundreds of thousands died from lack of food and medical attention. Now was the time for North Koreans to think about making a drastic change in their situation.

The Kim regime, realizing that it could not feed its people, temporarily relaxed its hold on them, making it possible in the late 1990s and early 2000s for defectors to cross into China to look for food. Although this travel went against official policy, starving North Korean border guards were willing to let people cross the border in return for payment of a small bribe or food brought back from China. Of the hundreds of thousands who crossed the border, most spent just a few days in China before returning. Some remained for a short period of illegal residency. Others traveled through China and eventually made it to South Korea, where they were officially counted as defectors.

In 2002, over one thousand North Koreans arrived in South Korea, and by 2007 over two thousand were arriving annually; the peak defection year was 2009, when almost three thousand North Koreans reached South Korea, even though by then the North Korean economy was improving. When Kim Jong-un took charge of the country in 2012, one of his priorities was to reduce the flow of defections by strengthening border controls, just as China was cracking down on defections on its side of the border. Beginning in that year, defections dropped below two thousand, and since then the annual count has been around one thousand.

Until the 1990s a large proportion of defectors were soldiers, who knew how to cross the DMZ with a fair chance of not getting killed. Diplomats traveling abroad found it relatively easy to defect, although few did so. Some of the more unusual defections included three North Korean pilots who flew their MiGs to South Korea in the 1950s, 1960s, and 1970s, receiving a warm welcome and a handsome financial reward. The highest-profile official known to defect was Hwang Jang-yop, a former cabinet member and the brains behind North Korea's *juche* philosophy. In 1997, Hwang and his associate, Kim Tuk-hong, defected in Beijing while returning from an official visit to Tokyo.

A few members of the Kim family have also defected, including Kim Jong-il's second wife, Song Hye-rim, and her older sister, who eluded their minders during a stay in Moscow in 1996. Kim Jong-il's oldest son, Kim Jong-nam, fell out of favor with his father and was allowed to live in exile in China and Macau for many years. In 2017 he was murdered during a visit to Malaysia, apparently on orders from his younger brother, the current ruler. Rumors of defections by other diplomats and officials have occasionally surfaced, but if the rumors were true, the defectors (and the South Korean government) have managed to keep the details out of the press. Whenever South Korea announces the defection of a noteworthy person, the North Korean media wage a vigorous campaign to denigrate the defector, not only calling him or her a traitor "for the ages" but adding so many unsavory details about the defector's personal life as to suggest that the North Korean bureaucratic vetting system is notoriously weak and that, in any case, the North Koreans should be happy to be rid of the scoundrel.

Some defectors have arrived in South Korea in groups. A hundred North Korean loggers working in Russia defected in a group in 1994 by taking refuge in the South Korean embassy in Moscow. In 2002 a number of groups of defectors rushed into foreign embassies, consulates, or foreign schools in China, where they were given asylum and then transported to South Korea. In 2007 a total of 468 North Korean defectors who had traveled through China to Vietnam in separate groups were flown to South Korea in two jumbo jets. And in 2016 twelve waitresses and their manager at a North Korean restaurant in China were spirited to South Korea by the South Korean intelligence service. In most of these cases the North Korean media accused South Korea of abducting their citizens.

The great majority of defections are by ordinary North Koreans who want a better life or simply to avoid starvation. Most defectors live in one of the provinces near the Chinese border, and they come from all walks of life: farmers, laborers, students, and the unemployed. About 70 percent of them are women, who find it easier to slip away unnoticed, and who also find it easier to secure illegal employment in China as servants or prostitutes. Many become the illegal brides of older Chinese farmers. In 2019 a human rights group estimated that 60 percent of North Korean women in China were involved in the sex trade: 50 percent as prostitutes, 30 percent sold into forced marriages, and 15 percent employed in cybersex operations.[5] Many of these women were single, but some were married and were simply trying to earn money to send back to their families. Life in China is difficult for all defectors because the Chinese government considers them to be illegal aliens rather than economic or political refugees. Defectors are sometimes caught by Chinese police or by roving bands of North Korean security agents and forcibly returned to North Korea, where they are imprisoned. While living in China illegally, they can be mistreated and blackmailed by their Chinese spouses or employers.

South Koreans have conducted surveys to learn why North Koreans attempt their difficult journey to freedom. As one would expect, in the latter half of the 1990s the main reason for defecting was to find food. Interestingly, many defectors were not originally planning to go to South Korea. Instead, they crossed the border into China to look for food, and while they were there, they learned that economic conditions were good in South Korea and that South Koreans were not impoverished and oppressed slaves of the Americans, as they had always been taught. As economic conditions in North Korea gradually improved (although to this day malnutrition is still a fact of life for millions), North Koreans defected simply because they wanted a better economic life. Many young defectors are lured by the glamour and excitement of life in South Korea as seen in videos smuggled into North Korea.

As more North Koreans fled to the South, a new motive emerged: the pull of those family members who had already defected. One of the first things defectors do upon arriving in South Korea is try to get their family members out. A 2006 survey found that almost half of North Koreans arriving in South Korea said they had been helped to defect by family members who had previously defected.[6] A system of brokers working in China and communicating with brokers in North Korea make it possible to set up an underground railway to bring family members out, with the cost running into thousands of dollars. By this method, wives can bring out children and spouses. Friends and neighbors hear about the successful defection and begin to realize that escaping from their predicament is possible.

Defection from North Korea is not something to be taken up lightly. Apart from the logistical difficulties and the emotional strain of leaving family and friends behind, most North Koreans are attached to their homeland, and most even seem to believe that their country's economic problems are not necessarily inherent in their political system but are caused by foreign embargoes. Defectors know that the family members they leave behind are likely to be viewed with suspicion by the police and may even be evicted from their home and sent to live in an even more remote part of the country. Family members face extortion threats from the police, who realize that the family now has a "wealthy" relative living in the South.

The route that most North Koreans take to South Korea is long and dangerous. Fleeing across the Yalu or Tumen Rivers to China is relatively easy, although more difficult than it was before Kim Jong-un took power. Once in China the defector needs to find food, housing, and employment, perhaps arranged by a broker or provided by a sanctuary church. Then arrangements must be made to travel three thousand miles from the northern part of China down to the southern border. This trip is a project that requires contacts and an amount of money that may take several years to accumulate.

Defectors generally travel south through China in small groups led by professional guides. They head for Vietnam or Laos, where payment of bribes enables them to cross into Thailand, which recognizes them as legitimate refugees. Once there, they surrender to the Thai police, are placed in temporary camps, and, after they have been granted a visa, are flown out by the South Korean government. Once in South Korea, they are taken into custody by the National Intelligence Service and placed in a Hanawon (One Community) facility for several months, during which they are interviewed about their background and given an orientation about life in South Korea. After completing their orientation, they are released into the general population with a modest stipend and housing allowance and an official contact who acts somewhat like a benign parole officer. Various defector and church organizations help them if they do not have family already in the country.

Most South Koreans look down on North Koreans as country bumpkins and avoid becoming involved with them. For that matter, the attitude of the South Korean government toward defectors varies depending on whether it is "conservative" or "liberal." Liberal governments, which have held office from 1998 to 2008 and since 2017, are solicitous of the feelings and concerns of the Kim regime in the North and consider defectors to be a hindrance to improving inter-Korean relations. Yet many defectors have thrived in their new home, and in the 2020 national election, two defectors even became members of the National Assembly—as representatives of the political party opposing the liberal administration.

Defectors face a host of problems in their new country. They need to find a job, make friends, and perhaps get married. They speak with a distinctive accent and use a somewhat different vocabulary than South Koreans, so they are immediately identifiable. Most defectors suffer from a variety of chronic diseases that were not treated in the North, including parasites and tuberculosis, and they may develop psychological problems including depression and anxiety. The majority discover that life in individualistic South Korea is more difficult than they had expected, but very few would want to return to North Korea until its government has changed.

The flight of over thirty-three thousand North Koreans (by the end of 2019) to South Korea, with a very small number taking refuge in other countries (e.g., Canada, the United Kingdom, and the United States), is an indictment of the policies of the North Korean regime as well as a test of how South Korea will be able to cope with eventual Korean reunification. The South Korean government considers all Koreans living on the peninsula to be South Korean citizens. Compared to the four and a half million East Germans who fled to the West between World War II and German unification (about half of them coming before the Berlin Wall was built in 1961), the number of North Koreans reaching the South is a mere trickle. Should that trickle become a flood, it will put severe strains on both North and South Korean societies—strains that the South Koreans, at least, are not yet prepared to cope with.

HUMAN RIGHTS REPUTATION:
AN INTERNATIONAL DISGRACE

As illustrated in the review of North Korea's political class system and its treatment of defectors, North Korea's human rights situation is dismal. This is to be expected insofar as the country is run for the benefit of the leader, not the people. The regime's human rights policies are embedded in the structure of its dictatorial rule. The people live under the authority of the government, which serves the party, which is controlled by the leader. Before the 1990s, foreigners could only get a glimpse of the regime's oppression of its people; however, once North Koreans began to defect, they were able to tell their stories. With over thirty-three thousand North Koreans now living in South Korea, the stories have accumulated and validate each other. Despite the regime's claims that North Korea is a paradise on earth for its people, the facts of the case clearly show otherwise.

At least through the 1970s, the Kim regime adequately promoted what have been called collective human rights. All able-bodied males had an assigned job, most received a minimum of daily necessities distributed free of charge (in return for working), and basic health care and education were available at little or no cost. True, people had no freedom of choice, but as long as they obeyed the party they could survive. Yet there was a darker side, insofar as several hundred thousand Koreans languished in prison camps, often for political crimes. By the late 1980s the system of collective social security was disappearing. People began to gain a measure of freedom while the regime was distracted by its economic problems.

Every year, even when South Korea is under the administration of a left-leaning president, the government's Korean Institute for National Unification publishes a book-length *White Paper on Human Rights in North Korea*, with evidence based largely on the testimony of defectors.[7] In its chapters "The Reality of Civil and Political Rights" and "The Reality of Economic and Social Rights," which parallel the UN's two human rights covenants, the white paper discusses the serious shortcomings of individual rights under the Kim regimes, including deficiencies in the rights to life, liberty, security, fair trial, humane treatment in detention, privacy, movement and travel, and freedom of residence. Also lacking are freedom of thought, conscience, expression, and religion; freedom of the press and publication; freedom of assembly and association; and the right to political participation. Even the most basic human rights, such as the right to food, health, work, education, and social security, elude many North Koreans. The white paper also discusses grave shortcomings in the rights of women, children, and persons with disabilities. Even though the North Korean constitution explicitly grants North Koreans all of these rights, they hardly exist in everyday life.

The UN has frequently criticized North Korea for its human rights practices. In 1981 North Korea joined the UN's International Covenant on Economic, Social, and Cultural Rights and its International Covenant on Civil and Political Rights. After submitting its first periodic report to the UN

Commission on Human Rights in 1984, North Korea delayed submitting its next report until 2000. In 2003, the commission adopted its first resolution citing North Korea for human rights violations on a broad range of issues. A second resolution, passed in 2004, requested the appointment of a special rapporteur to monitor the DPRK's human rights situation, and beginning in 2005 this office began issuing critical reports. The Office of the High Commissioner on Human Rights also publishes reports.

A third commission resolution on North Korea, which passed in 2005, recommended that the issue be taken up by the General Assembly, which adopted a resolution concerning North Korean human rights later that year. The draft resolution was supported by eighty-eight countries and opposed by twenty-one, with sixty abstentions (including South Korea) and twenty-two absentees. Virtually all the world's developed countries supported the resolution, whereas most of the countries that opposed the resolution had their own serious human rights problems, including China and Russia. Most African countries either abstained or were absent from the vote. Since 2005, the UN has continued to pass resolutions criticizing North Korea's human rights policies.

In 2013 the UN Human Rights Council appointed a three-person Commission of Inquiry to investigate North Korea's human rights situation. The commission's report received wide press coverage when it was released in 2014, although it cannot be said that the findings came as any surprise to those who had been watching North Korea over the years.[8] The UN high commissioner for human rights urged that the report findings be "treated with the greatest urgency, as they suggest that crimes against humanity of an unimaginable scale continue to be committed in the DPRK."[9] He also called upon the international community to "use all mechanisms at its disposal" to halt the violations, including referral to the International Criminal Court. Subsequent calls for Kim Jong-un to be brought before the court met with resistance from China, whose foreign ministry issued the usual meaningless advice on North Korea, namely that the issue "should be solved through constructive dialogue."[10]

Few foreign governments have pushed the Kim regime to improve its human rights policies. One might think that the South Korean government would be actively engaged in human rights initiatives, but this has only been true of conservative South Korean governments. The liberal governments in office from 1998 to 2008 and since 2017 have been less than enthusiastic about raising the issue. In a 2000 BBC interview several months after his summit meeting with Kim Jong-il, President Kim Dae-jung explained that he "would not press the issues of human rights and democracy at this early stage as it could be detrimental to building trust" between the two Koreas.[11]

In a 2003 interview with the *Washington Post*, Kim Dae-jung's successor, Roh Moo-hyun (who would meet Kim Jong-il four years later) said, "Rather than confronting the Kim Jong-il regime over human rights of a small number of people, I think it is better for us to open up the regime through dialogue. I think this will ultimately bring broader protection of human rights for North Korean people as a whole."[12] Roh's reference to a "small number" is particularly unfortunate. President Moon Jae-in, a former human rights lawyer who took office in 2017 and met Kim Jong-un three times in 2018, has continued his leftist predecessors' policy of not criticizing North Korea for its human rights practices.

Whereas American presidents have strongly criticized North Korea's human rights situation, they have been more focused on limiting North Korea's weapons of mass destruction (WMDs) than on improving the human rights of the North Korean people. Perhaps President George W. Bush's labeling of North Korea as a member of the "Axis of Evil" and charging it with starving its people was the highest-profile American criticism of North Korea.

President Barack Obama, who served for eight years after President George W. Bush, was not noted for his foreign policy initiatives, especially with regard to North Korea. He was well aware of the plight of the North Korean people and the danger that nuclear negotiations would leave them behind, but he felt constrained by the prevailing military situation: "Our capacity to affect change in North Korea is somewhat limited because you've got a one-million person army, and they have nuclear technologies and missiles. . . . The answer's not going to be a military solution."[13] Instead, President Obama opted for a "strategic patience" approach that included waiting for the regime to collapse and trying to hasten that collapse by providing funding to send outside information to the North Korean people. Even while the Obama administration increased economic sanctions on North Korea, the Kim regime seemed to be largely impervious to pressure.

President Donald Trump sidelined the policy experts and harbored the belief that he could change the Kim regime through his powers of persuasion. Mercurial in the extreme, he went from threatening war (boasting of the "red button" on his desk) to embracing Kim Jong-un. In his speech to the UN in September 2017, Trump said, "No one has shown more contempt for other nations and for the well-being of their own people than the depraved regime in North Korea. It is responsible for the starvation deaths of millions of North Koreans, and for the imprisonment, torture, killing, and oppression of countless more." President Trump continued his criticism in his 2018 State of the Union speech: "No regime has oppressed its own citizens more totally or brutally than the cruel dictatorship in North Korea. Past experience has taught us that complacency and concessions only invite aggression and provocation. I will not repeat the mistakes of past administrations that got us into this dangerous position."

However, after meeting with Kim Jong-un later that year, President Trump changed his tune. In September 2018 he told a crowd of supporters that after exchanging letters, he and Kim had "fallen in love."[14] In a February 2019 interview he described Kim as "a real personality. He's very smart . . . and he's a real leader. . . . He likes me, I like him. Some people say I shouldn't like him. Why shouldn't I like him?"[15] In December 2019, President Trump said, "Chairman Kim has a great and beautiful vision for his country, and only the United States, with me as president, can make that vision come true. He will do the right thing [in regards to nuclear and missile programs] because he is far too smart not to, and he does not want to disappoint his friend, President Trump."[16]

On the return flight home from his February 2019 summit meeting with Kim, a Fox News interviewer reminded the president that Kim was "a killer, he's clearly executing people." Trump replied, "Hey, when you take over a country, tough country, with tough people, and you take it over from your father, I don't care who you are, what you are, how much of an advantage you have. If you can do that at 27 years old, I mean that's one in 10,000 that could do that. So, he's a very smart guy. He's a great negotiator. But I think we understand each other." In the same interview, when reminded that Kim had done "some really bad things," the president said, "Yeah, but so have a lot of other people done some really bad things. I mean, I could go through a lot of nations where a lot of bad things were done."[17]

Every March, the US State Department issues its annual Country Reports on Human Rights Practices, and every year it singles out North Korea as one of the countries with an especially poor record. Adding to the pressure put on North Korea by international organizations like Human Rights Watch, Amnesty International, and Refugees International, various American groups such as the Committee for Human Rights in North Korea and Freedom House have lobbied for a stronger response to human rights abuses. In 2004 the US Congress passed the North Korean Human Rights Act, which has been renewed under later administrations. When it was first passed, North Korea warned that its passage was a hostile act and a virtual declaration of war.

When North Korea is criticized for its human rights policies, the Kim regime asserts that human rights standards are specific to each country rather than being universal. "All the countries of the world differ from each other in traditions, nationality, culture, history of social development; and human rights standards and ways of ensuring them vary according to specific conditions of each country. . . . The human rights standards in the DPRK are precisely what the Korean people like and what is in accordance with their requirement and interests."[18] The regime also insists that the most important right any people can enjoy is national sovereignty, and the governments of many other countries, especially autocratic governments in the third world, would agree on that point.

The Kim regime also criticizes the United States for its human rights failings and boasts that North Korea has absolutely no problems in this regard. At the end of 2019, in response to another American government criticism, KCNA charged that "the U.S., a cesspit of all sorts of human rights violations including murder, rape, racial discrimination, maltreatment of immigrants, can neither be justified in poking its nose into other's internal affairs, nor is it entitled to. Our country is a people-centered socialist state where the entire people fully enjoy genuine freedom and rights, being masters of the country."[19]

No significant improvement in human rights can be expected under a dictatorial regime such as North Korea's. Extralegal social control mechanisms are a part of its totalitarian society. Nor can one expect that other governments will vigorously press North Korea on this issue. China is governed by a communist party that sympathizes with the desire of the Workers' Party of Korea to monopolize power. Under three liberal pro-engagement presidents, South Korea has extended economic and moral support to the Kim regime, and in any case it has little leverage over Pyongyang. Japan's poor relations with both Koreas force it to keep its distance. The countries of the European Union are far away. The United States is preoccupied with the Kim regime's nuclear weapons program. The UN cannot take decisive action because many of its members agree with the Kim regime's argument that the first principle of international relations is national sovereignty. Consequently, the prospect of freedom for the North Korean people does not look good. Even if the North Korean economy recovers, the Kim regime is likely to imitate neighboring China and prevent its people from exercising any meaningful political or social power.

Chapter Five

The Military

"Pillar" of Society

WEAPONS AND STRATEGY: A PORCUPINE DEFENSE

From the day the Russians handed over North Korea to Kim Il-sung, a young guerrilla fighter, the country has characterized itself as a militarized state. An article in the party newspaper during the Kim Jong-il "military-first" (*songun*) era aptly characterizes the regime's view of the country: "The People's Army is the pillar and main force of the revolution and of the military, the party, the state and the people."[1] Kim Il-sung was first introduced to the North Korean people as a great general, although he was only a captain in the Soviet army. In the early 1960s, a decade after his troops lost the Korean War (only to be saved by a million Chinese "volunteers"), Kim explicitly set North Korea on the course that it follows today with his "Four Military Lines." His son, Kim Jong-il, who also styled himself as a great general although he had never served in the military, made military-first politics the centerpiece of his administration. And his son, Kim Jong-un, more sophisticated in public relations than his father, promoted a parallel-development (*byungjin*) policy of simultaneously pursuing guns and butter—until 2018 when he announced that the military goal of making North Korea a nuclear weapons state had been achieved.

The Kim regime embraces militarization for both domestic and foreign policy reasons. Domestically, a population organized along military lines is much easier to control than a free and open society. Moreover, people living

Political postcard from 2010, reading, "Let's solidly realize our military-first ideology." *Wikimedia Commons, by John Pavelka, CC-BY-2.0.*

in fear of foreign attack—and the North Korean people are told that their country is on the brink of war—will be less concerned about their poor living conditions than people who believe their country is peacefully secure. On the international front, it must be remembered that the Korean Peninsula has been invaded many times in its history, including by the United States and its allies during the Korean War. Even in peacetime, until very recently, South Korea officially viewed North Korea as its "main enemy" because of the Kim regime's military provocations and its threats to finish the job it started in the Korean War. For the same reasons, the United States remains hostile toward the Kim regime. American forces are stationed in South Korea, Japan, Guam, and the seas surrounding the Korean Peninsula, and the United States regularly conducts defensive and offensive drills against North Korea.

From a military standpoint, North Korea must deal with several challenges. It has only half the population of South Korea and an economy only about one-fiftieth as large. Its conventional weapons are mostly hand-me-downs from Russia and China or domestically produced weapons based on old Russian and Chinese designs. North Korea's perennial shortage of money seriously hinders military maintenance and training. During the Cold War, the Kim regime might have been able to count on China and the Soviet Union for military alliance support, as it did during the Korean War, but these two neighboring countries have grown impatient with the Kim regime's backward economic policies and its pursuit of nuclear weapons, making it unlikely that they would come to North Korea's aid except perhaps if the North were the target of an unprovoked attack. North Korea is essentially alone with its oppressed populace, depressed economy, and swollen military, defying both friend and foe alike.

Given its relatively small size and large but inferior military forces, the Kim regime requires military strategies that can deal with stronger adversaries. One strategy is defense in depth—both literally and figuratively. Kim Il-sung's Four Military Lines dictated four "people's defense" policies, replacing the traditional Soviet military policy that relied on powerful weapons. The first line called for training all able-bodied North Koreans to be soldiers. The second line called for building defenses throughout the country, with a special emphasis on deep underground installations, appropriate in a country with many mountains. These two lines would make it difficult for invading forces to overrun the country.

The third line called for the thorough political indoctrination of soldiers so that they would be loyal to the Kim regime even in the face of military adversity, and the fourth line called for adapting North Korea's military strategy and weapons to conditions on the Korean Peninsula. This meant building or obtaining weapons particularly suited to North Korea's rugged terrain and within the government's tight budget. The goals of the Four Military Lines were to defend the regime and the country while preparing to launch another military invasion of South Korea to finally unify the country under the Kim regime.

North Korea's military forces are collectively known as the Korean People's Army (KPA). The backbone of the KPA's forces is its large army, consisting primarily of lightly armed foot soldiers who do not require expensive weapons or extensive training. To counter an adversary's more advanced conventional forces, the Kim regime has boosted its investment in asymmetric warfare capabilities. For example, the North Koreans developed a large special forces command, whose soldiers, wearing South Korean uniforms and landing from the sea in small submarines or boats, crossing the DMZ (demilitarized zone) in tunnels or through minefields, or dropping from helicopters or light air transports, would create a second front within South Korea. Over the years, North Korean special forces have conducted several raids into South Korea, mostly unsuccessfully. Another North Korean strategy to counter an enemy's superior forces is to develop weapons of mass destruction such as chemical, biological, and nuclear weapons to be delivered by ballistic missiles. The Kim regime has poured billions of dollars into such programs, and while WMDs could be used only in a suicidal scenario (given the vast superiority of the American WMD force), they are possibly useful as a threat.

North Korea also employs a form of defensive psychological warfare that involves taking a violently belligerent attitude toward other countries, primarily South Korea and the United States. This porcupine-like defense (not to malign that cute little animal) is designed to keep potential adversaries at bay. The North Korean press has often warned that if the enemy "violates an inch of land, a blade of grass and a tree in Korea" it will be punished "mercilessly."[2] To back up this threat, an estimated 70 percent of North Korean ground forces are stationed within sixty miles of the South Korean border, ready to counter an attack before falling back to dug-in positions, and, by the same token, making it possible to rapidly advance on South Korea's capital thirty miles south of the border, thereby holding that city of ten million people (with another fifteen million in the metropolitan area) as a virtual hostage.

By the late 1960s North Korea was falling behind South Korea in the technology of its conventional weaponry, especially if the American forces stationed in South Korea were included in the weapons count. On the other hand, the North continued to maintain a quantitative advantage in equipment as well as manpower. The North Korean armed forces are estimated to consist of approximately 1.2 million soldiers (the world's fourth-largest army), including 200,000 in the special forces, 110,000 in the air force, and 60,000 in the navy. Active-duty soldiers are backed up by a reserve force of over six million, along with millions more in various paramilitary organizations. By comparison, South Korea fields an active-duty force of about 600,000 soldiers.

The KPA holds an advantage in heavy armor, including over 21,000 artillery pieces, most of them dug in within sixty miles of the southern border and many of them able to hurl shells into downtown Seoul. Self-propelled and towed artillery are complemented by over 5,000 rocket launchers, compared to South Korea's total of 11,000 artillery. North Korea has upwards of 3,500 tanks, most of them aging, along with 10,000 armored fighting vehicles, against South Korea's 2,500 tanks.

Lacking a shipbuilding industry, North Korea has not tried to acquire a blue-water navy. Its navy consists of eight older frigates, about eighty small submarines, and hundreds of patrol boats, landing craft, and semisubmersible boats for troop infiltration. South Korea, which does have a robust shipbuilding industry, has twelve destroyers, thirteen frigates, and sixteen submarines, all newer and in better operating condition than North Korea's naval vessels. In the air, North Korea has a quantitative advantage in military aircraft, with approximately 550 fighters dating back to the 1960s, primarily old Russian MiGs. The South Korean air force is qualitatively superior, with up-to-date aircraft including over two hundred F-15 and F-16 fighters, backed up by approximately one hundred US Air Force F-16s stationed in the country and many more American aircraft based in Japan. North Korean pilots get relatively little training because aviation fuel is scarce. The North's helicopter fleet is smaller than the South's and relatively old. In short, in terms of conventional forces, North Korea is prepared to fight a largely defensive mid-twentieth-century land war conducted in mountainous terrain. On open ground the North Koreans would be quickly defeated by superior allied airpower.

Since the North Koreans cannot count on their airplanes for air combat or bombing duties, they have concentrated on developing rockets. For defense, they field Russian-style SAM antiaircraft rockets. For attack, they have developed an impressive array of short-, medium-, and long-range ballistic missiles. Their Scud-type ballistic missiles can hit most of South Korea, while their Nodongs can reach most of Japan. In recent years the Kim regime has made significant strides in building longer-range ballistic missiles, even including a few intercontinental prototypes that could, at least in theory, reach the continental United States. To arm these missiles the North has conventional warheads, probably chemical warheads, and is trying to develop a nuclear warhead that would be light enough to fit on its larger ballistic missiles. North Korea has also developed electronic warfare capabilities, including GPS jamming, and a robust cyber warfare force.

Supporting an army of over a million soldiers and at the same time developing an expensive ballistic missile force is a serious drain on North Korea's state budget, not only in terms of supporting the troops but also in terms of the opportunity costs of all this lost labor and industrial capacity. Only a country as dedicated to militarization as North Korea would have pursued this line for its entire history. The most important role of the KPA is to protect the leader and his party: "To annihilate those who dare to thrust their claws to the headquarters of the Korean revolution and become lifeguards of the supreme commander is the first mission and great honor of our army."[3] Military units with the best-armed and most loyal troops are assigned to defend the leader and the capital city.

The army also provides labor for the nonmilitary sector of the economy. Since the 1960s the military has had first call on the country's increasingly scarce resources, including construction materials and fuel, so it makes sense that the army would be called on to participate in important economic projects. Military organizations operate their own foreign trade organizations to procure foreign supplies and earn money through foreign weapons sales. Until the 2000s, when private enterprise began to spread throughout the country, the army was the only organization with trucks and fuel to transport goods from one location to another. One consequence of this transportation monopoly was that the army was well positioned to help itself to foreign aid before it could be distributed to civilians.

Most of the country's major construction projects, such as dams, tunnels, roads, bridges, monuments to the Kim family, and even amusement parks, were built by the military, with drafted soldiers doing most of the work. While this is one way to make the soldiers useful in peacetime, it undoubtedly degrades military readiness. Moreover, labor performed by unskilled soldiers often results in shoddy construction and many occupational accidents. Much of the labor is done by hand because construction machinery is in short supply. North Korean defectors tell of hungry soldiers forced to carry earth and boulders on their backs in the dead of winter.

If the Kim regime should ever send its undertrained and outmoded military force to attack South Korea, only one attack strategy would seem practical. As in the early days of the Korean War, the attack would need to employ surprise, overwhelming firepower, blitzkrieg speed, and nighttime operations, all preceded by special forces operations and electronic warfare attacks to disrupt South Korean and American command and control operations. The only target within striking range would be the city of Seoul, just thirty miles south of the border. If North Korean troops could make it that far, they would presumably be safe from enemy bombardment. Recalling the disaster that North Korean troops suffered during the Korean War when they attempted to overrun the entire peninsula, North Korean forces might simply hold Seoul and in a battle of nerves demand that South Korea agree to its truce terms.

In the meantime, allied forces would be able to attack any point in North Korea that they chose, so the North would need to get a South Korean truce very quickly. One might expect that this would be the time for North Korea to threaten the use of nuclear weapons if the allies did not abandon their attacks. If nuclear weapons were used and the United States retaliated in kind, it would spell the virtual end of North Korea. A North Korean campaign against Seoul would be an exceptionally high-risk gamble, but if South Korea at that point were governed by a left-leaning president who was optimistic about the virtues of Korean unification, the odds of North Korea conducting successful truce negotiations might improve markedly.

When Kim Il-sung launched the surprise attack on South Korea that started the Korean War, he expected that many South Koreans would willingly join forces with the invaders to free themselves from "American domination." Of course, this expectation was entirely wrong. A second North Korean attack might expose the Kim regime to an opposite outcome. What if North Korean troops, once they saw the modern wonders of Seoul, decided to abandon their campaign and join the opposition? Such an outcome might not be inconceivable in light of the hardships that North Korean soldiers face even in peacetime.

SOLDIERS: WARTIME CANNON FODDER, PEACETIME SLAVE LABOR

Kim Jong-il's military-first regime (1994–2011) glorified soldiers as model citizens. "No other people in this land today are bigger, more precious, and more sacred than soldiers."[4] "The gun-barrel family is a new type of family for mankind, where all the family members regard wearing a military uniform and holding a gun as the greatest happiness and the best family tradition and where they all become soldiers."[5] The North Korean media even proclaimed that Kim himself came from the first gun-barrel family (his father, his mother, and little Jong-il were called the "three generals" of Mount Paektu). In reality, living conditions for soldiers are spartan, and during the famine of the latter half of the 1990s, which were Kim's first years as the supreme leader, living conditions in the military as well as in the civilian community became absolutely perilous.

All able-bodied males are required to serve in the military for ten years after graduating from senior middle school (high school) at the age of seventeen. Women are drafted for six years or until they reach the age of twenty-three. If there is a manpower shortage in a unit, a soldier's discharge may be delayed for a year or two. Students who are enrolled in a university are

Soldiers on holiday march to visit Kim Il-sung's alleged secret camp on Mount Paektu, 2012. *Wikimedia Commons, by Laika ac, CC-BY-SA-2.0.*

exempt from service, as are those who are physically unfit, although given the poor health of the general population, the physical requirements of service are extremely low. Payment of a large bribe can often buy an exemption from service. Bribery can also shorten the period of service, or at least get soldiers easier jobs or better treatment while serving. Recruits are treated harshly, and female soldiers are often subjected to sexual abuse. During their period of service, soldiers are not permitted to marry, and they may be granted home leave only a few times during their long years of service.

The single greatest challenge for enlisted soldiers is getting enough food to eat. Until the mid-1980s soldiers received the same kind of state food rations as everyone else, with the amount depending on their rank. Even then, the meals were of poor quality, generally consisting of a watery soup, a dish of corn or rice, and small side dishes of vegetables and peppers for seasoning. Occasionally a small piece of fish would find its way to a soldier's plate, and a couple of times a year soldiers could even enjoy a piece of fatty pork for dinner. When the state's Public Distribution System (PDS) ran out of supplies in the 1990s, soldiers along with everyone else, except top party officials, were forced to fend for themselves, and this remains the norm.

Meals for enlisted soldiers often consist of no more than a handful of corn, some small bite-size potatoes, and salt soup. A South Korean report from 2016 estimated that many North Korean soldiers received a ration of only 70 grams of food for each meal, far below the regulation 250 grams and also short of the UN's recommended minimum nutritional requirement of 600 grams a day.[6] Conditions are worse for soldiers than for civilians because soldiers are unable to move about the countryside in search of food, and they are not free to find ways to feed themselves on their own initiative.

Since the 1990s, military units in the countryside have been required to operate their own farms. Military newspapers offer instruction on how army units can feed themselves, with titles such as "Raising Rabbits in Summertime," "Smoke-Drying of Catfish," "Growing Bean Sprouts in Caves," "Pickling Mountain Garlic," "Ways of Cooking Cabbage," and "Beans Are Multiple Vitamins." There is no reason to believe that soldiers are particularly adept at farming, nor for that matter do they find it easy to get their hands on the tools and implements needed for successful farming.

Soldiers who become too malnourished to perform their duties are housed in special recovery barracks. Those facing death from starvation may be granted a few months of home leave to recuperate, thereby transferring the burden of feeding them to their families. Officers manage to get more food than enlisted men because they can siphon off the best of the rations and accept bribes from soldiers and their families in return for special assignments, promotions, and leaves. Soldiers sometimes go into the local markets and demand food. Acting alone or with the connivance of their officers, they erect highway checkpoints to shake down traders and travelers. A more direct means of obtaining food is simply to raid farms—sometimes the very farms they are supposed to be guarding.[7] On occasion, North Korean soldiers have even crossed over the border to raid Chinese farms.[8]

North Korean soldiers tend to be short in stature from years of childhood malnutrition, and they are invariably thin. This is true even of most military officers. Not only is food in short supply, but medical care is rudimentary at best. In 2017 a North Korean soldier serving near the DMZ (an assignment that is supposed to be given only to the healthiest and most loyal soldiers) made a dash for freedom across the truce line at Panmunjom. He was badly wounded when he was fired on by other North Korean soldiers but was finally pulled to safety by South Korean troops. Numerous surgeries saved him, and at the hospital it was discovered that his body was filled with parasites and he was suffering from tuberculosis. His poor health is not likely to be an exception among North Korean soldiers.

Except for the movie-star-quality soldiers who are stationed in the Joint Security Area (frequently referred to as "Panmunjom") and the soldiers prominently featured in North Korean military parades, the majority of North Korean soldiers look more like skinny Boy Scouts from the wrong side of town than the soldiers who are supposed to be the pillar of North Korean society. Military uniforms, including boots and shoes (many soldiers simply wear rubber-soled sneakers), are frequently in short supply. Soldiers dressed in T-shirts and baggy pants are difficult to distinguish from beggars.

Male and female draftees are not permitted to fraternize with each other or with civilians. A military lecture warns that "once soldiers become infatuated with women and start to have inappropriate relations with them, the soldiers lose interest in their military duties and in their army lives."[9] Still, "inappropriate relations" with female civilians, soldiers, and the prostitutes who ply their trade near military bases are apparently not uncommon for young North Korean soldiers.

Many reports from inside North Korea and from North Korean defectors attest to the low morale of draftees. Until the 1990s, one reward for ten years of military service was eventual membership in the Workers' Party of Korea, a membership that opened doors to a somewhat better civilian life. However, since the failure of the state's PDS in the 1990s, party membership has dramatically declined in value, and most North Koreans prefer to stay as far away from the government and the party as they can, instead seeking their fortune in the burgeoning private enterprise economy. The best that can be said for the fighting quality of North Korean soldiers today is that, thanks to the forced indoctrination they receive for ten years, on top of what they have learned in school up to that point, they harbor a hatred and fear of Americans and their South Korean "lackeys"—a hatred that should boost their morale if they ever engage in battle.

As was typical in former communist countries, North Korea's military has a dual command structure. At every level the military officer in charge shares leadership responsibilities with a political officer who reports to the party. The party ultimately controls the military through its Central Military Commission, although during Kim Jong-il's reign the National Defense Commission, which he headed, exercised ultimate command over the military and the rest of the government. It is the political commander who often receives deference, even if his expertise is inferior to that of the military officer in charge. The party watches the military through its hierarchy of agents in the Security Command, who report to party officials in the General Political Bureau. This extensive oversight is probably the reason why there appears to have been very few attempts at military coups, even though the generals have often chafed under the thumb of Kim Jong-il and Kim Jong-un.

Kim Jong-un seems to distrust his generals. Even though they live and work under the watchful eye of the party, they have command of the only organization that could depose the leader. Kim frequently replaces his top commanders to prevent them from establishing any independent base of power. In the first year of his reign, Kim went through four defense ministers, and since then he has replaced many generals, sometimes moving them to different commands, sometimes sending them to a reeducation camp for a few months, sometimes retiring them, and sometimes even having them executed by firing squad. Being a general in North Korea, even in peacetime, is a precarious occupation.

From the top generals down to the lowliest privates, the KPA is riddled with corruption, as is all North Korean society. As government employees, military officers receive salaries that, at the current rate of exchange, amount to just a few dollars a month. Officers are entitled to food and housing that is better than what enlisted soldiers receive, but even so they are not able to enjoy the lifestyle of even moderately successful private entrepreneurs. Thus, officers, like party and government officials throughout the country, engage in a variety of corrupt practices to supplement their income. In addition to skimming off whatever they can get from any "private" military enterprises their unit may be engaged in, such as farming, trading, and construction, they expect to receive bribes for promoting subordinates and giving them choice assignments. This bribery cascades down the chain of command so that the enlisted soldiers are the ones who ultimately pay the highest price in terms of their welfare.

NUCLEAR WEAPONS: THE PRIDE OF THE REGIME

The development of nuclear weapons is consistent with the Kim regime's long-standing militaristic policies. Kim Il-sung's Korean War attack on South Korea was an early indication that North Korea was willing to resort to force to achieve its goals. Kim's promotion of the Four Military Lines in 1962 made the development of military force the country's official priority. Kim Jong-il's choice of "military-first" as his guiding policy updated North

Portion of a tile mosaic at the Korean Film Studio outside of Pyongyang, 2011.
Wikimedia Commons, by Mark Fahey, CC-BY-2.0.

Korea's militarization to the second generation of dynastic leadership, and Kim Jong-un's aggressiveness is believed to be the reason that his father chose him to be the country's third-generation leader.

North Korea has never been an economically successful country. Its very existence under the Kim family regime rests on its military might. As the party newspaper put it (in 2004), "Our socialism is, first of all, a unique socialism with its root originating in the barrel of a gun."[10] Because nuclear weapons are universally acknowledged to be the most powerful weapons any nation can possess, it is hardly surprising that the Kim regime has sought them.

In 1956, only three years after a truce was signed ending the Korean War, and with the country still in ruins from allied bombing, several North Koreans were sent for training to the Soviet Union's nuclear science and research center at Dubna. In 1959 the Soviet Union agreed to provide assistance to North Korea in the construction of a nuclear research center, and in 1965 a small research reactor began operating at Yongbyon, a nuclear research complex sixty miles north of the capital of Pyongyang. By the late 1970s the North Koreans had acquired the necessary technology to begin building their own nuclear reactor, fueled by domestically sourced uranium. This small reactor, rated at five megawatts of electrical generating power (5 MWe), commenced operations in 1986.

Although the 5 MWe reactor did not generate enough electricity to be a useful source of power, once the uranium fuel was burned it could be reprocessed into plutonium for nuclear weapons. About this time American spy satellites photographed construction of a building at the Yongbyon nuclear complex that looked very much like a reprocessing plant that could convert spent reactor fuel into plutonium. The plant was the size of two football fields and six stories high, making it the second-largest reprocessing plant in the world at that time. The Kim regime insisted on calling it a "radiochemical laboratory." By 1990 the plant was ready to begin reprocessing a small amount of the spent fuel that was being produced by the 5 MWe reactor.

In 1984, construction was begun on a 50 MWe reactor, and in 1991 on a 200 MWe reactor (worldwide, most nuclear reactors generate upwards of 500 MWe of power). In 1985, the Soviet Union signed an agreement to provide North Korea with three reactors at a new facility in Sinpo. The 1994 Agreed Framework (discussed below) promised North Korea two proliferation-resistant light-water reactors capable of producing a total of 2,000 MWe of power. For a variety of reasons, none of these other reactors ever got beyond the early stages of construction. Thus, all the nuclear negotiations over the years between North Korea and the international community, and all the economic sanctions imposed on North Korea, concern one very small nuclear reactor whose only purpose is to burn fuel to be converted into weapons-grade plutonium.

The operation of the 5 MWe reactor, and especially the construction of the reprocessing plant, brought North Korea's nuclear program to the attention of the international community. The Kim regime must have had mixed feelings about this attention. On the one hand, the regime presumably wanted to continue its nuclear development in secret up to the point where it could produce a number of nuclear weapons. In a 1992 interview with the *Washington Times*, Kim Il-sung said,

> As far as the nuclear issue is concerned, our country does not have any nuclear weapons. . . . And, what is more, we don't need nuclear weapons. What is the use of producing one or two nuclear weapons while the big countries have

several thousand? . . . And we don't have a delivery system either. So, to be
honest, we don't need nuclear weapons. [11]

Not that Kim Il-sung was noted for his honesty. On the other hand, the Kim
regime was clearly eager to enter into political negotiations with its archenemy the United States, and for this purpose at least, a nuclear weapons threat
was eminently useful.

As a condition for receiving nuclear reactors from the Soviet Union,
North Korea signed the International Atomic Energy Agency's (IAEA) Non-
Proliferation Treaty (NPT) in 1985. It did not, however, sign the accompany-
ing safeguards protocol that would provide for IAEA inspections of its nucle-
ar facilities to ensure that they were not being used for weapons production.
Four years later, Pyongyang announced that it would sign the protocol if the
United States removed its "nuclear threat," which was generally interpreted
as a demand for the removal of American tactical nuclear weapons from
South Korea and an end to US–South Korea joint military maneuvers. In the
event, the document was not signed, although in 1991 President George H.
W. Bush announced that the United States was withdrawing all its tactical
nuclear weapons from overseas sites. Also in 1991, the two Koreas signed a
Joint Declaration of the Denuclearization of the Korean Peninsula, in which
both parties renounced the possession and use of nuclear weapons and facilities for nuclear fuel reprocessing and uranium enrichment—an agreement
that the North Koreans totally ignored.

In January 1992 North Korea finally decided to sign the IAEA's safeguards accord, opening the way for international inspections of its nuclear
facilities. As the IAEA inspections got underway, North Korea claimed that
its "nuclear problem" with the international community had been successfully resolved. To the contrary, documents obtained by the IAEA revealed
numerous discrepancies in North Korea's nuclear accounts, and in January
1993 the IAEA requested that it be allowed to inspect two sites that the North
Koreans had not listed on their nuclear disclosure statements. In response,
the North Koreans insisted that these sites were unrelated to their nuclear
program, and they threatened to withdraw from the NPT if the IAEA insisted
on conducting the inspections, going so far as to threaten that "if any special
inspection or sanctions are forced upon us, encroaching on our sacred land, it
will bring about a dangerous situation to throw the whole peninsula into the
ravages of war." [12]

Thus began a prolonged tug-of-war between North Korea and the IAEA. In March 1993 North Korea announced that in three months it would "withdraw unavoidably" from the NPT—the first country ever to do so. This threat opened a new phase in North Korea's nuclear weapons program. The United States feared that without IAEA oversight the North Koreans would unload spent fuel from their reactor and send it to the reprocessing facility to make plutonium. There followed three months of negotiations between officials in Pyongyang and Washington that resulted in North Korea's agreeing, three days before its threatened withdrawal, to stay in the NPT in return for various considerations from the United States. To motivate the United States to make the deal, the North Koreans began unloading spent fuel from their reactor. In July the two countries signed what was known as the "Agreed Framework"—a sort of guideline for North Korea's denuclearization, but less formal than a treaty.

In the agreement, the North Koreans promised to freeze their nuclear facilities and eventually dismantle them. In exchange, the United States would lead a consortium (largely financed by Japan and South Korea) that would build two 1,000 MWe light-water reactors for the North Koreans. The spent fuel that these reactors produced would be difficult to turn into weapons-grade plutonium. Until the reactors went online, the United States would annually provide half a million tons of heavy fuel oil to compensate the North Koreans for the energy they claimed would be lost by not pursuing their nuclear program. The United States also promised to improve diplomatic and economic relations with North Korea. The asymmetric aspect of this agreement was that the North Koreans were trading away a weapons program in exchange for a peacetime economic resource, leaving them without the kind of military deterrent they had always insisted they needed.

And so the construction of the reactors began, very slowly (dealing with North Koreans is always painfully slow), delivery of the heavy oil began, and North Korea's 5 MWe reactor remained dormant. Little happened in the way of improved diplomatic and economic relations because North Korea's policies were not in any way changed by this agreement. It was initially expected, but not promised, that the first of the two reactors would be completed by 2003, but by 2000 the reactors were still in the initial stages of construction. By early 2002 American intelligence got wind of a clandestine North Korean uranium enrichment program that would provide an alternative source of nuclear weapons material and thus satisfy the Kim regime's need for a nuclear weapon deterrent. In October 2002 the North Koreans (apparently) acknowledged the existence of this program, marking the beginning of yet another phase in the nuclear controversy.

The United States ended its support for the Agreed Framework and halted the heavy oil shipments. Construction of the two light-water reactors came to a standstill. The North Koreans began reprocessing the spent fuel rods they had removed from the 5 MWe reactor and began boasting of having a "physical deterrent," a "nuclear deterrent," and sometimes "something even stronger than a nuclear deterrent." In January 2003 they announced that they were withdrawing from the NPT. They continued to insist that they did not want to go nuclear but that the American threat forced them to do so, thereby blaming the United States for the existence of their nuclear program.

Now that the North Koreans presumably had sufficient plutonium to build a handful of bombs, the international community felt it necessary to try a new denuclearization approach. Neither the Chinese nor the Russians were concerned that they would be the target of a North Korean nuclear weapon, but they did not want to see any conflict on their doorstep. The United States, South Korea, and Japan, however, had every reason to worry about the bombs. In August 2003 these five countries, along with North Korea, began meeting in a new format, the Six-Party Talks, which would continue until North Korea finally walked out in 2008.

No lasting agreements were reached in the Six-Party Talks, although at times it looked like some sort of compromise might be reached. While the talks progressed, North Korea continued to develop its nuclear weapons and long-range missiles. In April 2005 the North Koreans briefly shut down their reactor in order to remove more spent fuel for plutonium processing. In October 2006 North Korea conducted its first (underground) nuclear test of a very small device estimated to be no more than one kiloton (the two American bombs dropped on Japan near the end of World War II were fifteen and twenty kilotons). As a result of this test, the UN began passing sanctions resolutions against North Korea. In May 2009 the North Koreans conducted a test of a nuclear device estimated at four kilotons. In March 2010 they began constructing a prototype light-water reactor, and during this period they were also pushing forward with their uranium enrichment project.

In February 2013 the North Koreans conducted their third nuclear test, this time of what they claimed was a "lighter, miniaturized atomic bomb," with an estimated yield of twelve kilotons. The fourth test, of a device of similar size, occurred in January 2016. In its fifth test, in September 2016,

North Korea exploded a twenty-five-kiloton device. In the sixth test, in September 2017, North Korea claimed it had detonated a thermonuclear (hydrogen) device. The claim was plausible as the yield was estimated to be at least one hundred kilotons. During this period North Korea's missile program was also making progress, with its longest-range missiles theoretically able to reach the US mainland.

In April 2018 Kim Jong-un announced that North Korea had achieved its goal of building a reliable nuclear deterrent and that it would henceforth concentrate its efforts on building its economy. After the June 2018 US–North Korea summit meeting between Kim Jong-un and Donald Trump, North Korea halted nuclear tests and long-range missile launches but presumably continued to develop both its nuclear and missile programs.

Despite hopes in some quarters of the United States that a deal can be found to permanently end North Korea's military nuclear program, the results to date are not the least bit encouraging. It seems that the North Koreans were always clearheaded about their nuclear needs. They could never trust the United States, and despite repeatedly calling for a "bold switchover" of American policy, they knew the United States would never trust them. This was unlike the situation in Europe after World War II when, after significant changes in the military governments of the Axis powers, they became friends and allies of the United States. No change of administration has taken place in North Korea. By 2020, North Korea was believed to have made twenty to sixty relatively small nuclear weapons, and it probably possesses enough plutonium to make an equal number in the future. There is little reason to doubt that the Kim regime will continue to make such weapons, and resume testing them as well.

MISSILES: POWER PROJECTION

Nuclear devices may be the ultimate weapons, but without an airborne delivery system they are of little military value. In order to project its military power, North Korea needs either airplanes or rockets to deliver its nuclear weapons. The North Korean air force is notoriously weak, especially when it comes to bombers, so the burden of delivering nuclear weapons has fallen on North Korea's missile force. Missile development has followed a general trend of advancement marked by periods of missile launches followed by periods of launch moratoriums. The principal reason the three successive Kim regimes have publicly offered for missile development is that North

Korea needs to deter the United States from initiating an attack that would trigger another Korean war. By this logic, North Korean missiles and nuclear weapons are preserving peace in the region and conferring a great benefit on South Koreans as well.

Whether the Kims have actually believed this explanation is hard to say. It could easily be argued that building long-range missiles might provoke the United States to launch an attack against the missile program, leading to the very conflict the North Koreans say they are trying to prevent. Given the pattern of launches and the rhetoric the Kim regime employs, one could surmise that the missile program is meant to serve a variety of purposes in addition to deterrence. For one, missiles are useful as a threat against the United States, not just for deterrence but possibly to prevent American forces from entering a future inter-Korean conflict. North Korea's missile development—not the entire program but improvements in the program—could also be used as a bargaining chip to gain rewards or concessions from the United States or other concerned countries.

Moreover, an advanced missile program confers international prestige on North Korea and personal prestige on the leading Kim. The problem with nuclear weapons as a symbol of military power is that they sit hidden in storage facilities waiting to be used, and nuclear tests are conducted underground where they cannot be seen. Missiles, on the other hand, can be fired into the air for all to see. Kim Jong-il and Kim Jong-un have often been photographed proudly pointing to missile launches. Missiles can also be carried on launchers in military parades. In short, for North Korea, missiles serve as a visible symbol of military strength.

An irony of missile development, and nuclear weapons development as well, is that employment in actual combat would almost certainly spell the end for North Korea. As Kim Il-sung publicly recognized decades ago, American weapons of mass destruction will always be able to overwhelm whatever weapons North Korea can develop, so in an all-out war North Korea will be defeated. However, missiles and nuclear weapons, collectively referred to as weapons of mass destruction (WMDs), may serve various purposes short of war, such as providing a deterrent to attack. A final irony is that missile tests, like nuclear tests, involve the destruction of weapons. The more missile tests North Korea conducts, the more missiles it needs to replace.

The origins of the North's missile program can be traced as far back as 1960, when the Soviet Union gave North Korea surface-to-air missiles. By the early 1970s, China was also supplying missiles. Sometime in the 1970s, about a dozen years after Kim Il-sung adopted his "Four Military Lines," the buildup of North Korea's conventional force was augmented by research into the development of a domestically manufactured short-range ballistic missile that could be used to attack South Korean forces and American forces stationed in South Korea. Whether North Korea really needed a missile capability, given that it had a long way to go to modernize its conventional forces, is another question. If for no other reason, North Korea would have felt the need to keep up with South Korea, which began its own missile research in 1971 and reached an agreement with the United States in 1972 that allowed it to reverse engineer the American short-range Nike Hercules surface-to-air missile. The South Koreans continued to develop their own missiles, within American restrictions that limited South Korean missiles to a range of 180 kilometers (112 miles). By the late 1980s South Korea fielded some two hundred short-range ballistic missiles.

The North's own ballistic missiles (that rise above the atmosphere and fall back to earth) went into development by reverse engineering a Soviet Scud-B missile, one of a dozen or more that the Soviet Union had sent to Egypt during the 1973 Arab-Israeli War. North Korea's first indigenously developed short-range ballistic missile, with a range of 320 kilometers (200 miles), was the Hwasong-5, which underwent six launch tests in 1984 before going into production. Incidentally, the North Koreans tend to name their missiles after celestial bodies (*Hwasong* meaning "Mars"), whereas foreigners usually name those missiles after the locale where they were first launched (e.g., Nodong or Taepodong). To further confuse things, foreigners use different spellings for these locations, for example, either *Nodong* or *Rodong*. The Hwasong-5 missiles were also sold to Iran during the Iran-Iraq War, and since then, missile exports have also reportedly gone to the United Arab Emirates, Syria, Iraq, Libya, Yemen, Pakistan, and Myanmar.

Not facing any political restrictions on their missile ranges, the North Koreans then developed a medium-range missile, the Nodong (also known as the Hwasong-7), with its first test launch apparently in 1993. The Nodong has a range of a bit over one thousand kilometers (620 miles), sufficient to hit all of South Korea and much of Japan. Assistance from Russian and Chinese technicians helped. Pakistan also became interested in the Nodong and began to cooperate with North Korea on missile development. During the Kim Il-sung era, North Korea launched about fifteen missiles. Kim was an old-school leader, mostly concerned about reunifying the Korean Peninsula and protecting his country from invasion by foreign countries. It seems unlikely that he spent much time thinking about how he might attack the continental United States with missiles.

North Korea did not launch any missiles during the first four years of Kim Jong-il's reign, a time when Kim lived mostly in seclusion and the nation was suffering from severe economic shortages. However, during this period research continued on longer-range missiles. Then in 1998 North Korea tested a new missile, the Taepodong-1, which attempted to insert a satellite into orbit. According to the North Korean government, the Kwangmyong-song (Bright Star) went into orbit and began broadcasting "The Song of General Kim Il-sung" and "The Song of General Kim Jong-il."[13] According to foreign intelligence services, the payload crashed into the Pacific Ocean about four thousand kilometers (2,500 miles) to the east. With a lighter payload, the rocket could have reached the American Midwest, although its exact target of impact would certainly have been a matter of pure chance.

The Taepodong's potential range rang alarm bells in Washington. And since the missile had flown over Japan, the Japanese, who are no friends of the North Koreans, became even more alarmed than the Americans. In the final year of his presidency, Bill Clinton sent his secretary of state, Madeleine Albright, to Pyongyang to meet with Kim Jong-il, who hosted a performance at the May First Stadium that included a theatrical depiction of a North Korean missile launch. Hoping to promote a beneficial relationship with the United States, Kim turned to Secretary Albright and quipped, "That was our first missile launch—and our last."[14] North Korea did indeed initiate a moratorium on missile launches that lasted until 2006, which was also the year that the North Koreans detonated their first nuclear device.

In some respects, 2006 was a watershed year. Beginning in the early 1990s the United States and North Korea conducted a dialogue to explore the possibility that foreign economic assistance and political recognition might serve as a substitute for the Kim regime's nuclear and missile programs. An agreement was reached in 1994 and then failed, and a new dialogue in the form of the Six-Party Talks began in 2003 and continued for several years, making little headway. The nuclear test and missile launches in 2006 were the Kim regime's way of putting pressure on the United States to reach an agreement, but the pressure failed to achieve its intended effect. North Korea launched seven short- and long-range missiles in 2006 and another eight in 2009. By the time he died in late 2011, Kim Jong-il had tested about the same number of missiles as his father, with an emphasis on the development of long-range missiles.

Kim Jong-un took over where his father left off, overseeing two launches in 2012, one of which finally placed a small satellite into orbit. Needless to say, the "satellite rocket" launches were also a means of testing the North's intercontinental missile capability. Under the young Kim, the North's missile program improved by leaps and bounds: six launches in 2013, nineteen in 2014, fifteen in 2015, twenty-four in 2016, and twenty-one in 2017. The only discernible effect these tests had on the US government was to prompt it to impose increasingly strong economic sanctions on North Korea.

In early 2018 Kim sensed a promising change in the political atmosphere, with the possibility of opening beneficial dialogues with the United States and South Korea. To push things along—and especially to make a bid to reduce the economic sanctions imposed on his country—he announced in April 2018 that North Korea would discontinue nuclear and missile tests and concentrate on economic development. As an explanation for this decision, and to keep foreigners from forming the impression that North Korea might be bowing to international pressure, he claimed that his country had completed its development of a powerful nuclear deterrent and the means to deliver it. In 2018 President Donald Trump decided to deal directly with Kim, meeting him in Singapore in June, in Hanoi in February 2019, and stepping across the DMZ into North Korea for a brief conversation with Kim in June 2019. In 2018 Kim also received three visits from South Korea's left-leaning president Moon Jae-in. The North Korean moratorium on launches of long-range missiles continued throughout 2019 but brought North Korea no political or economic gains. From the beginning of 2019, North Korea warned that if no progress was made in negotiations by the end of the year, it would adopt a new policy, and therefore "it is entirely up to the U.S. what Christmas gift it will select to get."[15]

The frequent tests conducted during the Kim Jong-un years served to increase the range of North Korea's intercontinental rockets, although at this stage they still had to be considered experimental rockets with little practical use. Perhaps more important, North Korea made progress in operationalizing its short- and medium-range missiles. Missile launches were made from numerous locations around the country. Mobile launchers were tested. Cruise missiles were tested, as well as elementary submarine-launched missiles. Simultaneous multiple launches were made, as would be necessary in wartime. North Korea also began using solid-fuel rockets, which can be launched with more stealth and less warning than liquid-fuel rockets because the fuel does not have to be loaded just before launch. In short, under Kim Jong-un, North Koreans promoted what they termed "combat application" and "operational deployment" of their missiles. What remained was for North Korea to perfect long-range missile targeting, reentry, and the miniaturization of nuclear weapons to put on missiles. These accomplishments would require many more missile tests but should be well within North Korea's capabilities.

By the end of 2019, North Korea had a reasonably large arsenal of short- and medium-range missiles that could reach anywhere in South Korea and most of Japan (and of course large areas of neighboring China and Russia, to no obvious purpose). The costs of the missile program have been enormous—not just the direct costs of developing and launching the missiles, but the far greater costs incurred through international sanctions on its economy. The benefits have been less clear. Missile launches and nuclear tests have brought the United States to the bargaining table, but no bargain has been reached—just as years of economic sanctions from the UN, the United States, Japan, and South Korea have done little or nothing to slow the North Korean missile program. The missiles, especially the long-range ones, have created a certain amount of fear in Japan, less fear in the United States, and seem to be hardly noticed in South Korea. Domestically, the missile launches have increased national pride among some North Koreans; the majority, however, seem to be uninterested and would much prefer to have a strong economy freed from international sanctions.

The Kim regime has always considered itself to be a first-world country in terms of its military strength, even though it has a third-world economy. A highly developed missile program, along with nuclear weapons, is absolutely essential to claim first-world military status. Given this fact, it is unreasonable to expect that the Kim regime will negotiate away its arsenal of missiles in the foreseeable future.

THREATS AS A WEAPON: THE FIRST LINE OF DEFENSE

North Korea has a well-earned reputation for belligerent rhetoric. The Kim regime deploys verbal threats to augment or substitute for physical force. While these verbal threats are inexpensive to deploy, they will have limited impact if they are not, at least occasionally, reinforced with military action. The Kim regime's launch of the Korean War lends some credibility to its threats, but that war was many years ago, and contemporary threats need to be backed up by contemporary violence if they are to have much of an impact.

North Korea's threats are most often directed at the United States, South Korea, and Japan. In some cases, an entire country is the threatened target; at other times, the threat is directed at specific individuals or institutions. The threats tend to follow a standard script and employ a repertory of favorite phrases. The source of the threats varies. Sometimes the threat comes from the ruling Kim. Other times the threat is issued by a military or party organization. Some of the threats are intended to compel another country to do something, such as lift economic sanctions or issue an apology. More often the threats are meant to deter another country from doing something, such as staging a military exercise or launching an attack on North Korea.

North Korean threats against the United States are common, most often coming after the United States has criticized the North Korean leader, censured North Korea for its human rights policies, criticized North Korea's missile or nuclear programs, or boosted its economic sanctions against North Korea. North Korea also routinely issues threats when the United States is about to stage one of its joint military exercises with South Korea. In 2016 North Korea's delegate to the UN unleashed the following threat in response to American criticism of Kim Jong-un: "The Obama administration went so far as to have the impudence to challenge the supreme dignity [Kim Jong-un] of the DPRK. . . . The United States has crossed the red line in our showdown. . . . We regard this thrice-cursed crime as a declaration of war."[16]

In March 2017 the North Korean government's news agency warned that "the U.S. imperialists and their stooges should clearly bear in mind that the nuclear treasured sword of the DPRK, keeping highly alert, will more mercilessly deal anytime a sledge-hammer blow to the enemies resorting to desperate moves for igniting a nuclear war despite our repeated warnings. The Korean People's Army makes no empty talk."[17] In addition to mixing its metaphors, the threat admits that previous warnings have gone unheeded. As North Korea has developed its nuclear and missile capabilities, threats to the continental United States have become more frequent and plausible. In February 2016: "We have all sorts of powerful ultra-cutting-edge attack means—which never existed previously in the world—with which we can beat the land of the United States at will anytime and anywhere."[18] The following month the party newspaper *Nodong Sinmun* reminded Americans that "the U.S. mainland is not the safe haven for the worst aggressors and provocateurs," citing North Korea's alleged "access to nuclear miniaturization and technology for ballistic rocket atmosphere re-entry" and its alleged ability to "manufacture the latest strategic weapons and H-bomb."[19]

Another threat was taken more seriously in the aftermath of several North Korean long-range missile launches in 2017. North Korean radio quoted a spokesman of the KPA Strategic Forces (SF) command as warning that "the KPA SF is carefully reviewing an operation plan to execute an encircling fire around Guam with [the] medium- to long-range strategic ballistic rocket Hwangsong-12 in order to contain and check key military bases in Guam, including Andersen Air Force Base. . . . [The plan] will be executed simultaneously and consecutively at any moment once a decision is made by Kim Jong-un, commander in chief of our Republic's nuclear armed forces."[20]

Such threats are analyzed by American intelligence organizations based on a variety of factors, including the history and specificity of the threats, the context, the harshness of the rhetoric, and the authoritativeness of the source—and the threats are generally dismissed as propaganda. A typical American response, if there is one, might come from a State Department spokesperson. For example, the response to the above-mentioned 2016 threat from North Korea's UN delegate ran thus: "I think what I would say is the same thing we've said, that it's time for the DPRK to cease rhetoric and to cease actions that only, you know, serve to destabilize the peninsula and do nothing to improve the lives of the North Korean people."[21]

When Donald Trump became president, the United States lowered (or raised?) itself to the rhetorical level of North Korea. An almost comical exchange of threats occurred in January 2018 when Kim Jong-un, in his annual New Year's statement, said (as translated into English by KCNA), "Our country's nuclear forces are capable of thwarting and countering any nuclear threats from the United States, and they constitute a powerful deterrent that prevents it from starting an adventurous war. In no way would the United States dare to ignite a war against me and our country. The whole of its mainland is within the range of our nuclear strike and the nuclear button is on my office desk all the time; the United States needs to be clearly aware that this is not merely a threat but a reality."[22] The next day President Trump tweeted, "North Korean Leader Kim Jong-un just stated that the 'Nuclear Button is on his desk at all times.' Will someone from his depleted and food starved regime please inform him that I too have a Nuclear Button, but it is a much bigger and more powerful one than his, and my Button works."[23]

In October 2017 President Trump had begun referring to Kim as "Rocket Man" or even "Little Rocket Man." The North Korean press in turn called Trump a "dotard" (literally, "a mentally deranged old man"). Strange as it may seem, when Trump and Kim met in 2018 and 2019, President Trump seemed to think that he had developed a special and positive relationship with Kim, despite the past name-calling. No nuclear deal was reached at those meetings, and in late 2019 the name-calling resumed on both sides.

North Korean threats against South Korea are as common and long-standing as threats against the United States, and as often as not include the United States, following the official North Korean line that South Korean governments are simply puppets of the Americans. For example, in March 2001 North Korea's *Youth Front* newspaper threatened that if a war developed, all US military bases in South Korea would become a "sea of fire in a stroke," and that "all U.S. bases surrounding the Korean peninsula like those in Guam and Okinawa, as well as in South Korea, will be blown up in the sky."[24]

From February 2013 until March 2017, when she was impeached, South Korea's conservative president Park Geun-hye proved to be a bitter enemy of the Kim regime, which specifically targeted her and the presidential mansion with threats. In March 2016, North Korea's KCBS radio station issued a strong threat in the aftermath of a spectacular demonstration of its long-range artillery: "The long-range artillery force of our large combined unit on the front, which is waiting for a future order to strike from the highly dignified Supreme Command [Kim Jong-un], issues an ultimatum as follows: . . . The matchless traitor Park Geun-hye and her gang should make a formal apology. . . . Nothing but their public execution before the eyes of all Koreans will offer the last opportunity for the Blue House . . . to escape a fiery baptism of punishment. . . . Our Mount Paektu army does not engage in empty talk."[25] No apology was issued, no one was executed, and the artillery did not fire on South Korea.

Japan is not threatened as often as South Korea and the United States, and when it does come into North Korea's sights, it is usually because it hosts American military bases. A typical threat, this one coming in September 2004, was lodged by *Nodong Sinmun*: "The U.S. ruling circle once boasted of the Japanese island as a 'nuclear-powered carrier that cannot be attacked.' However, in the event that the United States starts a nuclear war today, as U.S. military bases in Japan are a huge time bomb that threatens Japan's existence, [they] will not be able to avoid becoming the fuse for turning the Japanese land into a sea of fire of a nuclear war."[26] By way of explanation, it should be noted that in 1983 Japanese prime minister Yasuhiro Nakasone had referred to Japan as an "unsinkable aircraft carrier" from which American forces could launch a defense against the Soviet Union.

Someone not familiar with North Korea might be alarmed by these threats. However, students of this strange country understand that the threats are rarely carried out. Sometimes the threats are so superficial that the Kim regime will turn around and accept dialogue and negotiations with the very party it has sworn to destroy. When North Korea does stage a military attack, it does so by surprise, which is a traditional military tactic used by weaker powers against stronger adversaries.

An interesting case study of threats in relation to actions concerns North Korean warnings of military retaliation if South Korean forces approach too close to the disputed West Sea border, called the Northern Limit Line. North Korea occasionally sends fishing boats and small naval craft across the line in minor provocations or by accident, and on a few occasions North and South Korean naval vessels have fired on each other. After one such confrontation in 1999, the North warned that "the warmongers should bear in mind that there is a limit to our tolerance and that if they provoke a war indiscriminately, they will truly be submerged in a dreadful sea of fire and will only accumulate shameful death and corpses."[27]

North Korea finally backed up its long-standing West Sea threats by torpedoing a South Korean naval ship in West Sea waters in March 2010. The North denied committing the attack, which, considering the frequency and gravity of their threats over the years, seems cowardly. Then, on November 23, 2010, after the South Koreans began a live-fire exercise from one of their border islands, North Korean shore batteries opened fire on the island, killing one marine and two civilians. The North Koreans blamed the South for beginning the firefight, claiming that the South had fired into North Korean waters. To quote the North Korean military command, "Should the South Korean puppet group dare intrude into the territorial waters of the DPRK even 0.001 mm, the revolutionary armed forces of the DPRK will unhesitatingly continue taking merciless military counter-actions against it. It should bear in mind the solemn warning of the revolutionary armed forces of the DPRK that they do not make empty talk. There is in the West Sea of Korea only the maritime military demarcation line, set by the DPRK."[28]

The South Korean forces were caught by surprise and made only a limited response to the North Korean shelling. The South Koreans then announced plans for more military exercises, to which the North Koreans responded with another round of threats: "If [they] enforce the shell firing from Yon-pyong Island in the end despite our military's prior warning, an unpredictable self-defensive blow will be imposed for the second and third time to adhere to our Republic's sacred territory just as [we have] already declared to the world."[29] The South Koreans went ahead with the exercise, and this time the North Koreans did not make good on their threat. In the last chapter of this sad little saga, the North resumed its threats, claiming that their army was "getting fully ready to launch a sacred war of justice" against South Korea "based on the nuclear deterrent."[30] But this did not happen either.

As illustrated in this case, North Korea's threats usually fail to deter their target. Certainly, their threats against the United States have not softened American policy, and in the above case the threats did not prevent the South Koreans from staging more military exercises. Conversely, almost none of the military attacks that North Korea *has* made against South Korea and against US forces in South Korea over the years (e.g., commando raids, bombings) were preceded by any specific threat.

In the absence of any obvious change in the policies or behaviors of North Korea's adversaries, it is fair to ask why the Kim regime continues to issue threats that border on the ludicrous. Any number of answers are possible. Perhaps the North Koreans believe that the threats have made its adversaries a bit more cautious than they would otherwise have been. Perhaps the threats are a symptom of North Korea's frustration at not being accepted as a re-spectable member of the international community. Maybe the Kim regime (and it must be assumed that the leader signs off on all threats) is simply trying to get the world's attention. Perhaps the threats bolster morale in North Korea or divert the people's attention from their miserable lives and provide them with an explanation for why their government devotes so much of its resources to the military rather than toward improving the economy.

At the end of the day, a threat is defined by how it is perceived by the threatened target. Most North Korean threats hardly make a dent in the tar-get's considerations because the threats are so common. They fail to signal anything. In this sense, they are not true threats. Rather, they are perhaps better viewed as an unfortunate characteristic of North Korea's political cul-ture, a self-defeating habit that relegates North Korea to the status of a rogue state and convinces many foreigners that the North Korean regime is crazy.

Chapter Six

Foreign Relations

Of a Hermit Kingdom

FOREIGN POLICY PRINCIPLES: INDEPENDENCE FIRST AND LAST

North Korea's foreign policy goals can be easily described. First, the policy must protect the Kim family regime. Second, the policy must preserve the country's independence—especially from South Korea. Third, the policy must enable the regime to keep its people from coming into contact with foreigners. These three policy goals have been so thoroughly implemented that the Kim regime essentially rules over a hermit kingdom.

In August 1945, when Russian troops introduced their proxy, Kim Il-sung, to the North Korean people, it is probably safe to say that Kim's first priority was to establish a political position from which he could outmaneuver other politicians and at the same time please his Soviet advisors. Kim was essentially a country boy who had proved himself skillful at fighting and eluding Japanese troops in occupied China. He had only a limited education and virtually no knowledge of international politics. In short, the last thing he could afford to think about was how to position the new country of North Korea in the international arena. By default, North Korea became a client state of the Soviet Union and a minor member of the emerging communist camp.

In the months and years that followed, Kim could hardly ignore the fact that the Soviet Union had taken over Eastern Europe, including the eastern half of Germany. This domination must certainly have alarmed Kim because Korea had only recently been freed from Japanese domination. At the same time, Kim needed the economic assistance that the Soviet Union and its client states in Eastern Europe were providing, and he wanted the Soviet Union to support his goal of unifying Korea under his government. Besides, communism was spreading around the globe, so his allegiance to the communist model of politics and economy seemed to put North Korea on the winning side of history.

Stalin died in 1953, the same year that Kim had to accept the failure of his wartime campaign to bring South Korea under his control. A further disappointment was Khrushchev's "peaceful coexistence" policy and his acceptance of a two-Korea solution, which did not bode well for Kim's hopes of unifying Korea at a later date. Kim was also presumably alarmed by Khrushchev's 1956 political attack on the legacy of Stalin, who had served as Kim's political model. In 1955 Kim began to distance himself from the Soviet Union by making his famous *juche* independence speech, in which he is said to have proclaimed, "We are not engaged in any other country's revolution, but solely in the Korean revolution."[1]

In 1961 North Korea signed treaties of friendship with China and the Soviet Union that committed them to come to the North's aid if it were attacked, but this form of support fell far short of the United States' alliance and military assistance to South Korea. During this period, Kim's Korea became closer to neighboring China than to Russia. Koreans shared a cultural affinity with China, even while Koreans tended to be prejudiced against the Chinese people. Kim visited China almost every year, but he rarely made the longer trip to Moscow. During the Chinese Cultural Revolution in the late 1960s, when the Red Guards criticized Kim Il-sung as an old-style dictator, Kim temporarily distanced himself from China.

By the 1970s, Kim's rule over North Korea was a fact of life. North Korea's hostility toward South Korea, the United States, and Japan was at its height. The North Korean economy was slowing, and Kim's hope for another invasion of South Korea was dead. To bolster his country's independence from both China and the Soviet Union, Kim made a play to become a leader in the Non-Aligned Movement of third-world states, but North Korea was considered too strange and too closely allied to the communists to be fully accepted by these countries. In 1972 Nixon visited China, complicating North Korea's political relationship with the Chinese, and at the end of the decade Chinese leader Deng Xiaoping initiated an era of economic realism that began to move the Chinese economy away from the socialism that Kim Il-sung clung to. The Cold War stabilized, and North Korea became a political and economic backwater.

In the 1980s South Korea's importance to China as a trade and investment partner increased. South Korea was also a growing military power, and by the middle of the decade the Kim regime in the North (now mostly being run by Kim Jong-il) had decided that developing nuclear weapons would be much less expensive than trying to match South Korea's conventional arms budget—a decision that would complicate North Korea's diplomatic relations for decades to come. In the waning years of the decade, political changes in Eastern Europe and the Soviet Union heralded an international realignment in the socialist countries, moving them toward the West and leaving North Korea out in the cold.

The 1990s almost finished Kim's Korea. In September 1990 the Soviet Union and South Korea established full diplomatic relations, prompting North Korea's party newspaper to charge that "the Soviet Union sold off the dignity and honor of a socialist power and the interests and faith of an ally [North Korea] for 2.3 billion dollars," referring to Seoul's promise to provide Moscow with loans and trade credits.[2] At the same time, Moscow notified Pyongyang that henceforth their bilateral trade would be conducted in hard currency at international prices (which North Korea could not afford). Two years later China and South Korea established diplomatic relations.

In its search for new friends with money, the Kim regime invited the hated Japanese for a visit, and in 1990 a Japanese political delegation representing two of Japan's major political parties visited Pyongyang and met with officials of the Workers' Party of Korea. Although this was not an official government-to-government meeting, it did open dialogue between the two longtime enemies. Soon, however, the budding relationship broke down, leaving the North Korean association of Koreans in Japan ("Chosen Soren" in Japanese) as the main link between the two countries. When North Korea fired a ballistic missile over Japan and out into the Pacific in 1998, relations between the two countries turned overtly hostile.

North Korea's government-run economy completely broke down in the mid-1990s, but the Kim regime, headed by Kim Jong-il after his father's death in 1994, had a powerful diplomatic card to play in the form of its nuclear weapons program. After a series of high-level meetings with US officials, the two governments signed an "Agreed Framework" in 1994 that promised the Kim regime American and American-backed aid and two new "peaceful" nuclear power reactors in return for a promised end to North Korea's nuclear weapons–friendly program. This agreement with North Korea's archenemy gave Kim Jong-il a measure of diplomatic credibility, although it did not result in diplomatic ties or even a peace treaty with the United States, which still deeply distrusted the Kim regime.

Going into the new century, North Korea both benefited and suffered from its official military-first policy, which was the centerpiece of Kim Jong-il's politics. From 2003 to 2007 the two Koreas, Japan, China, Russia, and the United States met in the Six-Party Talks to seek a formula to stop North Korea's nuclear weapons program. Although the talks ultimately failed, they did serve to keep North Korea in the political spotlight and gave Kim Jong-il the kind of international credibility (although not respectability) that he longed for.

In 2000 the two Koreas held their very first summit meeting. Two years later, Japanese prime minister Junichiro Koizumi traveled to Pyongyang for the first-ever Japan–North Korea summit. In 2004 Koizumi returned to Pyongyang for a second visit, but relations did not improve. As North Korea built up its missile and nuclear forces, Japan instituted ever stricter economic sanctions, and the Japanese people remain strongly prejudiced against North Koreans. For its part, the North Korean press continued to castigate Japan for its past and present behavior, claiming that Japan was preparing to reinvade Korea.

On the Russian front, in July 2000, President Vladimir Putin met with Kim Jong-il in Pyongyang, marking the first (and at this writing the only) time that a Soviet or Russian leader had visited North Korea. A month later Kim took the train to Moscow for another meeting, and in 2002 he traveled by train to Vladivostok for a third meeting. After Kim Jong-un took power in 2011, he waited until 2019 to meet with Putin—in Vladivostok. In many respects it is hardly surprising that these two neighboring countries are not closer. North Korea was founded by the Soviet Union and copied many of its political and economic structures but never became an important participant in the communist bloc. The Kim Il-sung brand of dynastic rule is almost as alien to communism as it is to democracy, and the two countries share only a short border in a region that is remote for both of them. North Korea is a penniless trading partner. As long as North Korea does not start another war, its importance to Russia is mainly as a pawn in the renewed Cold War.

The sixth participant in the Six-Party Talks was the United States, an honorary member of the region by virtue of its long-standing alliances with

Japan and South Korea. Like Japan and South Korea (except when it is governed by left-leaning "unification presidents"), the United States has remained hostile toward North Korea, criticizing the Kim regime for its confrontational tactics, its nuclear weapons program, its human rights policies, and a host of state-sponsored crimes, including international smuggling, drug dealing, cybercrime, and counterfeiting. Relations have remained distrustful, and even two summit meetings between President Donald Trump and Supreme Leader Kim Jong-un in 2018 and 2019 have done nothing to change the US–North Korea relationship.

Seventy years after it was founded, North Korea remains a strange and lonely country of twenty-five million people. It no longer calls itself communist, and the Kim regime still resists moves toward capitalism. North Korea has no close friends, but it has kept its longtime enemies. Kim Il-sung's famous 1955 *juche* speech of independence and self-reliance was more prescient than he might have known.

NORTH KOREA AND SOUTH KOREA: DEADLY COMPETITION

The existence of two separate Koreas is a serious problem for the Kim regime. North and South Korea are close in so many ways, yet the Kims must keep them far apart—or conquer and rule over the South. The two Koreas have the same people—historically there are no cultural differences between them. They speak the same language (although after years of separation their dialects have diverged), share the same history, and eat the same food. What separates them is that the people of the North have been captured and imprisoned by the Kim regime, which needs their support to stay in power. Without this artificial division, the Northerners would be happy to live the same life as the Southerners.

Because the Kim regime completely dominates its people and their politics, the regime has always favored "people-to-people" contacts with South Koreans, meaning that the regime's people, who are completely under its control, would be free to meet with antigovernment groups in the South in an attempt to form a united front against the South's democratic government. Another long-standing North Korean campaign has called for the South Korean government to sever its alliance relations with the United States (in line with the principle of "Korean independence") so that the South, with its multiple parties and smaller armed forces, would be forced to deal politically and militarily with the united North—without any American support. For

several decades after the two Koreas became separate states, their governments had virtually no contact with each other, and they both claimed jurisdiction over the entire peninsula. Then, beginning in 1972, sporadic diplomatic contacts occurred. Since the late 1990s the contacts have become
somewhat more frequent, even while both governments prevent their citizens
from freely contacting one another.

The first official contact between the two Koreas was not actually between their governments but between their Red Cross organizations. In 1972,
officials from the two governments signed the July 4 Agreement, which laid
out three principles to guide eventual Korean reunification: negotiations
without foreign interference (e.g., from the United States, China, or the Soviet Union), peaceful overtures (despite the North's continuing military provocations), and acceptance of "multifaceted North-South exchange of information," by which the Kim regime meant that its propaganda could be sent to
the South but information from the South (and elsewhere) would still be
barred by the North. The July 4 Agreement did nothing to bring the two
Koreas closer together, and soon the North was resuming its terrorist attacks
on the South.

In 1988, with communist governments in Europe beginning to collapse
and China well on the road to capitalism, South Korean president Roh Tae-
woo initiated his own version of the *Ostpolitik* strategy that was bringing the
two Germanys together. Under his *"Nordpolitik,"* Roh extended a hand of
friendship to North Korea's allies, the Soviet Union and China. As it related
to North Korea, *Nordpolitik* permitted ordinary South Koreans to contact
citizens in the North (after receiving South Korean government permission),
authorized trade between the two Koreas (also requiring government permission), and initiated occasional dialogue with the government in the North.
After extensive intergovernment talks, two agreements were initialed in late
1991. The first was the Agreement on Reconciliation, Nonaggression, and
Exchanges and Cooperation, whose title was self-explanatory and overly
optimistic. The two governments also initialed the Joint Declaration of South
and North Korea on the Denuclearization of the Korean Peninsula, which
failed to slow North Korea's march toward nuclear weapons.

The first meeting of the leaders of the two Koreas took place in Pyongyang in June 2000 (postponed from a planned meeting in 1994 that was
canceled after North Korean leader Kim Il-sung died suddenly). The two
leaders, Kim Jong-il and South Korean president Kim Dae-jung, signed a
joint declaration that, once again, committed them to work toward unification

without other countries interfering, and promised to promote "balanced development" of the national economy, a code term referring to massive South Korean aid to North Korea. Although numerous economic projects were proposed, North Korean suspicion, red tape, and lack of knowledge of capitalism severely limited cooperation.

The second inter-Korean summit meeting, this one between Kim Jong-il and South Korean president Roh Moo-hyun, took place in Pyongyang in October 2007. A Declaration on the Advancement of South-North Relations, Peace, and Prosperity was signed, promoting again the idea of balanced development and, in particular, proposing that South Korean companies establish small assembly plants in the North to benefit from its inexpensive labor. Most recently, at the time this is written, South Korean president Moon Jae-in has met three times (in 2018) with North Korean leader Kim Jong-un, signing declarations in Pyongyang that reiterated what had been previously agreed to. No North Korean leader has ever visited Seoul. The diplomatic results of these agreements, spanning decades, have been limited to a North Korean willingness to conduct sporadic dialogue with the South Korean government, choosing its own time and place, and frequently canceling meetings. On the economic front, most South Korean businesses entering North Korea have failed. North Korean government suspicion and hostility toward the South has continued, and North Korean citizens are still forbidden to travel to the South (or anywhere else outside their country) except in groups under the watchful eye of North Korean security agents, nor are they permitted to communicate with South Koreans.

In the absence of diplomatic contacts with their neighbor to the south, the three Kim regimes have resorted to threats and armed provocations, the most notable of which was the massive North Korean attack on June 25, 1950, that launched the Korean War. Since then, North Koreans have initiated dozens of provocations against the South by land, sea, and air. The purpose of these attacks is hard to divine, and none had any chance of changing the South Korean political system. Rather, the attacks hardened the South Korean government's opposition toward the North. Notable incidents included the 1958 hijacking of a South Korean airliner, the 1968 commando raid on the South Korean presidential mansion, the 1968 naval landing of 120 commandos on the east coast, and the 1970 bombing attempt to kill the South Korean president at the Korean National Cemetery.

Even in the era of occasional dialogue since 1972, the North continued its attacks. In 1974 another North Korean assassination attempt was made while the president visited the National Theater. In 1983 North Korean agents attempted to kill the president and his entourage during their state visit to Burma (now Myanmar). In 1987 North Korean agents bombed a Korean Air Lines plane in Southeast Asia. In 1996 and 1998 North Korean submarines sent to infiltrate commandos were captured on South Korea's east coast. In 2010 a South Korean naval ship was sunk, presumably by a North Korean submarine, and a South Korean island was shelled by North Korean artillery.

In June 2020, during the administration of South Korean president Moon, who was very sympathetic toward the North, the Kim regime became angry that defectors living in South Korea were sending large balloons north carrying leaflets and demanded that the South Korean government stop this from happening. When the government proved unable to do this in the face of constitutional freedom of speech guarantees, the North Korean government blew up the unoccupied South Korean–built four-story office building housing the North-South liaison office in the North Korean city of Kaesong. The explosion also damaged a few nearby buildings. As the North Korean press laconically announced, "the liaison office was tragically ruined with a terrific explosion."[3] North Korea followed up the explosion by threatening military action against South Korea.

In good times and bad, both Korean governments have pledged that reunification is their ultimate goal. South Korea has its Ministry of Unification, and North Korea has its Committee for the Peaceful Reunification of the Fatherland, whose name belies the hostile statements it occasionally issues. For example, in 2016:

> The Committee for the Peaceful Reunification of the Fatherland, upon authorization [of Kim Jong-un?] proclaims as follows in connection with the prevailing dangerous situation: From this hour on, every act and every move of our revolutionary armed forces . . . will be directed at a retaliatory war of justice to resolutely remove the [President] Park Geun-hye gang of traitors from this land and from under this sky. . . . We do not hide that our retaliatory war may kick off inside Cheongwadae [the South Korean presidential residence] or may be carried out near Cheongwadae.[4]

Apart from North Korea's continued belligerent attitude toward the South, the essential challenge to reunification is that the two governments have different political systems—a democracy versus one of the world's strictest dictatorships. It is hard to see how the two Koreas could unify, short of one defeating or swallowing up the other. The Kim regime would never tolerate democracy. In its own words, "Reunification under a 'free democratic system' is, needless to say, aimed at harming our idea and system and extending [South Korea's] rotten fascist ruling system to the North. It is, in fact, as good as a declaration of war on us."[5]

The Kim regime's unification principles were embodied in the July 4 Agreement and repeated in later agreements. In 1980 and 1993 Kim Il-sung proposed a "10-Point Program of the Great Unity of the Whole Nation for the Reunification of the Country" that expanded on the three principles. The proposal was essentially for the two Koreas to become a federation of "one nation, one state, two systems and two governments." Thus, on paper the two Koreas would be unified, but in practice they would remain separate countries. South Korea envisions a true reunification of the two systems under democracy, preferably occurring in stages over a period of decades: first, arms reduction (including North Korea's denuclearization), then economic and social exchanges, and finally complete unification.

It can only be surmised what kind of unification the North Korean people want since no surveys are published in the North, but it can be safely assumed that they would be delighted to become truly unified if they could share in the economic benefits of South Korea. In 2018 a small survey of North Korean defectors living in South Korea found that over 90 percent of them, when they still lived in North Korea, wanted unification, although only half had thought it was possible.[6] New surveys of attitudes toward unification and estimates of when unification will occur are conducted almost every year in South Korea, and the trend in recent years has been for younger South Koreans to put less emphasis on reunification and more on peaceful coexistence. The obvious costs of unification have put a damper on their desire for early unification, and these younger generations have few ties with the people of the North. For example, in a 2018 survey, only 41 percent of people in their twenties considered reunification necessary at some point in the future, compared to 58 percent in their forties, 62 percent in their fifties, and 67 percent over sixty.[7]

Most Koreans in the South and in the North strongly identify as members of one Korean people, yet in many respects they are further apart from each other than they are from citizens of other countries. Emotionally, Koreans desire to be unified. Practically, most South Koreans, as well as the Kim regime elites in the North, are more sensitive to near-term costs than long-term gains. Most foreign observers of Korea predict that unification will eventually come, but not for decades unless some extraordinary event such as a change in the North Korean regime triggers it. And even when the Kim regime as an obstacle to reunification is finally overcome, the South Koreans will likely try to control and prolong the unification process in order to reduce economic and social costs to their own society.

NORTH KOREA AND CHINA: BEWARE OF THE DRAGON

The people who originally populated the Korean Peninsula moved down from what is now China. Over the millennia different groups swept over China from the north, most notably the Mongols and the Manchus, establishing dynasties and eventually becoming intermixed with the native Han people. These groups also expanded their influence into the adjoining Korean Peninsula, at times defeating the people living there and then, as China's rulers, establishing a suzerain relationship over them.

To this day the Koreans, especially the North Koreans, keep a wary eye on the Chinese for fear that they might again expand their influence over Korea. North Korea's 880-mile-long border with China is today fairly well demarcated by two rivers, but even so, the two countries don't always agree on the exact borderline. The most controversial section of the border straddles Paektu Mountain, a volcanic peak that is considered politically sacred by both countries but especially by the North Koreans, who claim that their founder, Kim Il-sung, had a guerrilla camp on the mountain slope.

Centuries ago both China and Korea exercised jurisdiction over land in the border region. The Korean Koguryo kingdom in the fifth to eighth centuries spread across what is now northeast China. On the other hand, the Chinese Yuan dynasty of the thirteenth and fourteenth centuries dominated much of the Korean Peninsula. Today approximately two million ethnic Koreans live in several northeastern Chinese provinces, thereby providing a ready-made trading link with North Korea as well as a refuge for North Koreans fleeing from their country—and a reminder that, depending on which historical era one cites, both countries have claims to the area.

Within two years of becoming the ruler of a separate state, Kim Il-sung wanted to invade South Korea. In order to do so, he had to consult with Mao Zedong and Joseph Stalin, both of whom gave their grudging consent. When the war went badly for Kim, China sent several million soldiers to his aid, 180,000 of whom died in the war. Without these Chinese "volunteers," North Korea would probably have been wiped off the map. Instead of showing gratitude, the North Koreans have, for the most part, tried to hide this Chinese assistance, claiming instead that they defeated the United States single-handedly. But on those occasions when they want to advertise their political ties with China, they claim that North Korea and China are as close as "lips and teeth" and that their political relationship is "sealed in blood." The Chinese and North Korean political systems were initially similar. In its economy, North Korea tended to favor the industrial development model of the Soviet Union while feeling greater affinity toward the culturally similar Chinese. Like Mao (and for that matter Stalin), Kim Il-sung intended to remain the ruler of his country indefinitely. But Stalin died in 1953 and Mao in 1976, leaving only Kim holding on to the reins of power. By the time he died, in 1994, he had transformed North Korea's communist system into a personal dictatorship "in the Korean style." As North Korea distanced itself from China and Russia, it had to perform a skillful balancing act because it needed economic assistance and political and military support from both countries. When in the early 1960s the Chinese objected to the Soviet Union's putative role as the leader of global communism, North Korea sided with China. During the Chinese Cultural Revolution later in that decade, the Red Guards attacked Kim Il-sung as a "revisionist," causing North Korea to draw away from China. Kim was also angered by China's invitation to Richard Nixon in 1972, and he became even angrier when China supported South Korea's request to join the UN before the two Koreas reunified, thereby forcing North Korea to join as a separate state as well. In 1992, a year after the two Koreas joined the UN, China and South Korea established diplomatic relations—without any "cross-recognition" that would have granted North Korea diplomatic relations with the United States. North Korea became something of an orphaned communist country.

The Chinese Communist Party under Deng Xiaoping permitted the Chinese people to develop a market economy, which became a great success. Kim Il-sung refused to take China's advice to do likewise, and from the early 1980s the economies of the two countries diverged. By 1985 China's trade with South Korea was larger than its trade with North Korea, in 1990 it was ten times larger, and in 1997 it was thirty-six times larger. By 2018, China's total trade with South Korea (its fourth-largest trading partner) was approximately one hundred times greater than its trade with North Korea (some China–North Korea border trade is not reported, but the total amount is relatively small by international standards). North Korea became a financial drag on China, running trade deficits in the hundreds of millions of dollars year after year. Fortunately, this was a trade gap that the rapidly growing

Chinese economy could easily absorb. Perhaps the Chinese government's greatest regret has been that the Kim regime refuses to develop its economy in a way that would help the economically backward northeastern Chinese provinces, which for years have been hoping for a trade windfall from across the border.

Another political and diplomatic balancing act was required, this time from China, after North Korea began its serious pursuit of nuclear weapons. In 1994 China welcomed an agreement among the United States, Japan, South Korea, and North Korea to provide an energy-producing substitute for North Korea's new nuclear program. That agreement ultimately failed. Beginning in 2003 China hosted the Six-Party Talks (China and Russia joining the other four states) to come up with another solution to the North's campaign to produce nuclear weapons. That effort failed as well. It became clear that nothing within reason was going to stop the North's nuclear program, and when in 2006 the UN began imposing sanctions on North Korea for its nuclear and missile programs, China reluctantly went along. In its attempts to uphold a series of UN economic sanctions imposed over the years and at the same time prevent the North Korean economy from collapsing, China tends to relax some of the sanctions and to ignore Chinese entrepreneurs who bypass them.

It is difficult to divine exactly what the official opinions of the two governments are toward each other because, like most governments, their pronouncements are guarded, and in neither country is there a free press that can interpret or comment on government positions. For years the assumption has been that China is firmly opposed to North Korea's developing nuclear weapons. In the absence of informative official news, it is necessary to rely on opinions that appear in the Chinese press, making the assumption that those opinions are not likely to be diametrically opposed to official government positions. For example, a February 2016 editorial in China's *Global Times* asserted that "the North Korean nuclear issue lies fundamentally with the hostility between North Korea and the United States. . . . We have to say that the US factor is the major driver that has exacerbated the North Korean crisis time after time. . . . That is to say, the key that can unlock the North Korea nuclear crisis hangs on Uncle Sam's belt."[8] But the editorial then continued, "China is the United States' real overall target on the west coast of the Pacific Ocean; North Korea is only a short-term concern."

Even though China may blame the United States for creating a situation that induces the Kim regime to develop nuclear weapons and the missiles to deliver them, China does not approve of the regime's nuclear response to American pressure. A 2017 academic opinion piece in the *Global Times* was highly critical of North Korea: "North Korea possessing nuclear weapons has become a major and real threat for peace and stability on the Peninsula. This is an indisputable fact. . . . China's role is to prompt North Korea to come to its senses and change its tune."[9] The Kim regime has never accepted criticism humbly, whether coming from friend or foe. Three months after the appearance of this criticism in the *Global Times*, the official North Korean press published a lengthy response, reading in part, "*Renmin Ribao* and the *Global Times*, widely known to represent the official positions of the party and government of China, are pouring out articles covering large sections of their newspaper pages. . . . These commentaries argued that [North] Korea is threatening the security of the northeastern region by conducting nuclear tests . . . and providing the United States with 'an excuse for strengthening its strategic deployment' in the region. . . . China should better ponder over the grave consequences to be entailed by its reckless outrageous act of chopping down the pillar of [North] Korea-China relations today."[10]

This heated exchange supports the long-standing assumption among foreigners that China and North Korea are uneasy neighbors. In a meeting with American congressmen back in 1997, Chinese premier Li Peng reportedly said, "North Korea is neither an ally of the PRC [People's Republic of China] nor an enemy, but merely a neighboring country."[11] In late 2017, the editor of the *Global Times*, presumably as a way of defending China from the American charge that China was not doing its part to combat North Korea's nuclear program, explained on a popular Chinese blog that "many Chinese people think we are North Korea's 'big brother' and [North Korea] should carry out every order we give. But the reality is, China and North Korea have never been 'brothers' to begin with. We can choose to become hostile toward North Korea, but we cannot make Pyongyang do whatever we say."[12]

Another way of gauging the closeness of the two governments is to look at their official visits. Although Mao could not have been happy with the outcome of the Korean War, the two veteran fighters who ruled China and North Korea seemed to enjoy a close relationship, and Kim Il-sung visited China almost every year. Their successors have not shared the same wartime background. China has never approved of dynastic succession—a decidedly noncommunist political practice. Kim Jong-il became the official ruler of North Korea when his father died in 1994, but he did not make his first visit to China until six years later. After that, Kim traveled to China almost every other year, witnessing the Chinese economic miracle but refusing to imitate it, to the chagrin of his Chinese hosts.

Much like his father, Kim Jong-un was in no hurry to visit China after he took over the country in late 2011—or perhaps he was simply not invited to Beijing. If the Chinese did not favor the leadership succession of Kim Jong-il in 1994, as seems likely, they certainly could not have liked the Kim Jong-un succession of 2011, although by then they must have been resigned to the North Korean tradition of dynastic succession. Kim Jong-un did not make his first trip to China until seven years after he took office, but then he made two more visits in the same year and one the following year. It is impossible to say what he talked about on those visits, but there is no reason to believe that relations between China and North Korea measurably improved. Chinese leader Xi Jinping paid a visit to Pyongyang in 2019, his first visit to Pyongyang since taking office in 2013 (he visited South Korea a year after taking office).

North Korea is an economic burden and a political embarrassment to China, which wants to be seen as a respectable world power rather than the ally of a disreputable neighbor—and, what's worse, a neighbor that in some ways reminds people of China's own political system. North Korea is important as a neighbor that eventually may come under Chinese influence. North Korea is also a useful buffer to keep American troops away from the Chinese border. In Beijing, the United States is the main concern, with North Korea more of a pawn in a bigger game. If North Korea distracts the United States in this game of big-power politics, so much the better. But the last thing China wants is for North Korea to trigger American aggression on China's doorstep.

NORTH KOREA AND JAPAN: AGE-OLD ENMITY

For two countries separated by only a few hundred miles of water, North Korea and Japan have an exceptionally distant relationship. North Korea's major eastern port, Wonsan, is only 418 miles from the important Japanese port of Fukuoka. Opposing political systems have separated the two countries during the last seven decades, and today there is strong animosity on both sides.

Several thousand years of history have witnessed many hostilities between Korea and Japan, as has been the case between so many neighboring nations. The Mongol rulers of China enlisted the Koreans to join them in two unsuccessful invasions of Japan in the thirteenth century. The Japanese, on their way to attack China, invaded Korea twice in the sixteenth century, killing tens of thousands. As a trophy and proof of their victory, the ears and noses of at least thirty-eight thousand Koreans were brought back to Japan and buried in the Mimizuka (Ear Mound) in Kyoto. In these campaigns the Japanese also took many Korean national treasures and carried back with them Korean artisans who taught the Japanese cultural skills such as pottery making, mostly originating in China.

Memories of the bitter Japanese colonial period still shape Korean views of the Japanese. The Japanese did not even have to defeat Koreans in order to incorporate them into the Japanese Empire. Japan expelled the Chinese from Korea in the 1894–1895 Sino-Japanese War and eliminated Russian influence in the 1904–1905 Russo-Japanese War, after which the Japanese began to take administrative control of the Korean government. In 1910, Korea was forced to become part of the Japanese Empire and remained so until the Japanese were defeated by Western forces in World War II.

During the colonial period the Japanese tried to make Koreans loyal second-class Japanese citizens by obliterating Korean culture. In resistance, Koreans staged a few anti-Japanese revolts that were easily quelled. Some Koreans, like Kim Il-sung, left the country to fight the Japanese in China. During the occupation, the Japanese built modern industrial infrastructure in Korea, bringing the country into the twentieth-century economy. Yet the Koreans have not forgotten the decades during which the Japanese tried to make them into Japanese. In 1965 Japan and South Korea signed a Treaty of Basic Relations. Japan wanted to move in this direction with North Korea as well, but the North demanded that it be compensated not only for purported economic damage inflicted during the colonial period but also for the years since the occupation, and this demand met with firm opposition from Japan. The two governments have never signed a "peace treaty," and the people of North Korea and Japan remain mutually hostile to this day. The Kim regime's media frequently warn that the Japanese are preparing another invasion of the Korean Peninsula, an illusion shared by no one else.

North Korean contact with Japan is extremely limited. During the colonial period thousands of Koreans went to Japan for education and employment. In the run-up to the Pacific War, two million Koreans were drafted to work in Japan, including "comfort women," who were forced to work as prostitutes for the Japanese army. In the late 1950s and early 1960s, some ninety-three thousand Koreans living in Japan emigrated to North Korea under the mistaken impression that they were going to a worker's paradise. Some members of the North Korean organization of Koreans living in Japan, Chosen Soren, traveled back and forth to North Korea on the *Mangyongbong* and *Mangyongbong 92* ferries until the service was banned by Japan in 2006.

A particularly strange and unfortunate form of contact between the two countries involved North Korean abductions of an undetermined number of Japanese in the late 1970s and early 1980s. The Japanese government officially recognizes seventeen abductions (five of the individuals were allowed to return to Japan), whereas the Japanese police have listed 866 people missing that they think may have been abducted from coastal areas of the country. Most of the abductees were young, and some were just youths. In North Korea, some of the abductees were required to become language teachers and wives of Japanese already living there. Although the number of abductees was small compared to the number of Koreans drafted by Japan during the colonial period, this human rights issue has become one of the strongest barriers to better Japanese relations with North Korea.

For many years the Kim regime adamantly denied any knowledge of the abductions. Then in 2002 Kim Jong-il acknowledged that the North had abducted thirteen Japanese. For this he apologized and said that the abductors, whom he called rogue elements of the military, would be punished. He also claimed that eight of the thirteen abductees had died of natural causes, a claim that further angered the Japanese public. Kim denied that any other Japanese had been abducted, and despite subsequent agreements to conduct further investigations, North Korea continues to insist on this point. The poster child of the abduction issue has been Megumi Yokota, a Japanese girl who was abducted in 1977 at the age of thirteen, and who the North Koreans claim committed suicide in 1993, although this claim cannot be verified. The five Japanese who survived after their abduction were later repatriated.

Yet another strange link between the two countries is that the mother of the current North Korean dictator, Kim Jong-un, was born a Korean resident of Japan before moving to North Korea as a young child. She became an entertainer and as an adult, before she married Kim Jong-il, traveled to Japan with a North Korean entertainment troupe. Moreover, in the early 1990s, it appears that a young Kim Jong-un and his older brother Kim Jong-chul traveled to Japan as tourists under assumed names. The oldest of the Kim boys, Kim Jong-nam, also traveled to Japan in 2001. He was arrested and deported by Japanese authorities. The North Korean people have never been told of any of these Kim regime connections with Japan.

Until the mid-2000s, Japan was North Korea's third-largest trading partner. Japan had the technology that North Korea desperately needed, and Chosen Soren facilitated trade through its many companies. In the early 1970s North Korea went on a purchasing spree, buying goods from noncommunist countries. Several hundred million dollars' worth of goods were purchased on credit from Japan, a clear indication of how much North Korea could benefit today from economic relations with Japan. North Korea's default on its payments ended any possibility of future trade with reputable Japanese companies. In addition to the legitimate goods it has imported, banned items have also found their way to North Korea. Beginning in 2006, a year that saw several North Korean ballistic missile tests and the country's first nuclear test, the Japanese government instituted stricter trade sanctions on North Korea, and these sanctions have strengthened over the years, essentially eliminating Japan as a trading partner. Yet every year North Korean fishing boats by the hundreds poach in Japan's exclusive economic zone despite the efforts of Japan's coast guard to drive them out, and every year hundreds of dilapidated wooden "ghost boats," presumably from North Korea, wash up on the Japanese shoreline, sometimes carrying dead fishermen.

Politically, Japan and North Korea have rarely talked to each other. An exception occurred in 1990 when a delegation representing two of Japan's major political parties visited Pyongyang and met with officials of the Workers' Party of Korea. In 1994, after prolonged negotiations, the United States signed a nuclear agreement with North Korea that called for the North's eventual abandonment of nuclear weapons development in return for economic aid provided by the Korean Peninsula Energy Development Organization (KEDO). Japan agreed to help fund KEDO and provided half a million tons of food aid during North Korea's mid-decade famine.

Japan–North Korea dialogue resumed in 2000, with Japan granting additional food aid, and the two sides fruitlessly discussed normalization of relations. In 2002, Japanese prime minister Junichiro Koizumi met Kim Jong-il in North Korea, and he returned for another meeting in 2004. Neither meeting was cordial or productive. When North Korea conducted its first nuclear test in 2006, relations became even more strained, if that was possible. Subsequent nuclear tests and missile launches, including numerous missiles that have landed in or near Japan's special economic zone, have prevented any improvement in relations between the two neighbors.

The North Korean media publish a constant stream of threats against Japan for its historical animosity, its economic sanctions against North Korea, its talk of reformulating its "peace constitution" into one that permits Japan to mount a stronger defense against countries that threaten it, and of course Japan's military alliance with the United States. To take only one of countless examples, in 2017 the (North) Korea Asia-Pacific Peace Committee, responding to a new round of UN sanctions, criticized Japan for cooperating with them: "The behavior of Japs, sworn enemy of the Korean nation, are enraging us. . . . A telling blow should be dealt to them who have not yet come to [their] senses after the launch of our ICBM over the Japanese archipelago. The four islands of the archipelago should be sunken into the sea by the nuclear bomb of *Juche*. Japan is no longer needed to exist near us."[13]

Japan can get along without North Korea, although a reduction in the North Korean threat would be much appreciated. North Korea, on the other hand, could mightily benefit from better relations with Japan, a wealthy advanced nation with the resources to help one of East Asia's poorest and most backward countries. Unfortunately, there is little reason to expect that relations between these two neighbors will improve in the foreseeable future.

JAPAN'S CHOSEN SOREN: A FIFTH COLUMN IN ENEMY TERRITORY

Almost since the day it became a state, North Korea has been able to call on the assistance of a substantial community of sympathizers living in Japan, North Korea's long-standing enemy. The great irony of this circumstance is that these Koreans have for decades been free to aid North Korea, while in North Korea no one is free to do anything.

From 1910 until 1945, when Korea was a colony of Japan, thousands of Koreans emigrated to Japan to take advantage of its relatively advanced economy. As the war years approached, the Japanese government drafted over two million Koreans to come to Japan to work in industries for a period of a few years at a time, including thousands of Korean women who were recruited to work as prostitutes for the Japanese forces—a fact that many Japanese still deny and most Koreans cannot forget. Immediately after the war ended, the majority of Koreans returned to their homeland, now divided into north and south, and those who remained in Japan found themselves ostracized from Japanese society, which has never been accepting of foreigners. Unable to assimilate easily, the Korean residents (known as Zainichi Koreans, meaning foreign-resident Koreans) formed their own communities and associations. By the early 1990s, the number of Koreans in Japan numbered some eight hundred thousand.

Korean residents of Japan organized themselves into two social-political groups. The organization that eventually professed political loyalty to South Korea was Mindan, a Japanese-language abbreviation of "Korean Residents Union in Japan." A more active organization of Koreans, loyal to the Kim government in the North, was established in 1955. This was the "General Association of Korean Residents in Japan," abbreviated in Korean as Chongryon and in Japanese as Chosen Soren or Chosoren. Interestingly, most Chosoren members had originally come from the southern part of a unified Korea, but as leftists they were more attracted to the communist government of the North. This group was also more nationalistic than the Mindan group and more hostile toward the Japanese government. Needless to say, Chosoren was not looked upon kindly by the government or by most Japanese citizens. Nonetheless, since Japanese culture seeks to avoid conflict, the popular attitude toward Chosoren was benign neglect, even while the Japanese police tried to keep the organization under surveillance.

In the late 1950s, as the initial stage of recovery from the Korean War was completed, the Kim Il-sung regime decided to invite Koreans living in Japan to return to their native land and help with the rebuilding. Although North Korea at the time was desperately poor, the regime's propaganda made out that the country was a paradise where Koreans could live in peace and prosperity and not be looked down upon by their Japanese neighbors. The Japanese government was eager to get rid of their Korean residents, and the Japanese Red Cross Society organized emigration trips for any Koreans and their families who wanted to leave the country.[14] Beginning in 1959, some ninety-three thousand Koreans made what turned out to be a one-way journey to North Korea before the program ended in 1984, with most Koreans emigrating in the first few years of the program. Some settled well and received good treatment, but the majority were discriminated against as Koreans who had been "polluted" by foreign life, and many ended up in labor camps. The immigrants were not permitted to return to Japan, but they could correspond with their friends and relatives in Japan, who sent them money and gifts to help them survive in the harsh North Korean economy and bribe North Korean officials to give them better treatment. More than 1,800 Japanese family members, mostly wives of Korean men, also ended up in North Korea. Only a handful of these wives have ever been able to return for a visit to their relatives in Japan, and that was only thirty years later as a result of political negotiations between the Japanese and North Korean governments.

Mindan and Chosoren have their own schools and social organizations. The North Korean government boasts of providing millions of dollars to support the Chosoren schools, but in fact most of the money moves the other way, with Chosoren soliciting funds from its members to send to North Korea, along with technology and Japanese goods. Much of the money was carried by Chosoren members making visits to their homeland to see relatives, traveling on a North Korean ferry that made monthly trips between the two countries. The original ferry, the *Mangyongbong* (named after the hill in Pyongyang where Kim Il-sung is said to have been born), began sailing in 1971; its replacement, the *Mangyongbong 92*, sailed from 1992 until the Japanese government banned the vessel in 2006. Estimates of the amount of contributions flowing to North Korea by the early 1990s, much of it on the *Mangyongbong*, are as high as half a billion dollars a year. It is likely that a considerable amount of Japanese technical equipment, some of which aided the North Korean weapons program, was smuggled on the ships as well. It is also likely that some of the Japanese women who were abducted by North Korean agents in the 1970s and 1980s were carried on board the ships to a lifetime of exile in North Korea. Chosoren has also presumably been an excellent cover for North Korean spies operating in Japan.

As North Korea's fortunes declined in the 1990s, and as the original Koreans living in Japan were succeeded by later generations, Chosoren went into decline. At the first Japan–North Korea summit meeting in 2002, Kim Jong-il admitted to the visiting Japanese prime minister that North Koreans had indeed abducted a small number of Japanese and taken them to North Korea as Japanese instructors. This was something the Japanese had long accused the North Koreans of doing, and Chosoren, along with the North Korean government, had vigorously denied it. Now Chosoren was revealed as lying. The Japanese public turned even more strongly against North Korea and Chosoren when Kim claimed that a number of the abducted Japanese had died (prematurely) of natural causes.

Chosoren schoolchildren, who wore distinctive North Korean–style school uniforms, were harassed, and membership declined dramatically. As the Japanese public became more frustrated with the failure of the North Korean government to divulge credible information about the abductions, the Japanese government instituted harsher embargoes against North Korea and decided to tax Chosoren organizations as non-charitable entities. The exact size of Chosoren membership is difficult to determine. For years the organization did not publish any membership numbers, although it was assumed that in the early 1990s the organization might have about half a million members. In 2016 the Japanese government counted thirty-four thousand registered Chosoren members. If unregistered members were included, the number might have reached eighty thousand. [15]

Because Koreans living in Japan were frequently discriminated against in the job market, many resident Koreans started their own businesses, and to serve those businesses, Chosoren established a network of credit unions to serve as banks. These banks, along with many others, suffered serious financial losses during the 1997 Asian financial crisis, and about half of them failed. Since they were part of the Japanese banking system, the government rescued them with billions of dollars of taxpayers' money, at the same time taking a closer look at how the Chosoren banks were run. It appeared that over the years much of the Chosoren banks' money may have been remitted to North Korea, and the Japanese government demanded that Chosoren reimburse it for approximately half a billion dollars, which the organization did not have. To collect the debt, the government began auctioning off Chosoren property, including the organization's Tokyo headquarters.

Chosoren schools have also run afoul of the government. At one time they numbered over two hundred and taught forty thousand students, from elementary grades through college. As one would expect, the ideological content of their classes was high. Public hostility toward North Korea and Chosoren prompted the government to restrict the financing of these schools. Subsidies that are routinely granted to parents of Japanese schoolchildren were withdrawn, along with local subsidies to some of the schools. After the turn of the century, total enrollment fell to ten thousand and has continued to decline. [16] As far back as the 1990s, Kim Jong-il had instructed Chosoren to make its schools less distinctively North Korean in order to keep them from provoking negative Japanese comment. Pictures of the two Kims were taken down from the classrooms, and students were no longer required to wear North Korean–style uniforms. Similar instructions continued under Kim Jong-un.

The existence of Chosoren in Japan as an enduring fifth column was made possible, and perhaps even necessary, by the slave-labor policies of the former Japanese Empire and by the ethnic exclusiveness of Japanese society. Chosoren served many functions, some bad and some arguably good. The organization's sponsorship of spying and smuggling to benefit North Korea has been a decided threat to the Japanese nation. On the other hand, Chosoren provided educational and occupational opportunities for thousands of Koreans who were stranded in a foreign and somewhat hostile land. The education offered at Chosoren schools, especially during the Cold War, included not only instruction in communist principles but also indoctrination of a Korean nationalist spirit that helped make Korean students in Japan proud of themselves and their heritage.

It might seem puzzling that so many Koreans in Japan remained loyal to Chosoren even after it became public knowledge that those who had gone to North Korea were treated badly and that Chosoren officials had lied when they denied that Japanese had been abducted by North Korean agents. Part of the reason for this continued loyalty is probably that many Chosoren members had relatives in North Korea who were essentially being held hostage; Chosoren members were pressured by Chosoren and North Korean officials to stay in the organization and send funds to relatives in North Korea. The gradual demise of Chosoren was inevitable as newer generations of Koreans assimilated into Japanese society and as Japanese society and government gradually became aware of how detrimental it was to allow Chosoren to function with virtually no restrictions.

NORTH KOREA AND THE UNITED STATES: THE ULTIMATE ENEMY

Relations between the United States and North Korea started out badly and over the years have continued badly. In 1866 an American merchant ship, the *General Sherman*, sailed up the Taedong River toward Pyongyang with the intention of opening the Korean market to trade. Korea was then known as the "hermit kingdom" because it refused to have relations with foreigners, except of course the Chinese. When the ship's crew made contact with Koreans, the Americans were instructed not to approach Pyongyang without the authorization of higher officials. They sailed ahead anyway. Trading proved to be impossible, and after several hostile encounters the ship made its way back downriver toward the sea. On its way out it ran aground and was set on fire by the Koreans, resulting in the death of all crew members. Americans were unsuccessful in learning about the fate of the missing ship until 1871, when a squadron of American naval vessels forced its way in and defeated Korean resistance. A treaty between the two governments was signed in 1882.

In 1895 the United States signed another document, this one a memorandum with Japan that put Korea firmly in the sphere of the Japanese Empire, where it stayed until the end of the Pacific War. In September 1945, US forces landed in Korea to accept the surrender of Japanese troops south of the 38th parallel, a line of division between Soviet and American postwar jurisdictions drawn by the United States without any input from Koreans. American support for South Korea meant that the United States and North Korea were enemies from the day the two Koreas became separate states. On June 25, 1950, when North Korean troops attacked South Korea, the United States and other allied countries quickly came to South Korea's aid. Bitter fighting over the next three years left a legacy of American hatred toward North Korea and a deep resentment in North Korea over American intervention in what the North Koreans considered to be a civil war launched to reunify their country. Ever since the signing of the 1953 truce ending wartime hostilities, North Koreans have been taught that they won a great victory over the Americans and that their army will surely finish the job if the United States ever attacks them again.

Throughout the rest of the 1950s and into the 1960s, North Korea was transformed into a controlled society beyond what even Stalin had accomplished in the Soviet Union. North Korea's one-party dictatorship, its socialist economy, and its cultlike culture based on medieval Confucianism and the worship of Kim Il-sung combined to make it not only different from the United States but virtually the opposite. The Kim regime, recognizing that the United States was opposed to its very existence, kept its political distance from Americans, even while the armies of the two countries faced each other along the demilitarized zone (DMZ).

North Korea became particularly hostile toward the United States in the late 1960s, although why this happened is hard to tell. Perhaps the increased hostility had something to do with the fact that the United States was becoming involved in, or distracted by, a war in Southeast Asia. Or maybe it resulted from the realization in Pyongyang that forced reunification of the country had become impossible. In 1969, two days after a thirty-one-man North Korean commando team tried unsuccessfully to attack the South Korean president's mansion, the North Koreans seized the American spy ship *Pueblo* off the coast and held its crew for a year before releasing them. The ship itself remains in North Korea as a trophy of war. In April the following year, two North Korean MiGs shot down a US reconnaissance plane over the

East Sea, resulting in the loss of all thirty-one crew members. In neither case did the United States retaliate militarily.

North Korea's hostile provocations continued into the 1970s, interspersed with occasional attempts to engage the United States in dialogue. In 1976 a small contingent of American soldiers attempting to trim a tree that was blocking their view in the DMZ were attacked by North Korean soldiers, who hacked two of the Americans to death. Yet the very next year, and again in 1979, North Korean officials attempted to meet with US officials who were attending international meetings, and in 1983 North Korea sent an open letter to the US Congress proposing talks. These approaches fell on deaf ears.

Lines of communication were finally opened in 1988, when the Reagan administration, presumably responding to South Korea's tentative opening to North Korea, relaxed a few restrictions on trade and people-to-people exchanges with North Korea and permitted American diplomats to meet with North Koreans in third-country venues. Over the next few years, while most communist bloc countries were undergoing sweeping political and economic changes, low-level diplomats from the United States and North Korea met several times a year, usually in Beijing. What specifically brought the United States to the talks, to judge by their agendas, was North Korea's nuclear weapons program, which had come to light by the late 1980s. That is, as North Korea became more of a threat, the United States decided it was better to try to address the threat with dialogue than resort to force.

Bilateral talks in 1993 and 1994, and a trip to Pyongyang by former president Carter in June 1994, led directly to the signing of an agreement by which North Korea promised to abandon its nuclear weapons program in exchange for two powerful "peaceful" nuclear reactors and interim shipments of fuel oil. The United States also provided a "formal assurance" that it would not threaten North Korea with nuclear weapons. President Bill Clinton, whose administration negotiated the deal, sent a letter to "His Excellency Kim Jong-il" promising to "use the full powers of my office" to facilitate the agreement. The agreement was widely criticized in the US foreign policy community for providing North Korea with more than it deserved. Whether or not that criticism was justified, the agreement, which ultimately failed to achieve its denuclearization goal, dramatically boosted the political stature of North Korea's new dictator, Kim Jong-il. In the final year of his presidency, Bill Clinton sent his secretary of state, Madeleine Albright, to Pyongyang to meet with a smiling Kim Jong-il, who hosted a mass performance of young children drafted to dance and sing. The show also included a depiction of a

North Korean missile launch, which could be considered a slap in the face of the visiting secretary. President Clinton also hosted North Korea's top general at the White House and reportedly was himself considering a trip to Pyongyang.

US–North Korea dialogue continued sporadically, and in 2003, when it became clear that North Korea was cheating on the 1994 agreement (which was being implemented by the United States and its allies very slowly), a new dialogue was initiated in the form of the Six-Party Talks (including also South Korea, Japan, Russia, and China). These talks struggled on through 2007 and were formally ended when North Korea quit them. Like the 1994 agreement, the Six-Party Talks failed to stop Pyongyang's nuclear program while earning the North more time to develop weapons and missiles. Contact with the Kim regime continued. In 2008 the New York Philharmonic gave a performance in Pyongyang, and in August 2009 former president Bill Clinton traveled to Pyongyang to effect the release of two imprisoned American journalists. In August the following year, former president Carter traveled to Pyongyang on a similar mission.

None of these contacts slowed North Korea's nuclear or missile programs or softened the Kim regime, which in 2010 sank a South Korean naval vessel and bombarded a South Korean island. North Korea's first nuclear test was held in October 2006, followed by tests in 2009 and 2013, two tests in 2016, and another in 2017, interspersed with test launches of long-range missiles. The high-level American diplomatic visits arguably conferred on the Kim regime a degree of international respectability and proved to the North Korean people that their leader was held in high esteem by their archenemy, the United States. During the eight years of Barack Obama's presidency, the US government adopted a policy of "strategic patience" coupled with stronger economic sanctions, which did nothing to slow North Korea's nuclear campaign. Kim Jong-un, who had taken over when his father died in December 2011, repeatedly threatened to launch nuclear missiles at American bases in Asia and at the US mainland, and he taunted President Obama personally.

After President Donald Trump took office in 2017, he dubbed Kim Jong-un the "little rocket man," while Kim threatened to "surely and definitely tame the mentally deranged U.S. dotard with fire." North Korea's nuclear arsenal continued to grow. With boundless confidence in his negotiating skills and the power of his personality, President Trump decided to personally take charge of diplomacy, meeting with Kim in Singapore in June 2018, again in Hanoi in February 2019, and stepping across the DMZ into North

Korea for a brief conversation with Kim in June 2019. These meetings with a dictator that Trump claimed he actually liked (he had frequently demonstrated a liking for dictators), were best considered to be his personal initiatives and not part of the foreign policy agenda of the US government. During this period North Korea halted its nuclear and long-range missile tests but continued working on its nuclear weapons and missile programs.

Looking back over three decades of political contacts between Pyongyang and Washington, several themes become clear. First, Pyongyang's positions have been consistent. The Kim regime, no matter who was in charge, has always insisted that it will not abandon its nuclear weapons, which it considers to be a deterrent to US aggression, until the United States makes a "bold switchover" in its attitude. In other words, the United States must consider North Korea to be its friend, and moreover, a friend who has been unfairly injured by decades of American mistreatment. In 2010 North Korea estimated that it was owed $65 trillion for damage caused by the United States, including compensation for the deaths of North Koreans.[17] In 2003 North Korea estimated that the United States owed South Korea $43 trillion for similar damages.[18]

If the United States were to consider North Korea to be a friendly nation, there would be no reason, according to the North Koreans, to station American troops in South Korea, or for that matter anywhere in Northeast Asia. Nor should there be any occasion to criticize the Kim regime for its political or economic policies or to object to its human rights policies. Moreover, the United States would be expected to support international economic assistance to North Korea, for example, through the Asian Development Bank. Until such time as the two nations became fast friends, the Kim regime would presumably consider that it needed to keep at least some of its nuclear weapons deterrent and a large part of its conventional forces. *Trust* is not a word in the Kim regime's vocabulary.

A mistake that some naïve American foreign policy makers tend to make is to assume that economic inducements offered to the Kim regime to improve the lives of the North Korean people can convince the regime to reduce its military arsenal. To the contrary, the primary concern of the Kim regime is to stay in power, and to do so it needs a strong military to defend the country from foreign attack—and to control its own people. In fact, it could be argued that any foreign economic incentives that further the creation of a North Korean middle class would be considered an absolute threat to the Kim regime. Hence the American emphasis in recent years on trying to squeeze the Kim regime's elite supporters—who might put pressure on their leader—rather than focusing on the welfare of the North Korean masses.

Finally, although diplomatic negotiations between the United States and North Korea have almost exclusively focused on nuclear disarmament, many other issues are or should be of serious concern to the US government, including North Korea's chemical and biological weapons, its large conventional forces, its counterfeiting and cybercrime programs, and its human rights abuses. Whatever agreements might be reached between the two governments, the two countries will still remain on opposite sides of the world. Or, as the Pyongyang press said many years ago, "the [North] Korean people cannot live under the same sky with the U.S. imperialists who have inflicted immeasurable suffering upon them."[19]

TOURISM: CAUTIOUS AND CONTROLLED

Whereas international diplomacy is the most recognizable form of "high" foreign relations, people-to-people contacts define "low" foreign relations. The Kim regime is eager to promote tourism as a means of earning hard currency. Prices charged to foreigners are based on the official rate of exchange, which is grossly inflated compared to the illegal rate on the street. A secondary reason for welcoming tourists is to convince foreigners that North Korea is a "normal" country, not a hermit kingdom or a totalitarian state. Yet the campaign for tourism directly conflicts with the regime's desire to keep foreigners from learning too much about North Korea, and with the goal of preventing the North Korean people from learning too much about the outside world. For the most part, this social control consideration has outweighed the economic consideration.

The Kim regime is still trying to find a way to reap the economic rewards of international tourism while keeping itself politically secure. In recent years the government has built (with forced labor) a few ski resorts, water parks, and a golf course, mostly to draw in foreign tourists. In many years, mass gymnastic displays at the 150,000-seat Rungrado May First Stadium entertain a small number of foreign guests for several weeks in the summer. The annual Pyongyang marathon attracts a few hundred to a few thousand foreign runners each year in April, depending on the prevailing political climate. Tour companies operating out of China organize specialty tours to North Korea for such things as bicycling and train spotting.

Western tourists enter North Korea by train or by air in tour groups originating in Beijing and organized by one of half a dozen or so tour agencies that have long-standing relationships with the North Korean government. Hotels and transportation are arranged by the tour operator under the government's guidance. What this means is that tourists cannot choose their hotels or travel itinerary, and most tourists see pretty much the same sites in and around Pyongyang. Travel into the countryside is forbidden, except to reach a designated tourist site. Diplomats, aid workers, and a few foreigners who have developed a relationship with North Korean officials are given more freedom to move around the city and, occasionally, to travel to the countryside, usually escorted by "minders."

The two Pyongyang hotels that host tourists are the 47-story Yanggakdo Hotel, built on an island in the Taedong River by a French company and opened in 1996, and the twin-towered Koryo Hotel, built downtown in 1985. Tourists should expect that their rooms are bugged. Hotel service personnel are undoubtedly instructed to report on their guests. Much larger than either of these hotels is the pyramid-shaped, 105-story Ryugyong Hotel, begun by the North Koreans in 1987 but never opened, reportedly because of serious structural problems.

It has been estimated that only about five thousand Western tourists visit North Korea each year (tens of thousands of Chinese come on tour buses, mostly for day trips near the border). According to the Lonely Planet travel website,

> A visit to North Korea offers a glimpse of the world's most isolated nation, where the Internet and much of the 21st century remain relatively unknown, and millions live their lives in the shadow of an all-encompassing personality cult. The compromises required to travel here are significant. You'll be accompanied by two state-employed guides at all times and hear a one-sided account of history while being bussed from sight to sight. Those who can't accept this might be better off staying away—but those who can, will undertake a fascinating journey into another, unsettling world.[20]

Tourists are kept away from ordinary North Koreans by their tour guides. The small band of foreign-aid workers in the country are permitted to come in contact with ordinary Koreans, but in order to continue their charitable work without displeasing the government, these foreigners rarely tell the world anything negative about the country. Sometimes a physical barrier is erected between tourists and North Koreans, as was the case for visitors to the former Mount Kumgang resort, where a fence separated the tour bus road from the North Koreans trudging along the paths beside the road. One South Korean tourist paid a high price for straying out of bounds. Early on a July morning in 2008, a middle-aged South Korean woman left her Kumgang hotel and wandered into an off-limits beach area. All that is known for certain is that she was shot twice in the back by one or more North Korean soldiers. The South Korean government's request for a joint investigation was refused, and as a consequence, ten years after the Kumgang tours began and after almost two million tourists, mostly South Korean, had visited the Hyundai-built reservation, the tourist visits were suspended by the South Korean government.

More often, the barrier between tourists and the local people is in the form of "minders"—ever-present government tour guides who tell their charges what they can and cannot visit and photograph. Ordinary North Koreans know enough to keep their distance from these tourists, although in recent years this invisible barrier has been breaking down. Still, tourists quickly learn that if they try to slip away from their minders, they will be scolded and their minders will get in trouble.

Although by numbers most tourists are curious Chinese from just across the border, it is not difficult for citizens of other countries to obtain a visa. Most people travel to North Korea simply because it is an unusual travel destination. They are not expecting to see beautiful scenery or lively cities; they simply want to experience something different and strange. Their general impression of Pyongyang and the nearby tourist sites is that North Korea is clean and orderly. Few return. Tourist impressions of North Korea can be gleaned from comments left on travel websites such as Tripadvisor and on YouTube videos.

For many years the US State Department advised citizens not to travel to North Korea because of the arbitrary nature of the country's legal system. Over the years, more than a dozen visiting Americans have been arrested and imprisoned, usually for unspecified crimes such as "committing hostile acts against the DPRK" or "espionage." Detained American tourists are given a trial in a closed court and confess to whatever crimes they are charged with. After being imprisoned for several months at hard labor, they are released when an American government official travels to Pyongyang and makes a formal apology. In the most notorious case in recent years, an American college student, who apparently became drunk and disorderly in his hotel and tore down a propaganda poster, was arrested just before his plane departed from Pyongyang in January 2016 and was sentenced to fifteen years' hard labor for "hostile acts." When he was released in June the following year, he was in a vegetative state and died a week later. The North Koreans disclaimed any responsibility for his injury and death. Since then, the US government has prohibited travel to North Korea by US passport holders, except in special circumstances.

For the most part, Westerners visiting North Korea are treated well. North Korea wants to be liked, on its own terms. Given the sorry state of the country's economic infrastructure and the regime's concern to keep its people from being "polluted" by foreign influences, there is little prospect that North Korea will become a tourist mecca—or that North Koreans will be permitted to travel as tourists to other lands. Isolation remains one of the regime's principal weapons of social control. Even those few adventurous foreigners who make the long journey to Pyongyang are unable to see the "real" North Korea.

Chapter Seven

The Economy

From Socialism to Capitalism

THE OLD ECONOMY: SOCIALIST IN PRINCIPLE

During their occupation of the Korean Peninsula from 1910 to 1945, the Japanese controlled much of the Korean economy and exported hundreds of thousands of Koreans to work in the homeland. Anyone wishing to open a business in Korea had to submit a request to the office of the Japanese governor-general. A few Korean businessmen became highly successful, but during this period the Japanese increasingly dominated industry, farming, and trade in Korea.[1] They also developed Korea's economic infrastructure— for the benefit of the Japanese homeland. When Soviet troops arrived in Korea to take over from the defeated Japanese, the northern half of the peninsula possessed 76 percent of Korea's mining production, 92 percent of its electrical generating capacity, and 80 percent of its heavy industrial facilities.[2] Overnight the entire economy above the 38th parallel became the responsibility of the new North Korean government to manage.

Kim Il-sung's elementary school education had not prepared him to direct the country's economy, and his trusted colleagues, soldiers like him, had no more economic expertise than he did. Following the advice and example of his Soviet sponsors, who knew little about Korea and, for that matter, not a whole lot about economics, he imposed centralized management on the economy and put all property under the ownership of "the people," which is to say, under the ownership of the state. The brute force of centralized organization and the high motivation shared by Koreans emerging from years of colonial submission were sufficient to jump-start the economy, which established itself in the 1950s and continued to function adequately into the 1960s and even the 1970s.

The Soviet economic model that Kim followed required that the bulk of the country's resources be devoted to building up heavy industry. Farmers were gradually deprived of the land they had recently been granted and were forced to work on collective farms under the control of the state and the party, with the goal of eventually turning the farms into large state organizations, run like state factories. In the early 1960s, Kim decided to "militarize" the entire country, which meant giving preference to industries that supplied weapons. Light industries that made goods for the people were starved of resources. Like the Soviet Union, North Korea introduced multiyear economic plans that focused the country's resources on achieving the party's economic goals. People worked for the good of the country and received "wages" in the form of pocket change and daily necessities from the local Public Distribution System (PDS) stores, which in principle allocated equal shares to everyone but in fact favored party cadres.

By the late 1960s Kim's militarization was beginning to take its toll on the economy. Officials in Pyongyang found it impossible to manage the entire economy effectively. Corruption crept into operations, with factory and farm managers taking more for themselves and reporting inflated output to the central authorities. The motivation of workers declined as they saw that some were getting more than others and that diligence at work was not rewarded as much as party membership and influence. The government stopped publishing economic statistics. Multiyear economic plans had to be extended to meet their goals.

The annual New Year's editorial, North Korea's version of the American president's State of the Union address, boasted of great economic accomplishments under the party's wise leadership over the previous year—yet it called for exactly the same goals for the next year. This pattern has continued to the present day. The message format and list of economic goals from the 2019 message (no message was delivered in 2020) are virtually identical to what was published decades ago:

> Last year all the people further consolidated the foundations of the self-supporting economy by turning out in the struggle for carrying out the Party's new strategic line of concentrating all efforts on economic construction. . . . We should direct primary efforts to relieving the shortage of electricity. . . . Only

when coal is mass-produced can we resolve the problem of electricity and satisfy the demand for fuel and power. . . . A greater development should be achieved in establishing the *juche* orientation in the metallurgical and chemical industries, the two pillars in economic construction. . . . Rail and other transport sectors should launch an intensive campaign. . . . The agricultural front, the major point of attack in socialist economic construction, should conduct a campaign for increased production.[3]

Kim Il-sung and his son tried to find remedies for the defects of socialism, but without abandoning the socialist model. To replace the deficit in individual worker motivation, they turned to "speed battles," which lasted for months, years, or even an entire decade (the "speed of the '90s"). In a speed battle, workers were pulled off their regular assignments, including military duties, and thrown, unprepared, into a new project, in circumstances closely resembling slave labor. Red flags would flutter at the work site, and a party-sponsored cheerleading squad of women would bang drums and chant slogans. Workmanship tended to be shoddy, workers became exhausted, and workplace injuries skyrocketed.

In an attempt to alleviate the problems of centralized management, the government gradually devolved more responsibility on local jurisdictions and industries, which were assigned quotas to fill, along with the freedom to fill them however they wanted. The "rural question," which was supposed to be answered by converting collective farms into state farms, was instead addressed by assigning farming tasks to smaller groups of farmers, giving them a feeling of ownership in their work. Kim Jong-il's "August 3" initiative sought to shift the burden of manufacturing consumer goods down to the local level, ordering people to find their own resources.

During the 1970s, South Korea's economy began to surpass the North's. By the 1980s some North Koreans were undergoing hardships as the PDS began to run low on food and daily necessities. Economic disaster struck in the 1990s when the Eastern bloc of countries, which had long been North Korea's main source of trade and foreign aid, turned to capitalism, leaving North Korea stranded. Neighboring China, which had also been an important source of aid and trade, likewise embraced capitalism. Kim Il-sung and his son were urged by their foreign benefactors to adopt a modified capitalist economic model, but the Kims held fast to centralized socialism, which enabled them to keep personal control of the country. Nor could the Kims turn to their fellow Koreans in South Korea, toward whom they continued to harbor implacable distrust and hatred.

Kim Il-sung died in 1994, and his son, Kim Jong-il, entered a strange three-year period of mourning and virtual seclusion. Severe floods in the summer of 1995 devastated much of the country. PDS rations stopped for almost everyone except high-level officials living in Pyongyang. Having no other source of food, people began to starve. During the next three years, which the Kim regime referred to as the "Arduous March" (adopting a phrase referring to his father's struggles against the Japanese, decades earlier), as many as one million North Koreans may have starved, and a large segment of the population became undernourished. This period served as a wake-up call to everyone who survived. Only by taking personal responsibility for their economic survival, despite what the government wanted them to do, could they have any future. The end of socialism had come to North Korea—but not the end of the government's official commitment to socialism. And a new, unofficial economy based on private enterprise was born.

THE NEW ECONOMY: CAPITALIST IN PRACTICE

North Korea's new market economy, created in the 1990s out of the people's dire need for food and household goods, has largely replaced the dormant socialist economy. True, the party newspaper, *Nodong Sinmun*, continues to publish articles extolling the virtues of socialism and forecasting the end of world capitalism, but no one believes what the party tells them. The new economy is capitalist, anti-socialist, anti-regime, and off-plan. To what extent, if any, it was inspired by what the neighboring Chinese had been doing for two decades is a matter for future research. It seems that North Korea's version of capitalism was largely homegrown, true to Kim Il-sung's principle of *juche*—but this time what suited North Korea's situation was decided by the people, not the leader.

The immediate and obvious goal of the new economy was to replace the government's failing PDS, which was no longer able to deliver goods to most people. As a replacement, people gathered along country roads, on city street corners, and in empty lots to sell whatever of value they could lay their hands on, including household possessions, handmade goods, garden produce, and items pilfered from their workplace. This was marketing at its most basic, comparable to what would have been found in European countries during the Middle Ages. Because men were still required to show up at their government-designated places of work, it was the women who established the new marketplaces.

These markets were a new phenomenon for North Korea, where public gatherings other than party-sanctioned meetings had always been prohibited. Local authorities could not ban the markets because they needed them for their own survival as much as ordinary civilians did. Market norms gradually developed, including bribery payments to local police. In the countryside, the markets, which might consist of only a few women squatting on the ground with their wares spread out in front of them, moved whenever the police came to disperse them, gaining the name "grasshopper markets." In the cities, spaces were set aside where vendors could congregate, supervised by local police who demanded a small fee for their management and protective services. Kiosks soon appeared along city streets, selling all kinds of food and convenience items.

Marketing evolved from the sale of homemade goods and garden produce to the sale of inexpensive consumer products smuggled in from China. This smuggling route quickly took shape in a more professional manner, with North Korean sales agents developing relationships with Chinese sources, bribing border guards, arranging for transportation to various places inside the country, and then selling to local vendors. The rise in popularity of cell

Pyongyang street scene with kiosks, 2014. *Wikimedia Commons, by Laika ac, CC-BY-SA-2.0.*

phones made it much easier to coordinate activities in the distribution chain and to monitor prices in different parts of the country.[4]

The next stage of capitalism witnessed the private exploitation of the government's largely defunct industries. The manager of a factory or mine, along with the party officials in charge and other local officials who might get wind of the operation, would agree to contract out some or all of the factory's production to private individuals who had acquired substantial capital in the new economy, a class of people that dramatically grew in numbers and became known as *donju*, or "masters of money." These individuals would essentially take over management of the factory while operating on paper as employees, thus providing a veneer of legality to the business. The factory would resume operations or begin producing alternative products, generating income for the workers and hefty bribes for local officials.

If the factory could no longer be utilized for production because of decrepit equipment, lack of raw materials, inadequate power supplies, or a change in market demand, it might simply be dismantled, with the useful parts being purchased by capitalists. A notorious case of factory stripping was mentioned by Kim Jong-il to members of a visiting delegation from Japan's North Korea organization, Chosoren, in 1998. Kim informed his visitors that rumors of an army unit mutinying and taking over the famous Hwanghae steel mill were false. What really happened, he said, was that when the mill stopped operating for lack of electricity, "some rascals turned into a gang of burglars and brought out more than half of the machines and equipment in the plant and shipped them aboard a Chinese boat for sale as scrap iron."[5] Kim added that party cadres overseeing the mill operations, along with relevant security personnel, accepted bribes to condone the looting, and when officials in Pyongyang discovered the problem, the army was sent in to surround the mill and arrest everyone involved. The story sounds highly plausible and is probably only one of many similar cases.

The private black-market service sector, which had always operated in North Korea to provide maid service, day labor, and prostitution, among other things, became more organized. To complement the capitalist goods economy, most of the services that exist in a market economy appeared, including transportation services with taxis and buses. For example, unauthorized intercity transportation, which had existed for years in the form of government and military trucks called *ssobicha* (service cars), which picked up hitchhikers in return for the payment of a few packs of cigarettes, now became professionally managed, with private buses and trucks carrying passengers and goods for set fees. To complement the new transportation services, a host of supporting services appeared, such as vehicle repair, gas stations, and illegal arrangements to issue travel passes and pay bribes at police and military checkpoints.

Small entrepreneurs paid bribes to local police and government officials to avoid being arrested for "nonsocialist" activities. Services on a larger scale, such as fleets of taxis, used the same procedure as goods companies (i.e., they operated under the authority of a government or military organization). By 2010, wealthy *donju* were even entering the real estate market by building condominiums and "selling" units for hundreds of thousands of dollars, even though the ownership of private property remained prohibited.

And what of the Kim regime's response to the emergence of capitalism, even after the famine of the mid-1990s had subsided? Kim Jong-il wanted to bring the people back into the socialist economic system, but the new economy had gotten away from him. On June 1, 2002, an internal government document alerted top officials of an impending economic overhaul, with the explanation that, "at present, commercial transactions are rampant because state prices are lower than those of farmers' markets. As a result, we see a phenomenon in which goods are lacking in the state but are piled up for individuals. To be frank, the state does not have money at present, but individuals have money exceeding two years of the state's budget."[6]

To address this imbalance between private and state economies, Kim decided to move toward a cost-accounting practice within the socialist system. At noon on July 1, 2002, meetings were convened across the country to convey to the people the gist of a new set of economic measures that would take effect immediately. In line with the "July 1 Economic Management Improvement Measures," the government would no longer provide food and housing subsidies. The price of a Pyongyang city bus or subway ride increased twentyfold to cover operating expenses. Prices of other consumer goods and services were likewise rationalized. The government began to charge rent on houses and apartments and to tax farmers for the use of their private garden plots. According to one former North Korean, inspectors visited homes and assessed fees for electricity usage based on what lights and appliances were being used—and while they were there, they might also search for unregistered items such as radios and videotape players, forcing homeowners to pay bribes to stay out of trouble. State wages were increased from an average of three hundred to six thousand won per month, but that increase proved inadequate to cover the new costs in the marketplace, and people continued to spend as much time as possible engaging in private enterprise.

In 2005 the government tried to reinstate the PDS by banning the sale of food grains in the market. However, the PDS was unable to adequately stock its distribution stores, so people continued to shop at the markets. In 2007, women under the age of forty or fifty (depending on the locale) were prohibited from selling in the markets. In 2008 it was announced that, beginning the following year, markets would operate only three days a week. All of these measures proved to be temporary.

The regime's most vigorous attack on markets was launched in November 2009. On the last day of the month, authorities announced through the local wired speaker network (the Third Broadcasting System), speaker trucks, and speeches by party officials that within a week all existing currency must be exchanged for new currency, with one new won replacing one hundred old won. No more than one hundred thousand old won (or about thirty dollars) per person could be exchanged. The regime's rationale was that capitalists who had been making money in the markets would lose most of their savings and thus be taught a lesson. To reward those who had loyally stayed in their state jobs, their new wages would be the same as the old but would now be worth one hundred times more—assuming that the price of goods remained the same.

Public reaction to the currency conversion measure was hostile though unorganized. The government backed down and allowed up to five hundred thousand old won to be exchanged. People lost all confidence in the North Korean won and, even more than before, conducted high-value trades in dollars or Chinese yuan and kept their money out of the banking system, even though the use of foreign currency was officially banned in December. Prices quoted in won skyrocketed to reflect the lack of faith in the currency, and within months the markets were back to business as usual. Kim Jong-il died two years later, and when Kim Jong-un took power, he apparently decided not to interfere with the private economy, although no official recognition was ever made of it. In the years ahead, state factories began to turn out commercially viable products to compete with products made by private enterprise, and North Korea became a capitalist economy in all but name.

INDUSTRY: A NATIONAL RUST BELT

In its economy as well as in its politics, the newly established North Korea followed the Stalinist model, which mandated central planning and party control of the economy, with the party and state deciding what was to be made and consumers taking whatever the government provided for them. The first economic goal was to resume production in heavy industry for the building of essential physical infrastructure. Heavy industry was also needed to make the weapons that would enable the forced unification of the Korean Peninsula under communism.

Accordingly, in August 1946, a year after the Japanese surrender, the North Korean government began to nationalize all big businesses, most of which had been owned by the Japanese colonialists and Koreans who cooperated with them. The push for heavy industry was aided by the circumstance that the Japanese had built most of their Korean industrial facilities in the northern half of the country, along with the roads, railways, and ports needed to facilitate manufacturing, most of which had been devoted to supplying Japan. A few factories were sabotaged by the Japanese before they departed, and a few were stripped by the Russian troops who accepted the Japanese surrender, but enough was salvaged so that by 1949 the North Korean economy was producing as much as it had under the Japanese. [7]

It was fortunate that the North could inherit Japanese factories, because in most economies the capital required to build large factories is supplied over time by sales of products from smaller manufacturing facilities. The technology required to run large industrial facilities was supplied by Japanese, some of whom stayed on for a few years, and by technicians from Russia and Eastern Europe. Still, technology was, and to this day remains, in short supply in North Korea. Factory workers were drafted through the government's complete control over manpower. They were told where to work and when to work, and once they were assigned to a factory, they usually worked there for the rest of their lives.

The success of these early industrialization efforts put North Korea in a suitable position to attack the South on June 25, 1950. The war did not go the way Kim Il-sung planned, and the American air force quickly took control of the skies over North Korea, dropping 635,000 tons of bombs—more than were dropped throughout the recently concluded war in the Pacific. [8] Within two years, virtually all of the country's important structures were destroyed. The only factories that remained were located near the Chinese border, which the United States declared a no-fly zone. Some facilities were also moved underground, which is where many of the people had to live as well.

In 1953, after the armistice was signed, the North Koreans had to begin rebuilding their factories. This time they received considerable assistance from the Soviet Union and its Eastern bloc allies. Many of the Chinese troops that had fought on North Korea's side remained until 1958 to help with reconstruction as well. In an attempt to coordinate all aspects of its economy and assign budgets to the various sectors, the government laid out multiyear economic plans. How successful these plans were is impossible to say because the government was never noted for its openness or honesty, and by 1965 it had simply stopped publishing economic statistics.

The annual New Year's editorials provide an idea of the major weaknesses of the economy. Electricity was always in short supply. There was also an annual coal shortage, partly because some of North Korea's best-quality coal was exported to earn foreign currency. Hydroelectric dams were built, but not fast enough. The country has no domestic source of oil. So, without sufficient power-generating capacity, the rest of the economy inevitably suffered. North Korea's economic officials saw problems wherever they looked. Ko Yong-hwan, a North Korean embassy official who defected to South Korea in 1991, recounted an incident said to have taken place at a consultative meeting of the State Administrative Council in 1988 (before economic conditions went from bad to worse in the 1990s):

> The meeting participants discussed the causes of economic difficulties and groped for ways of solving them. Fountain pens, ones that university students use for writing, you know, were in short supply. The participants asked the director of a fountain pen plant why he had not produced fountain pens. He replied that he had not been supplied with metallurgical materials. They asked the director of a steel mill why he had failed to supply the fountain pen plant with materials. He said: Because I did not get any iron from the smelter. The director of the smelter said he had not gotten ore from the mine. The responsible official at the mine said: I produced some, but rail transportation was not available to the smelter. The railways minister was then summoned and asked: Why did you not transport the mineral ore? He said: Because we did not get any railroad ties from the Forestry Ministry. The Forestry Ministry replied that it did not have any gas to produce timber.[9]

As plants aged, they needed new equipment and technology. The equipment available from the Soviet Union and Eastern Europe was affordable but outdated. In the early 1970s, the North Koreans began to import from Western nations but soon defaulted on their debts, which closed that avenue of modernization. Then they turned to *juche* and tried to invent technology themselves, which proved to be a slow and inefficient process.

North Korea's emphasis on heavy industry shortchanged consumers. Between 1954 and 1976, over 50 percent of state investment went to industry, with 80 percent of that for heavy industry.[10] Even the most common daily necessities, such as toothpaste and toilet paper, were usually in short supply. To fill this vacuum, the Kim regime assigned the manufacture of consumer goods to small local factories and workshops, which were tasked with finding their own raw materials. In 1984 this local industry sector was named the "August 3" or "8.3" consumer goods movement, following instructions from Kim Jong-il. The locally made goods were generally of low quality, and after trade with China became legitimized at the turn of the new century, about 90 percent of North Korea's consumer goods were imported from China. Ten years later, it was even possible to obtain (relabeled) South Korean–made goods from China. Only with the coming of private North Korean entrepreneurs in the second decade did satisfactory domestically made goods begin to appear in the marketplace.

North Korea has never managed to produce the quality or range of products that are widely available in South Korea. Most of North Korea's capital goods, along with its durable goods such as motor vehicles and airplanes, continue to be imported from abroad. Energy shortages, obsolete technology, and lack of worker motivation at state factories have stymied the succession of economic plans the government has put forth. Only as the government has turned a blind eye to private entrepreneurs' taking over manufacturing facilities and making goods for profit has the North Korean manufacturing sector begun to recover, but by now the country is decades behind the rest of the world. In 2020 the estimated gross domestic product (GDP) of North Korea was probably somewhere in the $40 billion range, with per capita GDP at just over $1,000. This compares with South Korea's GDP of $1.6 trillion and per capita GDP of $30,000. The revenue from any one of South Korea's major conglomerates is five times more than the entire country of North Korea generates.

Even with the emerging private economy, it will be difficult for the country to overcome the effect of international sanctions on the import of technology and raw materials and the export of the minerals that are abundant in North Korea. If North Korea can make progress in developing its technology and service industries, it might be better, given the sad state of the country's industrial infrastructure, to entirely skip the industrial stage and concentrate on developing a postindustrial economy.

FARMING: PLANTING SEEDS ON ROCKY GROUND

The history of North Korea's farming sector parallels the history of its manufacturing endeavors. In both cases the guiding principles have been government ownership, party management, mass mobilization of labor, and localization of production when necessary to make up for failures in the state system. In one important respect, farming and manufacturing have been in opposition: the state budget must be allocated between the two, creating something of a zero-sum game. Since manufacturing, especially in the heavy-industry sector, has always received first priority, it should come as no surprise that the farming sector has been starved for funds. Agriculture is not considered essential to national defense or, more important, to regime security. People are viewed as work animals. As long as they are healthy enough to work, the regime is not overly concerned about how much they get to eat.

Ideally, these two economic sectors would be complementary. Manufacturing provides vital inputs to farming, especially in terms of fertilizers, electricity, and farm equipment. Farming in turn feeds the industrial workforce. In North Korea's case, both sectors have suffered. It is sad to say that millions of North Koreans have hungered and sickened because they could not get enough food. Until the 1990s, food shortages—which meant grain shortages, since people rarely had the opportunity to eat meat or fish—were made up by grain imports from fellow communist economies. Even in those few years when farming was able to match food demand, the people were kept on a subsistence diet, and the "surplus" food was put into storage. To this day, most North Koreans are short and banana shaped, whereas all three Kims have been decidedly pear shaped.

Over the years, North Korean party and government officials have made repeated attempts to increase production without providing farmers with adequate material support or work incentives. During the Japanese colonial period, most farmland was owned by Japanese landlords and by Korean landlords who collaborated with the Japanese. When Korea was liberated, one of the first things Kim Il-sung did was to break apart the large farms and distribute the land to 720,000 farmers, who did not gain title to the land but were nevertheless grateful to him. The harvests under these "private" farms improved greatly, and by 1950 the food situation was looking up. Then came the Korean War and the devastation of American bombing raids. Like everyone else, Korean farmers often had to work their fields at night and hide from the bombers during the day.

In August 1953, as soon as the war had ended, Kim Il-sung reversed his decision to rely on private farms and forced the farmers to form collective farms in which scores of people were assigned tasks by farm managers. The farms typically encompassed some three hundred households and were managed by party officials, not by a group of farmers. Collecting the farmers into large organizations was done presumably to increase their efficiency and to simplify the party's ability to control the people. It also made it easier to deliver crops to the state distribution system. Kim Il-sung hoped to eventually turn all cooperative farms into state farms, which, like state factories, would pay workers a wage rather than give them a share of the harvested crops.

It is hardly surprising that the collective farming strategy failed to live up to its promise. Party officials kept trying various means to motivate farmers without actually paying them for more production. For example, the Chongsan-ri movement of 1960 tried to inspire workers to emulate the farmers of the Chongsan-ri cooperative, who allegedly had made great strides under the leadership of their party managers. Over the years many similar propaganda campaigns would be mounted to convince the farmers that they could "grow flowers on rocks if the party wishes them to."[11] And yet farm production never managed to keep up with food demand.

In 1964 Kim Il-sung issued his "Theses on the Socialist Rural Question in Our Country," which sought to solve the problem of low agricultural production by employing four strategies to improve farming. The farming sector was ordered to dramatically improve electrification, irrigation, mechanization, and chemicalization. That is, provide more electricity to farms, irrigate more land, use more tractors in place of oxen, and spread more fertilizer. Unfortunately, the theses were issued just two years after Kim had proclaimed the "Four Military Lines," which called for fortifying the entire country and modernizing the military, an expensive undertaking. Not surprisingly, without funds to finance Kim's four farming recommendations, agricultural production failed to make dramatic gains.

One initiative that did produce positive results was the inauguration in 1965 of a "subteam" farm management policy, which broke farm teams into smaller groups. When these teams met their quotas (which might be in crop production or some other farm-related task), all team members received bo-

Oxen for transportation and farming near Sinuiju, 2012. *Wikimedia Commons, by Martin Cígler, CC-BY-SA-3.0.*

nus points, which in theory could be used to claim more crops at harvest time, the actual distribution being up to the farm managers.

North Korea's harvests improved somewhat in the 1960s and 1970s. On Kim's orders, the government committed more funds to producing tractors and trucks instead of tanks. Fertilizer production was increased, in part thanks to the import of a French-built fertilizer factory. The regime launched campaigns to enlarge farm fields (the better to use the tractors), drain tidelands, irrigate more fields, and cut terraced fields into hillsides, an expansion that ultimately resulted in erosion and river silting. At planting and harvesting times, city dwellers, including students, were sent into the countryside to assist the farmers.

During the 1980s the government continued to introduce grand schemes to uplift the farming sector. An extremely expensive five-mile-long dam at the mouth of the Taedong River, called the West Sea Barrage, was constructed to provide more fresh water for irrigating land, including land that was being newly reclaimed from the sea. Unfortunately, several violent storms hit the area during the following decade and severely damaged the newly reclaimed land. Farming continued to lag, and a wide gap in living standards remained between urban and rural workers. Even though most villages were electrified, the amount of electricity sent out to the countryside was often in short supply. Consumer products were hard to come by, as were entertainment opportunities and many other pleasures and conveniences of modern life. However, since people were not permitted to move their residence or change their job without special permission from the party, the country folk had little recourse other than to continue with their difficult and relatively boring lives. By the end of the decade North Korea's economic campaigns had been stretched to the limit, yet farming faced the same constraints it had encountered since the 1950s.

The 1990s were a decade of disaster triggered by international political events and cruel weather. For once farmers were better off than city dwellers because they were closer to the land and could find ways to grow extra crops to feed themselves. Farmers' markets, which had long existed on a small scale to sell produce that farmers had grown in their small private gardens or had gleaned from the fields and hills, were expanded to feed hungry people. People violated government restrictions by traveling from town to town to look for food. Farmers neglected their assigned tasks on the collective farms, which sent much of their crops to the cities, and worked private gardens carved out beside roads and railroads and up in the hills. Local authorities permitted these activities out of pity and in return for small bribes. In short, in the 1990s a new spirit of enterprise emerged in the rural areas, just as it was emerging in the cities, essentially changing the face of agriculture and the rest of the economy, even while the Kim regime clung to its traditional communist principles and commitment to a military-first policy.

The farming sector, along with the rest of the economy, clawed its way out of the 1990s depression, then reversed course in 2006 (when international sanctions were imposed), and regained its momentum up to 2012 before leveling off. The government has continued to reduce the size of work teams, which are now approaching the size of individual families. In 2012 the "6.28" measures, which were experimentally introduced (on June 28) in some parts of the country, reduced work team size, gave more responsibility to the work teams, and promised them 30 percent of their harvest quota plus anything above the quota.[12] In 2018 the party newspaper *Nodong Sinmun* introduced the Farmland Responsibility System, which apparently gave individual farmers responsibility for farming specific plots of land.[13] More farm produce was also being sold directly to consumers, eliminating the government as a middleman.

These are steps in the right direction. Still constraining the farming sector are international sanctions and the geography of North Korea. The greatest natural wealth of the country is not on the land but under the land in the form of huge deposits of minerals. Until such time as the country develops advanced mining techniques and gets out from under international sanctions that limit exports, this wealth will remain untapped. Ideally, North Korea would take heed of its economic advantages and trade with other countries to provide itself with sufficient food. That, however, would be a violation of the sacrosanct principle of *juche*.

THE LOCAL ECONOMY: TAKING UP THE SLACK

According to North Korean press reports, on December 28, 1955, Kim Il-sung gave a speech to assembled members of the party's Propaganda and Agitation Department bearing the title "On Eliminating Dogmatism and Formalism and Establishing *Juche* in Ideological Work." The term *juche* was not new in Korea, but beginning with this speech and continuing up to the present day, North Korea's leaders and propagandists have given it a variety of meanings, with the core idea being "independence and self-reliance." The most recent (2016) edition of the North Korean constitution opens with the sentence, "The DPRK is a *Juche*-based socialist fatherland that embodies the idea and leadership of the great Comrade Kim Il-sung and Comrade Kim Jong-il."

It is ironic and even comical that Kim, who had been put in power by the Soviet army ten years earlier, had recently been saved from total defeat in the Korean War by the intervention of Chinese and Soviet forces, still hosted thousands of Chinese soldiers engaged in reconstruction work, and continued to rely heavily on Soviet and Eastern European reconstruction aid, should make a virtue of self-reliance and independence. Clearly this was political theater rather than a description of political and economic reality. Over the years Kim would call on the idea of *juche* whenever he purged officials who had even a remote connection with another country, claiming that they were not truly North Korean. The idea would also be called upon as the Kim regime tried to motivate its people to work harder: "Achieving the strengthening and prosperity of the country and people is an arduous task. It can never be accomplished if we abandon our style and shift to another people's style to escape from ordeals and difficulties, or if we turn to another people for help without trusting our own strength."[14]

Juche remains to this day a declaration of North Korea's desire to preserve its national independence politically, economically, and culturally. To maintain the illusion of independence and self-sufficiency, the regime has routinely hidden or downplayed the economic contributions of other countries. Most of the country's vehicles and electronic products are manufactured by other countries. An estimated 90 percent of the country's consumer goods come from China. Most of the luxury goods enjoyed by the Kim family are purchased abroad. When the Soviet Union and China abandoned socialism and ended socialist foreign aid in the early 1990s, the North Korean economy simply collapsed. And since the 1990s, South Korea, the country that North Korea claims is subservient to the United States, has provided several billion dollars in aid to its northern neighbor, with the United States contributing over $1 billion in aid.

However, North Korea has adhered to the principle of *juche* in one important respect. Its foreign trade has been exceptionally small for a country its size. Then again, its limited trading relations may be more easily accounted for by its poor international credit rating and the limits imposed by unilateral and international trade sanctions, especially since 2006.

The domestic counterpart to the regime's desire for national self-sufficiency was publicly announced by Kim Il-sung's son almost thirty years after his father's *juche* speech. On August 3, 1984, Kim Jong-il—still ten years away from succeeding his father—conducted on-the-spot guidance at an exhibition of light-industry products in Pyongyang. He took the occasion to urge workers to use locally available resources, including scrap materials, to make consumer goods for the local community, with the goods to be sold in direct-sales stores rather than distributed through the PDS. The program was similar in some respects to Chairman Mao's disastrous Great Leap Forward program of the late 1950s and early 1960s, but proved to be less disruptive and, on the whole, more beneficial than Mao's program was for the Chinese.

Ever since Kim Jong-il made his appeal, the North Korean media have extolled the virtue of "8.3 goods," with an annual exhibition showcasing the products. For example, in 2016, the North Korean news agency KCNA announced that "the National Exhibition of August 3 Consumer Goods opened Wednesday with due ceremony at Pyongyang Department Store No. 2. On display there are at least 130,000 items of consumer goods of over 1,200 varieties, including garments, sundries for daily use, and foodstuffs produced by factories, enterprises, and housewives' work teams."[15] When the state economy collapsed in the 1990s, localized production became an absolute necessity. Many state enterprises, unable to operate for lack of materials and energy, turned to making 8.3 goods with whatever materials they could lay their hands on, and some workers were furloughed to work at home making such goods. By 2010, private entrepreneurs had largely taken over much of this localized production.

The August 3 movement is the most famous example of a more general attempt by the Kim regime to localize production in response to the failure of state production. Desiring to maintain some measure of control over the economy, the regime has favored localization at the level of the nine provinces. For example, in 2019 the party newspaper announced a new program with an editorial titled "Let Us Achieve the Country's Overall Full-Scale Development through the Hot Wind of Competition between Provinces."[16] It is not apparent that the people feel any special loyalty to their province, so the motivational basis of this approach was suspect from the beginning.

As a desperate measure to compensate for the collapse of the PDS, the localization initiative is both commendable and necessary. More important, as a potential bridge to privatization of the state economy, if that ever becomes state policy, localization is promising. But localization, as it exists now, poses tough political and economic challenges. Before the 1990s, the regime controlled the people by requiring individuals and families to present coupons distributed at state workplaces in order to receive the necessities of life at a nominal price. For this privilege the people were supposed to be grateful to the leader. Once the distribution system broke down, the regime no longer exercised this important economic control over its people. Kim still demands complete obedience and still wants to be seen as the head of the Korean family and the brains of the Korean body, but he now has little claim to such loyalty. Economic localization also severely complicates the regime's unreachable goal of achieving an efficient command economy. Kim is trying to remain in political control without commanding the economy, with Pyongyang as the political center and the provinces as economic centers.

Distributed production of goods is often inefficient. This is especially the case with manufactured goods. The disaster of Mao's rural industrialization program provides an apt lesson. August 3 goods produced by households and amateurs are unlikely to be of high quality. In the absence of well-developed communication and transportation systems, local production limits the distribution of goods. And then there is the question that the regime has been giving more attention to in recent years: what do the people want? Do they prefer August 3 goods over foreign-made goods? To take a specific example, South Korea's Choco Pie cookies have proved to be enormously popular in North Korea ever since they were first smuggled in from the South Korean–run Kaesong Industrial Complex (while it was still operating). The cookies sell for a premium on North Korea's black market.

Juche as self-sufficiency on the international and domestic levels may remain a founding principle of successive Kim regimes, but it has created problems as well as solutions. For now, it remains largely a necessity in the face of the country's strained relations with the outside world, but in the future, it will have to be discarded as unworkable, and the Kim family will no longer be able to exert any economic control over the North Korean people.

INTERNATIONAL TRADE: NOT EASY FOR A HERMIT KINGDOM

North Korea has never been a trading nation. Exactly how much it exports and imports is not known because the government has not published trade statistics for several decades. Instead, trade estimates must be based on statistics from its trading partners. North Korea's largest trading partner by far is China, and much of the Chinese trade is unofficial. Since the imposition of international sanctions in 2006, an increasing amount of North Korea's trade with other countries is hidden. For example, credible reports (and photographs) exist of imported oil being illegally transferred to North Korean ships on the high seas. The American CIA has estimated that for 2016, North Korea ranked 122nd in the world in exports, just ahead of Cyprus and behind Mali. For imports, North Korea's rank of 133 puts it ahead of Madagascar but below South Sudan.[17]

Adam Smith's theory of absolute advantage and David Ricardo's argument for comparative advantage mean little to the Kim regime, which is focused on keeping its people isolated, not on making them wealthy. Ever since Kim Il-sung made *juche* self-reliance the country's guiding policy, international relations of any sort have been suspect. This is not to say that the regime objects to receiving economic assistance: it has depended on it for the country's very existence.

A brief overview of the history of North Korea's trade would look something like this. In the aftermath of the Korean War, Kim Il-sung requested and received economic aid from China, Russia, and Eastern Europe. As North Korea rebuilt its factories and opened its mines, the country traded its commodities and third-rate goods for communist second-rate goods. This kind of trade had obvious limitations. In the first half of the 1970s, North Korea persuaded several noncommunist countries, mostly in Europe, to extend trade credits with which it purchased capital goods. This economic honeymoon ended when the North failed to repay its loans. In the 1980s, North Korea again turned to fellow communist countries, until they abandoned their socialist economies and expected North Korea to do likewise. The end of socialist trade resulted in the near collapse of the North Korean economy in the early 1990s. Since then a semblance of trade has gradually resumed, mostly based on North Korea trading its natural resources for finished goods and oil.

Another way of viewing North Korea's trading history is to look at the country's annual trade and trade balances. From 1946 to 1985, annual total trade (imports plus exports) rarely reached $3 billion.[18] From 1985 to 2010, annual total trade amounted to less than $5 billion. For just a few years, from 2011 to 2016, total trade reached a peak of $5 to $6 billion, before crashing after 2017 when China tightened its sanctions. Over the same decades, North Korea's trading balance has been negative almost every year, meaning that it buys more than it sells. Constantly running a trade deficit, without its being balanced by some form of foreign investment, raises the question of how North Korea manages to survive financially. The only obvious answer is that its continuing trade deficits are forgiven by its socialist trading partners—foreign aid among friends.

Over the years, North Korea's trading partners have changed. In the 1980s the Soviet Union was North Korea's largest trading partner, followed by China and Japan (which has a North Korean minority population). When Russia abandoned state socialism, its trade with North Korea virtually evaporated, and China became the largest trading partner, still followed by Japan. Once North Korea began testing nuclear weapons and launching ballistic missiles, Japan ended trade relations. By 2017, China, whose patience with its neighbor knows few bounds, dominated North Korean trade, accounting for over 90 percent of imports and exports. North Korea also imported about 2 percent of its goods each from Russia and India. Other countries that North Korea exported to in 2017, with each receiving about 1 percent or less of its exports, were Pakistan ($30 million in exports), India ($25 million), France ($12 million), and Sri Lanka, Saudi Arabia, Mexico, and the Philippines (less than $10 million each). North Korea conducts virtually no trade with the United States or the European Union.[19]

In 2008, North Korea's major economic journal published an article titled "The Great Leader Comrade Kim Jong-il's Economic Ideology of Expanding and Developing Foreign Trade *in Our Own Way*" (emphasis added), acknowledging that trade with other socialist nations was not likely to return to what it had been during the Cold War era. [20] The article's tone was defensive and hostile, cautioning that North Korea must not be "drawn into the capitalist economy" but instead must "penetrate into the capitalist market in order to crush" the imperialists' designs on North Korea. This is hardly a blueprint for participation in the international trading economy. Most important, "in a situation where the main target of our country's foreign economic relations has changed to the capitalist market as the socialist market has collapsed," North Korea needed to avoid the pitfall of primarily selling raw materials (which are especially vulnerable to international price fluctuations) and instead process those materials at home before export. To do this, North Korea would need to dramatically improve its domestic economy in order to develop or purchase the technology necessary to process raw materials.

This has not happened. By 2017, although the country's major class of export merchandise was basic clothing (25 percent of its exports), most of its other important exports were raw materials: coal (21 percent), iron (5 percent), lead (4 percent), and seafood (8 percent). Despite the fact that the country has large reserves of rare-earth minerals, they have proved too difficult to mine. On the import side, North Korea purchases cloth, broadcasting and video equipment, motor vehicles and bicycles, food (the country always runs a domestic food deficit), and petroleum products (North Korea has no domestic oil resources).

The situation is not much different even in terms of products that are simple to manufacture. It has been estimated that over 90 percent of the daily necessities that are purchased in domestic markets are imported from China, although in recent years, as private entrepreneurs have taken over much of the country's localized production, domestically produced daily necessities are gaining a foothold. In the absence of privately owned trading companies, North Korea's trade is conducted by state-owned trading companies. Exactly how many such companies operate is impossible to say, given the usual secrecy of North Korea and the fact that trading companies often change their names in order to avoid international sanctions on their activities. In 2011, one South Korean analyst estimated that North Korea might be operating about two hundred trading companies, based partly on how many companies participate in Pyongyang's trade fairs. These companies are operated by party, government, and military organizations in order to make money and, in some cases, market specific products (such as weapons) produced by their parent organizations.

A *South China Daily* newspaper article published in 2017 investigated one such trading company, then known as the Shinhung Trading Company.[21] The company, whose parent organization was believed to be the Ministry of State Security, had a history of selling whatever it could find to make money for the ministry and for the trading company's employees, and of course to pay loyalty fees to higher officials in the chain of command and to the Kim family in order to receive continued permission to operate. At the time of the report, the company was selling Korean herbal remedies, a special type of ginseng advertised to cure a variety of ailments including cancer. It was also selling cigarettes (there's an irony here) and tiger bone liquor. In previous years the company had sold computers, shellfish, produce, iron ore, and Japanese cosmetics.

Working for a trading company has always been one of the best sources of hard (i.e., foreign) currency for North Koreans. Trading company employees have a window on the outside world, and since their operations are often clandestine, they can earn money that even the North Korean regime is not aware of. As long as they pay off the right people, everyone benefits. However, if trading company employees are greedy (in the eyes of the regime), they may be accused of a variety of crimes, including spying for a foreign power and treason. In this sense, trading is a risky business.

For that matter, any North Korean who deals with foreigners places him- or herself in potential danger. In recent years, Jang Song-taek, the second most powerful figure in North Korea, served as an economic bridge between China and North Korea and, in the process, gained a significant amount of power and, presumably, money. He was arrested on numerous charges and executed in 2013. Years before, Kim Dal-hyon, North Korea's minister of external economic affairs in the early 1990s and a frequent traveler to foreign countries, including South Korea, was purged for unknown reasons and spent the rest of his days out of sight as a local official. And then there was North Korea's top official in charge of external economic affairs, Kim Chong-u, who was purged in the late 1990s.

For political reasons, North Korea has never been willing to enter the international arena. In this sense, it is indeed a modern-day hermit kingdom. In 2020, its economy and foreign trade are being crushed by international sanctions and, further, by border closures resulting from the COVID-19 pandemic. However, even without the sanctions and the temporary border clo-sures, it would have poor trading relations. Its guiding policy of *juche* is antithetical to international relations and trade. It lacks the capacity to make products that can compete internationally, and it still has not developed the means to mine its extensive mineral resources. Its credit rating has been in ruins since the 1970s, and its businesspeople and government officials have little experience in conducting reputable business dealings. Whereas the first order of business to enter the international trading community would be to get out from under the international sanctions regime, North Korea would still have a long way to go to realize its potential of absolute and comparative advantage in the world market.

FOREIGN INVESTMENT INFLOW: RISKY FOR INVESTORS

It is hardly surprising that a country that prides itself on self-sufficiency—even when that pride is largely an illusion—would still find it necessary to engage in foreign trade to make up for domestic shortfalls. What is surprising is that such a country would solicit foreign investment, which brings with it a measure of economic dependency and, often, an influx of foreign workers. Yet in 1984 that is exactly what the Kim Il-sung regime did with the promul-gation of its Foreign Joint Venture Law. Undoubtedly Kim (and his son) was hoping to tap into the foreign wealth that had begun to flow into China in the early 1980s. Initially most of the foreign investors who cautiously took ad-vantage of North Korea's joint-venture opportunity were the Chinese and pro–North Korean residents of Japan.

The Kim regime was extremely wary of letting in foreign investment because it would inevitably be accompanied by foreign influence, which would introduce what the North Korean press liked to call the "yellow wind of capitalism." An authoritative *Nodong Sinmun* article published in 1998 warned that "foreign capital is like opium."[22] Taking a page from the Chi-nese playbook, the regime decided to funnel foreign investments into desig-nated foreign trade zones that could be carefully managed. To maximize the economic impact of investment, one would expect that trade zones would be located near big cities and ports. But in North Korea, political considerations dictated that the trade zones be exiled to remote parts of the country, as far away from population centers as possible.

In December 1991 the government carved out a 240-square-mile trade zone encompassing the towns of Najin (Rajin) and Sonbong, over three hundred miles from Pyongyang in the undeveloped northeast corner of the country. After the two towns merged in 2000, the zone's name was changed to Nason (Rason). With tax incentives and cheap labor, the zone looked to be a fair imitation of China's new trade zones—with the crucial difference that China's zones were located close to the thriving capitalist center of Hong Kong and across the water from Taiwan. Before Nason opened for business, politically unreliable residents (i.e., members of the "hostile class") were expelled from the zone, and it was surrounded by a fence. Nason was part of a nascent industrial border region that is now called the Greater Tumen Initiative.

Nason lacked both an airport and a container port. The zone was connected to Russia only by a dirt road and a North Korean rail spur. Not until 2013 did the Russians build an extension of their own rail line to Nason. The dirt road to China crossed an old Japanese bridge on the Tumen River and was not renovated until 2010. Roads from Nason to Pyongyang were likewise unpaved, and the train trip to Pyongyang could take anywhere from twenty hours to several days. Almost from the start, investor interest was cooled when Kim Chong-u, the economic official who was the public face of the regime's foreign investment program, abruptly and permanently disappeared, along with several of his associates. The zone has continued to languish for thirty years.

Another foreign zone was established in the beautiful region of Kumgang (Diamond Mountain) in the far southeast corner of the country along the border with South Korea. The North Koreans fenced off the area and opened it to foreign (mostly South Korean) tourists, who began arriving in November 1998. By the end of 2007, over 1.7 million tourists had visited the mountain resort, with the Kim regime receiving $1 billion from tourist fees and business rights for the project. Unfortunately, in the early morning hours of July 11, 2008, a North Korean soldier shot and killed a female South Korean tourist who had wandered onto an off-limits beach near the hotel. When the North refused the South's demand for a joint investigation, South Korea stopped sending tourists. The North Koreans eventually took over the now-idled hotel facilities and in 2015 designated the area as part of the Wonsan-Kumgang International Tourist Zone. At a briefing given in China, the investment brochure claimed that it was "the unbending determination of the Workers' Party of Korea and the government to develop the zone into a globally recognized sightseeing destination."[23] This cannot happen until the South Koreans return, because the region is far from the Chinese border.

With the Nason industrial investment zone going nowhere and the Kumgang tourist zone closed down, the Kim regime looked for another doorway through which foreign capital could enter. Plans were announced in 2002 to make the border city of Sinuiju, in the northwest corner of the country, into a special trade zone. Sinuiju, with a population of four hundred thousand, lies across the Yalu River from the Chinese city of Dandong, which serves as the gateway for most of China's trade with North Korea. Pyongyang's selection for Sinuiju's first governor was not auspicious. Yang Bin, one of China's wealthiest businessmen, reportedly decided to make the zone a convenient gambling center to draw in Chinese punters, but apparently he didn't let

Mount Kumgang area, 2015. *Wikimedia Commons, by Uwe Brodrecht, CC-BY-SA-2.0.*

government officials in Beijing know about his plan. On the day Yang was to take up his governorship in Sinuiju he was arrested by Chinese police, charged with a variety of economic crimes, and sentenced to eighteen years in prison. Still, the North Korean government continues to voice hopes for this gateway zone and in 2013 designated it as the Sinuiju International Economic Zone. However, as long as North Korea remains under UN sanctions, Chinese companies will be reluctant to move into the zone.

North Korea's four-corners investment zone strategy was completed by another business zone, this one in the southwest corner of the country. Shortly after the first inter-Korean summit meeting in 2000, South Korea's Hyundai family of companies received permission to lease a twenty-five-square-mile zone outside the city of Kaesong, just north of the border with South Korea. The South Korean government and private investors provided the infrastructure for the zone, including electricity. Only North Korean workers chosen by their government were allowed to work in the zone, and South Korean managers and technicians were restricted to the zone and not permitted to enter the nearby city. By early 2009, over one hundred small- and medium-size South Korean companies had built factories in the Kaesong Industrial Complex. Because investment in North Korea comes with high risk, the South Korean government provided various investment guarantees and insurance coverage to those Korean companies willing to enter the zone.

It was difficult to keep the Kaesong project going. Whenever inter-Korean political relations soured, North Korea tended to hinder the operation of the complex. In 2016, in response to continued North Korean nuclear tests, the South Korean government announced that it was temporarily closing the Kaesong factories. North Korea responded by expelling all South Korean workers, and since then the complex has been closed, although some production may have continued, with North Koreans taking over and operating the factories.

Over the years the Kim regime has become more accepting of foreign investment outside the trade zones, especially for ventures that involve technology transfer rather than manufacturing. A few South Korean entrepreneurs have established joint ventures in Pyongyang and other cities, generally to their regret. North Korea's cell phone industry was established by a joint venture first with Thailand's Loxley Pacific Company in 2001, and then in 2008 with Egypt's Orascom Telecom Media, which has reportedly had trouble repatriating profits to the home office.

Chinese companies remain North Korea's largest investors and traders, although accurate estimates of their activity cannot be made because they usually keep a low profile, the better to avoid the scrutiny of Chinese and North Korean authorities. Chinese (and other) foreign investors complain that bribes must be paid at every turn and that North Koreans consider signed contracts to be merely the first step in continuing negotiations. When a foreign business begins to turn a profit, the North Korean partners, rather than rejoicing, try to squeeze out more profit for themselves. In a country where legal considerations are secondary to political and economic motives, almost anything goes. Despite the many difficulties that North Korea encountered in its four foreign trade zones, in 2013 the Kim Jong-un regime announced plans to open another dozen or so smaller zones spread throughout the country, but nothing has materialized in these zones.

Thirty-five years after North Korea was first opened to foreign investment, the results have been paltry, on par with the poorest African nations as an investment destination. Moreover, about 90 percent of the investments come from China, leaving North Korea in an uncomfortably dependent position. North Korea continues to be in desperate need of foreign capital, technology, and management expertise, even while it boasts of its self-reliance. Foreign investments in the country have failed for several reasons: first, because North Korea's foreign investment provisions have not been detailed enough to satisfy skeptical foreign investors; second, because the government has long since reneged on its foreign debt; and third, because the country's transportation, communication, and energy infrastructures are inadequate to support modern business ventures.

In 2012 Kim Jong-un announced a national policy of *byungjin*, which meant simultaneous pursuit of economic growth and nuclear weapons development. This policy was unacceptable to most foreign governments and led to a host of UN sanctions, which poisoned the North Korean business climate. Kim's 2018 announcement that the country's nuclear weapons goals had been reached and that the country would henceforth turn its attention to economic pursuits did nothing to change the investment climate. Meanwhile, Southeast Asian countries have become popular international bases for low-cost manufacturing, leaving North Korea as a desirable destination primarily for companies in neighboring China and South Korea, at such time as international sanctions are relaxed and the COVID-19 pandemic has abated.

WORKING ABROAD: HARD WORK FOR THE PRIVILEGED FEW

In the course of their travels, global tourists are unlikely ever to encounter a North Korean, for the simple reason that the Kim regime is as careful about who is allowed to leave the country as it is about who is allowed to enter. Only four categories of North Koreans travel abroad: defectors or temporary visitors to China who leave the country illegally, diplomats and government representatives, athletes and entertainers, and North Korean workers who are sent abroad to earn money for the regime. In addition, a small number of North Korean military advisors are assigned to foreign militaries in Africa and the Middle East, and a few North Korean students are sent abroad, including to the United States.

North Korea has diplomatic relations with 164 countries (as of 2019) but has embassies or consulates in only 54 of those countries (including four delegations to UN organizations). Asian countries host nineteen embassies, Africa and Europe each have thirteen, and the Americas have five. Only seventeen countries have embassies or consulates in Pyongyang; the other countries with diplomatic relations have their Beijing staff cover neighboring North Korea. North Korean embassies are expected to be self-supporting, which means they must find ways to earn money through local resources. Some embassies rent out part of their property or set up small businesses. It is assumed that most embassies avail themselves of the use of diplomatic pouches to smuggle goods such as drugs, counterfeit currency, gemstones, liquor, cigarettes, and ivory into or out of the host country; over the years dozens of diplomats have been expelled for these crimes. North Korean diplomats abroad are watched closely by their own security agents, while their family members are usually kept in Pyongyang as virtual hostages. Only a few diplomats have ever defected, usually because they feared they were about to be purged. Among the reported defections (some may never have been reported by the host country or by the North Korean government) are three embassy officials. Ko Young-hwan, the first secretary at North Korea's embassy in the Congo, defected in 1991. Thae Yong-ho, deputy ambassador in London, defected in 2016. Jo Song-gil, the acting ambassador in Rome, defected in 2019.

Likewise, North Korean athletes traveling abroad rarely defect. During their brief stays, they live in separate facilities from other athletes and are closely watched by security agents. Like diplomatic personnel, they are chosen in part because they are judged to be thoroughly loyal to the regime. And, also like diplomats, they lead a relatively privileged life in their country and know that their family, friends, and associates will be punished if they try to defect. It is not known that any North Korean Olympic athlete has ever defected, although a North Korean judo athlete defected at a competition in Spain in 1991, and a woman ice hockey player defected through China in 1997.

In several respects, the laborers that North Korea sends abroad for assignments of approximately three years are different from the diplomats and athletes. They are not nearly as privileged, although unless they are members of the "core" political class, they have no chance of being sent abroad. Estimates of the number of North Korean laborers working abroad (not counting those who left illegally for China) are in the range of fifty to eighty thousand.[24] Tens of thousands are employed in the Russian Far East at logging camps and construction sites and on fishing boats. Thousands more have been engaged in construction work in the Middle East. Several hundred workers have been employed in Eastern Europe, mostly in the garment industry, with several hundred more in various sub-Saharan countries, and North Korean waitresses staff hundreds of North Korean–owned restaurants in China and Southeast Asia. Most of these workers reside legally in the host country, where they earn less than other workers but more than they could get in their own country. There are also North Koreans involved in shady overseas operations (not including diplomats). For example, in 2014, Cambodian police arrested about a dozen North Koreans who were running an Internet gambling site, and it has been estimated that approximately 1,500 North Korean hackers in China and Southeast Asia make money from various computer scams and thefts.[25]

Workers are hired by foreign companies from a labor pool supplied by the North Korean government, with workers' wages paid to the local North Korean government agent. Monthly salaries range from $200 to $1,000, bringing in an estimated $500 million a year or more.[26] These monies go to the government and party organizations that send the workers abroad, with a significant part assuredly going into the Kim regime's private coffers (for example, through Offices 38 and 39). Despite the low pay, even difficult jobs such as logging in Siberia are much sought after by North Koreans. To be sure, the attractive singing and dancing waitresses employed in North Korean restaurants abroad are likely to be the daughters of high-level party officials in Pyongyang, not working-class women from the provinces. In addition to having a solid party background, it is necessary for prospective foreign laborers to pay substantial bribes to those who are in charge of overseas recruitment.

According to former workers, the process looks something like this: After paying bribes, generally amounting to a few hundred dollars (in foreign currency), prospective workers are enlisted in a training program that lasts one or two years, during which time their work skills are assessed and they are briefed on how to live and behave in a foreign country. Then, after payment of more bribes, they are chosen for either collective or contract work. Those who are put in the collective program are sent to a foreign country to work for a North Korean contractor. The more talented workers, who also have to pay bigger bribes, get into the contract program, which hires them out to foreign companies or sometimes even permits them to find their own foreign employment.[27] At no time in this process are they presented with a formal contract or given any guarantee of how much they will earn. In short, they go into the program blindly with the hope that foreign employment will be better than the dead-end work available in their own country. In choosing to go abroad, most recruits have probably heard about the experiences of those who have gone before them, so they are not entirely ignorant.

The trick to making money abroad is to find a good job, almost certainly in the contract program: that is, a job that pays well (compared to employment in North Korea), with a company that is not likely to declare bankruptcy or cheat its workers. All foreign workers have to expect that most of their pay will be taken away by the North Korean government in the form of various fees.[28] Approximately 70 percent of their wages go to pay a "state planning fee." Another 10 percent is deducted for the "entrance fee," which covers the costs of transportation to the foreign assignment, visa fees, work permits, any required physical examination, plus living expenses. The North Korean government also deducts 5 percent for "non-tax payments" for various ongoing projects at home. Periodically workers are required to submit a "loyalty offering" to the Kim regime. This leaves only about 10 percent for workers to take home. From this they will have to pay extra bribes as necessary.

When workers for some reason are unable to work (there is no worker's insurance) or if their employer fails to pay their wages, they will go into debt during their time abroad. Otherwise, they can expect to send home (or keep under the mattress) a few hundred dollars a year in hard currency, which is serious money in North Korea. Those North Koreans who are able to get into the foreign work program as supervisors can expect to make far more money, and to pay much more money in bribes and fees. Those who manage the work programs are probably making tens of thousands of dollars.

Foreign employers are enthusiastic about North Korean workers because they do whatever their government handlers tell them to do, typically working ten to twelve hours a day, six or seven days a week. North Korean guest workers live together in apartment houses or dormitories and are not permitted to associate with the local people or access local media (although many workers acquire cell phones with which they can get information about the outside world). If they don't live on-site, they travel to work in company vans or on foot, accompanied by North Korean security agents or agents hired by their foreign employer. This situation, where North Korean "slave laborers" are working in the midst of a democracy, is anomalous and, to many people in the host country, morally wrong.

North Korean workers, like diplomats, rarely defect, not only because they come from the loyal political class but also because their families are held hostage back home. After a few years abroad, they are required to return, bringing with them some hard currency and foreign-made goods. For them, the overseas work experience is only a taste of what the outside world is like, but that taste is better than nothing.

The UN Security Council has passed resolutions to try to reduce the amount of money the Kim regime earns to build its weapons of mass destruction. Resolution 2397 stipulated, among other things, that by the end of 2019 all countries hosting North Korean workers should send them home. Since the worker-abroad program benefits not only the North Korean government but also the workers (usually) and the host nations, the UN resolution has not been enthusiastically implemented. Both Russia and China, the two largest employers of North Koreans, signed on to the resolution. Russia stated that it did not want to hurt North Korean workers or the North Korean people and that it hoped events would occur before the 2019 deadline that would make it unnecessary to expel all the workers. No such events occurred. It appears that many North Korean workers in China were able to evade the sanctions by returning early to their country and then receiving a different kind of visa to return to their work. It is safe to say that any program that has continued for so long (since 1946) and that benefits so many parties is likely to continue in some form, sanctions or no sanctions. In the future the North Korean regime will continue to receive overseas work funds, and thousands of North Koreans will experience life in countries less oppressive than their own.

INTERNATIONAL SANCTIONS:
THE PRICE OF NUCLEAR WEAPONS

In the years since it became an independent country, North Korea has been targeted by numerous American sanctions: as a Marxist-Leninist state, as a sponsor of international terrorism, as a proliferator of weapons of mass destruction, as a violator of religious freedom, as an agent of human trafficking, as a counterfeiter and money launderer, and in recent years as a lapsed member of the Nuclear Non-Proliferation Treaty (NPT).[29]

Since 1950, when North Korea invaded South Korea, American trade sanctions have also been imposed under the 1917 Trading with the Enemy Act. The sanctions based on this act are directed at enemies in times of war, and North Korea and the United States have never signed a peace treaty ending the Korean War. These sanctions were lifted by President George W. Bush in 2008, but other American sanctions remained in place under the International Emergency Economic Powers Act. North Korea was also placed on the list of "state sponsors of terrorism" in 1988 after it bombed a South Korean Airlines flight the previous year, then taken off the list by George W. Bush in 2008, and then added again by President Donald Trump in 2017.

Over the years these unilateral American sanctions may not have had a great impact on the North Korean economy. North Korea had virtually nothing to offer developed countries in terms of manufactured goods, and its extensive mineral resources were difficult to extract given its level of technology. South Korea's almost total embargo on North Korea, first because of the North's Korean War aggression and after that because of periodic North Korean provocations, has arguably had a much greater impact.

North Korea traded with other communist economies, benefiting from favorable economic treatment, and thus was reasonably well protected from American and South Korean sanctions, except for the fact that the goods available from fellow communist countries were generally inferior to those manufactured by capitalists. The situation changed in 2003 when North Korea announced its withdrawal from the NPT—the first country ever to do so. After its withdrawal, the Kim Jong-il regime warned that imposition of UN sanctions would be considered an act of war, but later thought better of declaring war against the members of the UN.[30] The withdrawal, which was assumed to mean that the country was overtly arming itself with nuclear weapons, troubled many countries in the international community, including China and Russia.

Two sanctions enforcement organizations directly addressed the threat that North Korea might proliferate weapons. The international Wassenaar Arrangement, the successor to the Coordinating Committee for Multilateral Export Controls (COCOM), was established in 1995 to report on and restrict the transfer of conventional weapons and technology that could be used to manufacture such weapons. Participating countries must honor the NPT, the Missile Technology Control Regime (MTCR), the Chemical Weapons Convention (CWC), and the UN Register of Conventional Arms. And in 2003 the George W. Bush administration announced the formation of the Proliferation Security Initiative (PSI) aimed at interdicting shipments of WMDs. The PSI initially included eleven states and was subsequently expanded to include twenty-one states, with endorsements from eighty-four countries. Only a few interdictions of North Korean WMDs have been reported.

In 2006 North Korea test-fired several long-range missiles, and in October it conducted its first nuclear test. Responding to the test, the UN passed Resolution 1718, which prohibited the export of various military supplies and luxury goods to North Korea. After the country's second nuclear test in May 2009, Resolution 1874 broadened the weapons embargo. In February 2013 a third nuclear test was conducted, the first under Kim Jong-un's reign. In that year the UN passed two more sanctions resolutions, 2087 in response to a rocket launch and 2094 in response to the third nuclear test. The latter resolution was aimed at crippling North Korea's ability to tap into the international financial system.

In January 2016, North Korea's fourth nuclear test prompted the UN to pass Resolution 2270, which banned North Korean exports of minerals, including coal, which was a major export earner. In September, North Korea's detonation of a much larger nuclear weapon prompted the passage of Resolution 2321, which further restricted the country's mineral exports. Amid continuing nuclear threats, Resolution 2371, another financial sanctions measure, was passed in August 2017. North Korea conducted its sixth nuclear test in September 2017, and the UN responded with Resolution 2375, banning a variety of economic activities. After the North launched another intercontinental missile, the UN passed Resolution 2397, banning more exports and limiting the country's imports of oil.

This brief history suggests that sanctions are unlikely to dissuade the Kim regime from pursuing nuclear weapons and missile delivery systems. Viewed from another angle, it appears just as likely that the nuclear and missile tests may be responses to sanctions rather than the other way around. The ineffectiveness of economic sanctions comes as no surprise to political scientists and economists who have studied the impact of sanctions on other countries.[31] On the other hand, although sanctions are generally ineffective in coercing a target country, they do express a political and moral stance on an issue. If economic sanctions are applied by only one or a few countries, the targeted country can look elsewhere in the world for trade and aid. After all, North Korea has never expected anything from the United States or South Korea. China and Russia have reluctantly agreed to participate in the UN sanctions because they would prefer that North Korea not have nuclear weapons, but neither country is threatened by these weapons, nor is either country a friend of the United States. Despite the position that governments take on the imposition of sanctions, there are plenty of individuals and nongovernmental organizations willing to violate the sanctions in order to turn a profit. The Chinese border area is particularly porous when it comes to trade with North Korea.

For sanctions to change a country's policy, they must hurt the policy makers. In North Korea's case, the impact must be on the leader, who is well insulated from economic sanctions. He continues to live in luxury and, judging by his girth, is not having any trouble obtaining food. Many sanctions, for example, those on luxury imports, have targeted the Pyongyang elites who support Kim, but those people really have no choice but to remain loyal to him. As usually happens when a country is sanctioned, the effect is felt most heavily by ordinary people. Sanctions even restrict humanitarian aid, which is supposed to be exempt from interference. The way dictatorships work is that the people are held hostage by the leader, serving as human shields. While Kim does not want an unhappy or dissatisfied populace, he can live with that if necessary, as his father did during the famine of the 1990s. Nuclear weapons and missiles are to protect him, not the people.

Because the UN sanctions are an extension of those that the United States and South Korea have imposed on North Korea for decades, the North Koreans have had a long time to adjust, and they continue to come up with ingenious ways of skirting the increasingly heavy international sanctions. Smuggling by diplomatic pouches, oil transfers to North Korean ships at sea, frequently renaming those ships and operating them under foreign flags to confuse sanction enforcers, and smuggling across the Chinese border are tried-and-true methods that have provided the country with the minimum resources necessary to keep the economy going. One could say that sanctions evasion is a developed industry in North Korea.

Economic sanctions are not the only means, short of war, of trying to dissuade the Kim regime from pursuing a course of action. The country may be sanctioned in other ways, for example, by restricting cultural and personnel exchanges or by withdrawing diplomatic personnel.[32] The United States and North Korea have never exchanged ambassadors, although North Korea maintains an ambassadorial staff at the UN in New York City. Cultural relations between the two countries have been almost nonexistent. Only a handful of American humanitarian organizations work in North Korea. In the past, a few Americans traveled to North Korea as curious tourists, but since 2017 American passport holders have been prohibited from making the trip without special US government permission.

The Kim regime has always desired political recognition from other countries, yet it has obtained very little from the world's leading country, the United States. This form of political sanctions has arguably been an important card for the United States to play. The US policy of withholding recognition was weakened during the Clinton administration when the Agreed Framework was signed in 1994 and a smiling Secretary of State Madeleine Albright visited Kim Jong-il in Pyongyang in 2000. A trip by President Clinton was considered just before he left office, but he did not travel to Pyongyang until 2009, and then on a humanitarian mission. Former president Jimmy Carter visited in 1994 to promote what would become the Agreed Framework, and again in 2010, also on a humanitarian mission. It was not until 2018 and 2019 that a sitting president, Donald Trump, actually met a North Korean leader, lavishly complimented him, and thus destroyed any leverage that withholding American political recognition might have had.

With China just across the border and South Korea, under left-leaning presidents, eager to engage in economic cooperation with North Korea when international sanctions are lifted, the prospect of changing the policies of the Kim regime through either political or economic sanctions does not appear promising. By 2018 the Kim regime did seem to be eager to end the increasingly stringent UN sanctions, but not enough to give up its nuclear weapons or curtail its missile program.

Chapter Eight

Transportation and Communication

Necessary for the New Economy

DOMESTIC TRANSPORTATION: SLOWED BY YEARS OF NEGLECT

When the occupying Japanese surrendered to American and Soviet soldiers in 1945, they left not only most of their industries but also an extensive transportation network of roads, railroads, bridges, and ports. Before the Japanese had arrived, Korea was a rural land. Afterward, it was poised to become a modern nation, especially in the northern half of the peninsula. All that was lacking was technical and management expertise to run the infrastructure the Japanese had left behind. Unfortunately, North Korea had neither. The Japanese technicians returned to their war-torn homeland, while many educated Koreans fled south when the communists took over. The kind of infrastructure the Japanese had built, and the kind the new Kim Il-sung regime wanted, was almost exclusively industrial in nature. Kim viewed the people as communist workers, not as free individuals, so roads, railways, and bridges were needed primarily to carry freight, not passengers. Since virtually all motor vehicles were owned by the army, dirt roads served as well as paved roads for their slow-moving trucks, and trains did not have to hurry to arrive at their destinations in order to please passengers. Only since 2010 has this situation begun to change.

In modern life—in contrast to life in North Korea, which has much in common with how people lived in the nineteenth century—people travel for pleasure as well as for work. Even in third-world countries, cars, motorbikes, and buses are used to visit friends and relatives and to go to the cities for shopping. Until very recently, this has not been the case in North Korea. North Koreans lived in the same city or town that their parents lived in and were assigned to a workplace close to home. Special permission was required to travel outside of their county, and was granted only for weddings, funerals, and business travel. Walking or riding a bicycle was pretty much the only means of transportation they had. If it was necessary to travel any great distance, train travel was faster and more comfortable than truck beds or buses. Until recently, travel by private car was unheard of. Not only did the regime consider private cars to be an unnecessary expense, but people driving around in cars are harder to keep track of than people traveling on trains (watched over by train police) or on buses (stopped at police checkpoints).

Car ownership in North Korea is a recent phenomenon. Until the first decade of this century, all cars were owned and operated by government, party, or military organizations. As the market economy developed, a relatively small number of individuals (in the tens of thousands out of twenty-five million) amassed sufficient wealth to buy and operate a vehicle. As of 2019, the country's civil code (Article 59) permits the private ownership of cars, although it is not clear whether they can be registered under their owner's name or must be registered to a state organization. The first numbers on license plates indicate what organization a car belongs to. The highest officials in the country have license numbers beginning "727"—the date in 1953 that North Koreans claim they won the Korean War. Previously, these plates were numbered "216"—Kim Jong-il's birthday. How many motor vehicles operate in North Korea today cannot be determined, but the number has been estimated at a quarter of a million, one for every hundred people.

North Korea does not manufacture its own passenger cars except for a few hundred or thousand "Whistles," first produced in 2002 by a joint venture with South Korea's Unification Church; the company is now fully owned by the North Korean government. On the road one can see Volvos (including about a thousand 1970s models that were never paid for), Volkswagens, Audis, old Eastern European models like the Lada and Trabant, a few big Russian sedans, lots of Chinese imports including hundreds of yellow-and-green "Beijing taxis," and even some secondhand Japanese cars. Top officials have always preferred black Mercedes. Vans and SUVs are popular as well, with SUVs almost a necessity for traveling on country roads.

North Korean jeeps, originally made for the military, are also a common sight in the countryside.

With all the new traffic, the exceptionally wide streets in Pyongyang are beginning to fill up, although tourists frequently comment that the drive from the airport into Pyongyang is eerily quiet. Most of the country's passenger cars are found in Pyongyang, which now has something resembling rush-hour traffic, with a few traffic signals added to supplement the traffic control exercised by the city's traffic police, including the attractive "traffic ladies" in their smart blue- or white-jacketed uniforms. The police, in addition to demanding bribes for infractions, periodically stage crackdowns on drivers for the usual traffic offenses, while trying to keep pedestrians, who are not used to traffic, from jaywalking. It is impossible to know what the motor vehicle accident rate is because such numbers would never be published by the North Korean government. The growing popularity of private motor vehicles has spawned a new service industry of gasoline stations and repair shops.

Most city dwellers, even in Pyongyang, still use public transportation, which runs on electricity due to the chronic shortage of gasoline and diesel fuel. Trolley buses (from the Czech Republic and some domestically made), trams (many purchased secondhand from the Czech Republic), and a subway (with cars purchased secondhand from Berlin's subway system) are the primary public carriers. Pyongyangites have learned to patiently queue during morning and evening commutes. Private taxis, including call taxis, are becoming popular for the new middle class. Bicycles continue to be a transportation necessity for most families, and the venerable *dubalcha* (two-legged car, i.e., walking) still serves people well.

Transportation in the countryside and in smaller cities is more primitive. It might not be too much of an exaggeration to say that if transportation in Pyongyang resembles what was found in American cities in the 1930s (considering the amount of traffic and the sophistication of the road system), the rest of North Korea is stuck in the first decade of the twentieth century, when motorized transport was just beginning to replace horse-drawn vehicles. Most country roads are unpaved, and many of them run through mountains and valleys, requiring transportation by truck, jeep, or sport utility vehicle. Roadblocks set up by police and military organizations check on people's travel registration and demand bribes for the smallest infractions.

In North Korea the primary purpose of transportation is to move goods. In the 1990s, when the socialist state could no longer provide food and other

Directing traffic in Kaesong, 2008. *Wikimedia Commons, by yeowatzup, CC-BY-2.0.*

daily necessities for the people, military trucks began to be used as *ssobicha* (service vehicles) to carry people and goods on a commercial basis. Some of these open-bed trucks were even converted to burn charcoal that generated a synthetic form of gas to fuel the engine, in the process belching smoke like an old steam engine. Fortunately for other traffic and for those walking or living along the roads, most of these trucks have disappeared.

Bridges and tunnels are in no better shape than the roads themselves. Until 2019, the most heavily traveled bridge outside of Pyongyang was the China–North Korea Friendship Bridge connecting the bustling Chinese city of Dandong with the much smaller North Korean city of Sinuiju on the other side of the Yalu River. Like much of North Korea's transportation infrastructure, the bridge was built by the Japanese and was completed in 1943. Although it was only wide enough for one lane of traffic and one railroad track, it served as the major land gateway between North Korea and the rest of the world. In 2011 the Chinese began building a much larger suspension bridge just downriver. Although the bridge was completed in 2016, the North Kore-

Pyongyang metro station, 2015. Wikimedia Commons, by Mario Micklisch, CC-BY-2.0.

ans failed to connect it with roads on their side of the bridge. The prevailing opinion is that they wanted the Chinese to build these approach roads, but the Chinese were reluctant to get involved given the international sanctions placed on North Korea. The roads were finally completed (it is not clear who paid for them) and opened in early 2019. If South Koreans continue to elect presidential administrations that support North Korea, it might be wise for the Kim regime to wait until South Korea upgrades all of North Korea's infrastructure rather than spending money to upgrade it themselves.

Given the difficulty of building and maintaining roads in mountainous North Korea, it is hardly surprising that most freight and passengers are transported by the railroads originally built by the Japanese. The country has approximately four thousand miles of track, almost all of it single track. The railroads are in a notoriously poor state of repair, as proved by the fact that every year in the New Year's address, one of the first points mentioned in a discussion of the economy is the need to improve rail transport. When railroad tracks are repaired, it is usually by dragooned local laborers who work with picks and shovels and lack the skills and motivation to do a good job.

The road to the port of Nampo, 2015. *Wikimedia Commons, by Uwe Brodrecht,* *CC-BY-SA-2.0.*

Except for some local branch lines that still run steam engines, all railways have been electrified to cope with the chronic shortage of fuel oil. Since electricity is limited and train engines are old, the average speed on most rail lines tops out at thirty-five miles an hour. When the power goes out, trains can be marooned for hours or even days. In late 2018 the South Korean government was invited to send a team of railway experts into North Korea to survey the condition of the railroads. They estimated that the cost of bringing the North's railroads up to reasonable standards and installing one high-speed rail line to Pyongyang would cost $25 billion, which is almost as much as North Korea's annual gross domestic product. Whereas trains have been the main form of long-distance transportation in the countryside, local people get around on foot and by bicycle and move goods in carts drawn by oxen or people. With the rise of the market economy, trucks operated by private contractors are increasingly used to transport goods.

North Korea's rivers are mostly navigable only by small boats. The government owns a small fleet of aging cargo ships operating under other countries' flags of convenience and occasionally renamed to avoid international attention, especially in light of UN sanctions. Despite the fact that

North Korea has two long coastlines, these ships play only a limited role in domestic trade. In order to go from one coast to the other, they must make the long trip around South Korea. Moreover, North Korean commercial docks have a very limited cargo-handling capacity.

North Korea has a small fleet of mostly aging Russian-made airplanes that serve a handful of international routes, mostly to China, as well as a few domestic routes. Only the wealthiest North Koreans can afford to fly. At this writing, North Korean planes are not permitted to fly to airports in the European Union because of safety concerns.

The supreme leader has his own means of transportation. His fleet of automobiles includes a Rolls-Royce Phantom and a Mercedes-Maybach S600. When they visited other countries, even in Europe, Kim Il-sung and Kim Jong-il almost always traveled by private train. When Kim Jong-un traveled to Hanoi in 2019 for his second meeting with President Trump, he took a three-day train journey to the southern border of China and completed the remainder of the trip by car. When he traveled to Singapore for his first meeting with the American president, he flew on a Chinese government plane rather than trusting one of his own. For his travels, the leader can call on four Chinese-manufactured "presidential" trains with dark green railcars. On his trip to China, Kim Jong-un's train had fourteen carriages, with another seven added at the border for Chinese officials and security officers. In addition to Kim's private car, the train had a car for meetings, a car carrying his armored limousines, another with soldiers, another with medical personnel, and other railcars for his entourage.

Today, travel in North Korea can no longer be considered a luxury. Without a dramatically improved transportation system, the country has no chance of becoming a developed economy. Cities need to be tied together across difficult terrain. The emerging private economy requires that goods produced in one region be transported and sold in another region. Raw materials and machinery need to be delivered to factories if they are to reopen. When international sanctions are removed, trade with other countries will require a vastly improved transportation system. The cost to upgrade North Korea's roads, railways, bridges, and tunnels will be enormous, and at some point an entire airline industry will have to be created almost from scratch. So far, the Kim regime has been reluctant to spend much money on transportation. Americans, who enjoy a vastly superior transportation system but one that is in serious need of repairs, can recognize a similar reluctance on the part of their own government to fund improvements in infrastructure.

OLD COMMUNICATION CHANNELS:
GOVERNMENT TO PEOPLE

North Korea routinely ranks last in the world on the Reporters without Borders World Press Freedom Index and on the Freedom House Press Freedom Index. So far as knowledge of the world is concerned, North Koreans have lived like prisoners who are allowed to hear and see only what the warden allows. Total control of information is the regime's goal, and early on the regime took control of all public communication channels, the better to shape the worldview of its people in the direction of worshipping the Kim family. It is not accurate to say that the North Korean people were brainwashed, because that would imply that they had something else in their brains to begin with. Children are inculcated with the regime's propaganda almost from the day they are born.

All North Korean media are overseen by the party's Propaganda and Agitation Department, which in turn takes its orders from the leader. Successive Kim regimes have never been shy about the purpose of their media. *Nodong Sinmun*, the party newspaper, has likened the press to a "sharp ideological weapon dedicated to staunchly defending and safeguarding the leader," urging the press to "dye the whole society one color, the color of the revolutionary ideology of the great leader."[1]

The media publish little news about the outside world, and what is published is selected to make North Korea look like a paradise on earth, even with all its faults. South Koreans are depicted as prisoners of the American soldiers garrisoned in their country. The United States is portrayed as being in its death throes. When the media cover domestic news, virtually the only person ever featured by name is the leader. News stories boast of the progress the country is making in all fields of endeavor under the wise guidance of the leader and the party, even though people can see that the leader, party, and government are doing very little for them.

The premier news source in North Korea is the party newspaper, *Nodong Sinmun* (Daily Worker), whose editor holds a cabinet-level post. No alternative or conflicting news stories can be found in other government media. This uniformity of information presumably strengthens the impact of news stories, as one source reinforces another. On the other hand, most people are aware that they are receiving only the government's take on the news, so they are likely to ignore or discount whatever they read, see, or hear. Yet in every society there are some who will believe anything. *Nodong Sinmun* is only six pages long. Newsprint, and for that matter all paper, has always been a scarce commodity in North Korea. People read the paper as it is posted in public spaces or at their places of work. The paper is also available on the country's domestic Internet (intranet). Almost the only reason for reading the paper is to prepare for the mandatory political discussions regularly held at workplaces. The government's newspaper is *Minju Choson* (Democratic Korea). The military's paper is *Inmingun Sinmun* (Korean People's Army Daily). Provinces also have their own newspapers. All take their lead from *Nodong Sinmun*.

When Kim Il-sung was alive, he recorded a New Year's message that was broadcast on the radio and published in *Nodong Sinmun*. When Kim Jong-il succeeded his father, his stage fright prevented him from giving any speeches, so the New Year's message was replaced by a New Year's editorial published in the major newspapers. One year after Kim Jong-un took power, he resumed his grandfather's practice of broadcasting a New Year's speech. No item published in North Korea receives more attention from North Koreans or is read more carefully by foreign analysts than this editorial, which is comparable to the American president's State of the Union address. In the country, for weeks after its publication the editorial is discussed in political study sessions. At schools, prizes are given to students who have done the best job of memorizing the editorial, which usually runs to over five thousand words.

For all the attention it receives, the editorial is pretty much the same from one year to the next, which makes it easier to study and memorize. When it was only released in print form during the Kim Jong-il era, it was given a heroic title, for example, "Make a Higher Leap Full of Great Ambition and Confidence" (2006), "Usher in a Great Heyday of Songun Korea Full of Confidence in Victory" (2007), and "Let Us Glorify This Year of the Sixtieth Anniversary of the Founding of the DPRK as a Year of Historical Turn That Will Go Down in the History of the Fatherland" (2008).

Whatever the title and whichever the year, the editorial begins by boasting of the alleged progress made in the preceding year, no matter how badly things went for the country. The editorial then predicts even greater successes in the coming year, building on the alleged firm foundations of the preceding year. After this review and pep talk, the editorial presents the principal issues to be addressed in the coming year. The editorial then takes up ideology and politics, urging the people to follow the dictates of the party. The next major topic is the desirability of Korean reunification, followed by a brief discussion of the international situation, usually criticizing American attempts to intimidate or crush North Korea.

The editorial's tone is upbeat and militant. Every year the claim is made that a foundation for success has been laid and that now is the time to build on that foundation. The country is said to have reached a "turning point," after which things will get better. People are told that they have everything they need to achieve a brighter future if only they will faithfully follow the policies laid down by the leader and the party. Unfortunately, every year turns out to be pretty much like the year before, with little or no progress made in the economy. Consequently, people pay no more attention to the New Year's editorial than is absolutely necessary. Foreign analysts and reporters who place trust in the words of the editorial almost invariably discover that they have mistaken propaganda for news.

The government's radio station is KCBS, the Korean Central Broadcasting Station. Pyongyang Radio is a musical FM station. North Korean radios have their dials frozen to government stations, and for those who tinker with their radios to "unfreeze" the dials, the government jams foreign radio transmissions. Listeners who keep the volume low on their illegally tuned radios can receive spotty transmissions from such foreign services as Radio Free Asia and Voice of America, along with several South Korean radio stations targeted at the North.

There are four television stations, all state owned, with the primary station being Korean Central Television (KCTV), which broadcasts information, government-made entertainment programs, and instructional programs. The PAL television signal broadcast by North Korea (also used in Europe and China) is incompatible with the NTSC South Korean television signal (also used in the United States and Japan), so North Koreans cannot use their television sets to receive South Korean broadcasts. Owning an NTSC television receiver is illegal.

With the growing popularity of computers, smart phones, and tablets, the government established its own domestic version of the Internet called Kwangmyong (Brightness). The real Internet cannot be accessed in North Korea except by a small number of officials, research specialists, and foreigners. The domestic intranet service hosts academic and information websites, some entertainment, and social networking options. Use of the intranet is presumably closely monitored by the police, and it is not accessible from outside the country.

Two old-school information channels still function today. One is the Third Broadcasting System, which is a wired network of speakers in homes, public buildings, and outdoor spaces. Third Broadcasting messages differ from those on radio and television largely in being tailored to specific locales and in being less concerned about promoting a positive image of the country. People receive instructions on how to behave when a visiting foreigner is expected in the neighborhood, or they might be warned to be on the lookout for those responsible for a rash of local burglaries. The messages are sent out for about two hours a day, and the volume on home speakers can be turned down but not off. Power outages and the general deterioration of North Korea's communication infrastructure have hampered the operation of the speaker system.

And then there are the compulsory political meetings held in schools and workplaces two or three times a week, highlighting recent *Nodong Sinmun* articles, providing a forum for mandatory self-criticism, and attempting to boost morale. People try to bribe their way out of attending these meetings, which they do not take seriously.

The government hosts its own foreign news service, the Korean Central News Agency (KCNA), which carries its stories on the Internet (from North Korea and from an associated website in Japan). News items on KCNA for foreign audiences are similar to what is found in *Nodong Sinmun* but differ in that they sometimes deal with stories that would not be appropriate for the North Korean people to hear. For example, if large crowds gather in Seoul to protest South Korean government policies, the North Korean government would be pleased for its people to learn that many South Koreans are unhappy, but at the same time the government would not want their own people to know that South Koreans, who are supposed to be living under the thumb of the Americans and their "puppet government," enjoy the freedom of public assembly and protest, a freedom that North Koreans can't even dream of exercising for themselves. Foreigners get much of their news about North Korea from KCNA, with the understanding that it is a self-serving news service.

Through the 1980s the regime's media had the information environment well under control. When the economic disasters of the 1990s destroyed the government's socialist economy, the emergence of the people-led market economy gave rise not only to a private transportation industry but, more importantly, to a host of new forms of communication.

NEW COMMUNICATION CHANNELS: PEOPLE TO PEOPLE

In the 1990s, new modes of transportation and communication had to be developed to support the emerging people's economy, which unlike the centralized socialist economy could not be directed from above. The new freedom of transportation changed how people behaved, for example, in terms of where they went to buy food and how that food got to them in the first place. The new communication methods did more than that: they changed the way people thought. New ideas, values, and fashions began to circulate throughout the country, all without the consent or intervention of the Kim regime.

Two new channels of communication were created to supplement the old channel of government-to-people messages (in the absence of meaningful elections and in the face of stiff police control, there is no direct people-to-government channel). The more important of the two new channels was a people-to-people channel, something the regime had always resisted for fear it might facilitate the emergence of anti-regime organizations. The other new communication channel connected the people to the outside world, providing an alternative to the government's near total control over information.

It was formerly the case that the only time people could gather together was in state-monitored groups at schools, workplaces, and outdoor venues for organized activities. As people began to set up impromptu markets in the 1990s, they were able not only to exchange goods but also share information. At the same time, as travel restrictions were relaxed to allow hungry people to find food, travelers were able to talk with strangers on trucks and trains and while trudging along the roads from town to town. The country began to be connected in ways that were controlled by the people, not by the regime.

The easiest way for people to communicate with each other over any distance is by telephone or some other electronic device. Computer use has never become widespread in North Korea because of the cost of computers and the unreliability of the electricity supply. Schools have computers, as do government offices and businesses, but relatively few computers are found in homes. Until the widespread adoption of cell phones, around 2010, communication by telephone was pretty much limited to government offices. After all, a robust telephone network requires thousands of miles of well-maintained telephone lines, and North Korea has never had a good physical infrastructure. It is not known how many landline telephones there are in the North; in 1999 it was estimated that the country had between one and one and a half million phones, or about five for every hundred people.[2] Of these, it is believed that only about seventy thousand were in homes. Since the coming of cell phones, landline phones have become even more scarce. The country has only one telephone book, which is a classified document marked "secret," the better to keep people from learning about the structure of their government. According to a report leaked out of the country in 2018, six people had recently been executed for trying to sell a copy of the phone book to foreigners.[3]

Not only have home phones always been expensive, but getting them has required a considerable effort in terms of registering with the government and explaining why a phone was needed, so people who wanted to make a call would go to the local government communications office, present personal identification and a small deposit, and wait in line to use a public phone. It was always assumed that the phone call was being monitored by government agents, just as it had to be assumed that agents read letters that were put in the mail.

Cell phones (called "hand phones") came rather late to North Korea, and after they arrived, their adoption was interrupted. A foreigner who visited Pyongyang in 1999 reported that he saw a few officials using cell phones. To think about it, the Kim regime should have had serious reservations about allowing its people access to cell phones, which could be easily concealed and used anywhere within range of a cell tower. However, when Kim Jong-il visited Shanghai in January 2001, he was reportedly amazed at the economic and technological progress the Chinese had made, and in particular was shocked to see all the young Chinese using cell phones. It is said that, in his usual impetuous style, he ordered that North Korea establish a cell phone service the following year.[4] By this time Chinese cell phones had already been introduced in North Korea near the Chinese border, picking up signals from cell towers as much as thirty miles away in China.

In 2002 the North Korean government began a joint-venture cell phone service with Thailand's Loxley Pacific Company. This venture, called Sun-Net, was a blow to the South Korean government, which had hoped that one of its telecommunications companies could enter the North Korean market with the CDMA cell phone standard (licensed from the United States and used throughout the Western Hemisphere). Loxley used the GSM standard popular in Europe and parts of Asia (eventually Europe and the United States would provide service for both standards). Having one cell phone standard would make communication easier in the event of Korean reunification, but in the meantime it would make it more difficult for the North Korean government to keep its citizens isolated from South Korea.

The SunNet cell phones were extremely expensive by North Korean standards, making them affordable only for government officials. In any case, in 2004, before cell phones became widespread, their use was banned, and the government confiscated all the phones it could find. The reason for the ban, and even its timing, was somewhat of a mystery because the government never made any public announcement about it.[5] According to one rumor, the government suspected that a cell phone had been used to trigger a large explosion in a rail yard near the Chinese border at about the time that Kim Jong-il was returning by train from China. Another rumor was that the government was having second thoughts about the wisdom of letting people communicate outside of official channels, especially in regard to making phone calls into China (on the Chinese phones). Whatever the reason, for the next four years the expansion of cell phones in North Korea was stymied.

In 2008 the Ministry of Posts and Telecommunications signed a contract with Egypt's Orascom Telecom Media to provide a joint-venture cell phone service under the name Koryolink. The business flourished, although it appears that Orascom had trouble repatriating profits from the venture. By 2018, as many as six million phones, including many smart phones (called "touch phones"), were in use among a population of twenty-five million.

Like everything in North Korea, details about cell phone use are hard to come by, and the industry changes so quickly that it is difficult for the government, and for foreign analysts, to keep track of how people are using their phones. By 2018, two more cell phone services, these domestic, had been launched: Pyol (Star) and Kangsongmang (Kangsong Network). A former Orascom technician has reported that the country has at least three separate networks, each using a different phone number prefix, with no communication between them. One network serves the general public, another is restricted to officials, and the third is for foreigners.[6] Reception is said to be good in the major cities, especially in Pyongyang, but spotty near the Chinese border, perhaps because the government has spent a considerable amount of money purchasing jamming and detection equipment from China to try to stamp out the use of Chinese cell phones. Phone prices have come down, and thanks to the private market economy, many North Koreans can now afford them.

North Koreans have found many uses for cell phones. High school and college students consider the phones to be an important part of youth culture, just as in other countries. They communicate with their friends using North Korean versions of social networking systems, visit intranet sites, share photos, play video games, and watch movies on SD cards. Businesspeople need one or more phones to track merchandise shipments, check on the current price of goods in different places, and talk with their Chinese suppliers. The growing middle class in Pyongyang can call taxis and have even begun visiting a handful of domestic shopping sites. Cell phones provide a vital if tenuous link for those who have family in South Korea. Thanks to arrangements with Chinese brokers, South Koreans can place a call to Chinese cell phones that have been smuggled into the border area of North Korea, while their North Korean family members can call the border area on their North Korean phones. Then the two phones are held together ("kissing phones") to provide a primitive communication link. Since it is assumed that conversations are monitored by the North Korean police, they can't last more than a few minutes and their content must be disguised. The newer cell phones, manufactured by the North Korean government, contain chips that can keep a record of all numbers dialed, so users are never safe if the police check their phones.

With every student wanting to own a phone, the Kim regime is becoming concerned about the negative effects of these phones, yet the regime can't admit that anything is actually amiss in North Korea. In 2018, *Nodong Sinmun* published an article reviewing the alleged negative effects that cell phones have had on students in, of all places, France, adding that many other countries are also trying to figure out what to do about student use of cell phones in order to preserve "campus order and class discipline." The article concludes, "It is the view of the majority of teachers and students' parents in the world that various decadent and reactionary ideologies and cultures spreading via mobile phones create confusion in students during the formation of their outlook on life and their values. For this reason, various countries have created regulations on the use of mobile phones in school and keep them under control."[7]

Another channel of communication that has opened up since the mid-1990s links North Koreans directly to the outside world through the movement of people. North Korea's borders have always been closed. Traveling outside the country without government permission is a crime, and such permission is rarely granted. Visitors to the country are carefully screened and supervised. But when food ran out in the 1990s, thousands and then tens of thousands of starving people fled across the border into China to find food for themselves and bring some back for their families. Border guards were as hungry as civilians, and the payment of a small bribe was sufficient to make them look the other way. Thus, news and information began to flow both ways across the border.

Travelers not only brought back news of the outside world but also began smuggling in videotape players and then CD players, along with media to play on them. These became popular sources of entertainment, especially for young people, who were particularly attracted to South Korean music and TV dramas. Once cell phones became popular, SD cards, which were easy to hide from the police, brought in the same entertainment, along with the music, fashions, and lifestyles of the outside world. This information, by tape, CD, SD cards, and computer flash drives, was eagerly passed around among young people. When the police discovered and confiscated the media, it was passed around among them and their friends as well. Payment of small bribes was usually sufficient to keep offenders out of prison.

Thus, small gaps have appeared in the Kim regime's barrier to the outside world. In response, the regime regularly publishes articles about how capitalist information and entertainment will warp the "pure socialist minds" of the North Korean people, but few pay any attention to these warnings. Foreign entertainment is as popular among government officials as it is among any other segment of the population. And the former dictator, Kim Jong-il, was known (by top officials) to have a huge private library of foreign films.

The increased flow of information that arrives in North Korea has wide-ranging effects. People communicate to each other by how they speak (for example, by imitating the South Korean dialect), what clothes they wear, what foods they eat, and so forth. Foreign culture, especially from South Korea by way of China, has found a way to enter closed North Korea on the back of the market economy. The Kim regime is unable to control the thoughts and values of its people, although the regime is still able to control their public behavior. The North Korean people are no longer like frogs living in a well, but more like frogs living in a small pond surrounded by a broken fence.

Chapter Nine

Culture and Lifestyle

Trying to Live a Normal Life

EDUCATION: IDEOLOGICAL AND ACADEMIC

The Kim regime has set two goals for its education system: to make young people loyal supporters of the regime and to teach them the academic skills necessary to make North Korea economically successful. According to Article 43 of the DPRK constitution (2016 edition), "the State shall embody the principles of socialist pedagogy so as to raise the rising generation to be steadfast revolutionaries who will fight for society and the people, to be people of the new, *Juche* type [formerly reading "communist type"] who are knowledgeable, morally sound and physically healthy." The priority given to ideological education makes sense from the leader's point of view because an economically successful North Korea without a Kim at the helm is of no value to the Kim family. Better that people be poor and under Kim's thumb than prosperous and self-sufficient.

Korea's Confucian society has always put a high value on education, and under North Korea's "egalitarian" socialist system, twelve years of compulsory schooling have boosted the literacy rate to almost 100 percent. It also helped that in 1949 the Kim regime abolished the use of the complicated Chinese characters formerly supplementing Korean script, something South Korea has not completely done. North Korean youth attend one year of kindergarten, five years of elementary school, three years of middle school, and three years of high school (to use the American terminology). The school year starts on the first of April. In addition to occasional school holidays (including the two most important ones: Kim Il-sung's birthday, the "Shining Sun" day, and Kim Jong-il's birthday, the "Shining Star" day), students have a one-month vacation beginning in late July and another month during January. The school week lasts from Monday through Friday, with special assignments on Saturday.

In addition to regular schools, North Korea has special "number 1" or "first" schools for students who show promise in science and mathematics. Graduates of number 1 schools are not mobilized for annual labor assignments and head directly to universities after high school without being drafted into the army. By the 1990s, over two hundred of these schools had been established throughout the country, and promising students were being aggressively recruited. Another kind of school, far more exclusive, is the "revolutionary" school, of which there are only a few, Mangyongdae being the most famous. These schools are reserved for descendants of the original revolutionary leaders (i.e., compatriots of Kim Il-sung), children of war veterans, and children of important party, military, and government officials. Graduates of revolutionary schools can expect to become officers in the army or officials in national security organizations.

College education is not as common in North Korea as it is in South Korea due to a traditional need for laborers rather than thinkers (the party does all the thinking for the people). Since the turn of the century, the regime has dramatically expanded college education. North Korea now has a variety of colleges, universities, and professional schools, as well as trade schools and continuing education programs. Comprehensive universities such as Kim Il-sung University, Kimchaek Engineering University, and Koryo Songgyungwan University require four to six years of study. Professional schools such as teacher colleges, engineering colleges, and mining schools typically require three years of study.

Admission to universities and colleges is extremely selective. Students must take a preliminary selection exam and then a school's entrance exam. It has been estimated that only about 10 percent of high school graduates are accepted for further study. To get into schools of higher education requires good political class background, talent, and frequently the payment of bribes. An important part of education today is private tutoring, which is illegal but widely practiced. To get ahead in schoolwork and to improve test scores for college entrance, many parents spend hundreds of dollars a year on tutoring. This is a huge investment for North Koreans but only a fraction of what

South Korean parents pay. The tutoring is offered by moonlighting teachers and college students.

A typical school day begins as students head off to school at seven in the morning, sometimes marching in groups behind their homeroom leader. As they enter the school grounds, they must pass inspection to ensure that their school uniforms and grooming meet the school's standards. Students are required to wear uniforms (black or dark blue skirts for girls, dark trousers for boys, white shirt, red kerchief after they become "Young Pioneers," and Kim Il-sung and Kim Jong-il badges after they join the Youth League). The uniforms are supposed to be provided by the state but often must be purchased in the market. The first half hour of school is devoted to listening to the teacher read the news or present political messages—the same activity their parents are participating in at work. Classes begin at 8 a.m., with a lunch break at noon. Elementary school children do not attend classes in the afternoon; middle school students have classes until 3 or 4 p.m. In better times, children brought lunches of rice and vegetables; today some students in rural areas are lucky if they can bring a cupful of corn kernels.

Like adults, children are kept busy with group activities. After school they perform school and community service, and once or twice a week they participate in the children's version of political-criticism sessions, where they write down "mistakes" they have made and indicate how they will improve themselves. Children also engage in group sports activities. Students in Pyongyang are called upon to participate in gymnastic displays, parades, and mass rallies. Mandatory labor assistance is considered an essential part of education, despite the fact that Article 15 of the country's Socialist Labor Law prohibits children under the age of sixteen from working.[1] After school and on Saturdays students are assigned tasks such as cleaning the school, cleaning the neighborhood around the school, and assisting in labor projects in their area. Rural students are required to help out on collective farms. During the spring planting and fall harvest seasons, city students are sent away for several weeks to work on farms. Rows of red flags are posted by the fields to signal that this is a special patriotic mission.

One distinctive aspect of North Korean education is the amount of time devoted to ideological courses. As the Kim cult developed over the years, studies of the Kim family were added to the standard curriculum. Defectors have estimated that in the 1970s and 1980s (when Kim Jong-il's influence began to be felt), 40 to 80 percent of school time was spent on ideological lessons, with the tide turning back to academic subjects such as science and

Well-dressed schoolchildren, probably in Pyongyang, 2011. *Wikimedia Commons, by Mark Fahey, CC-BY-2.0.*

technology in the 1990s. This ideological tendency shows no signs of abating. For example, a 2017 *Nodong Sinmun* editorial, cited by KCNA in an awkward English-language translation, insists that "the Workers' Party of Korea remains unchanged in its stand to intensify the ideological work with firm grip on ideology as the revolution and construction are gaining in depth."[2]

In elementary school, one hour a week is devoted to the study of each of the three leaders, Kim Il-sung, Kim Jong-il, and Kim Jong-un, with another hour on socialist ethics. First-graders even get an extra hour on Kim Il-sung's second wife, the mother of Kim Jong-il. In addition to these explicitly ideological courses, school students study the usual subjects, with English-language training beginning in the fourth grade. It is difficult to say exactly how much ideological education students receive because academic subjects are suffused with ideology and the worship of the Kim family. In music class, little children are taught songs of praise for the Kims. In history class they study the alleged military victories of the Kims. In math class, they calculate how many American soldiers North Korean soldiers can kill. In art class they draw pictures of the Kim family home. A first-grade reader shows little children gleefully playing with a toy tank, accompanied by the ditty, "Mini-tank advances / Our tank advances / Crushing American bastards / Mini-tank advances" (Americans are almost always referred to in a highly derogatory manner).

North Korea's traditional isolation has cut it off from many advances in knowledge available in developed countries, although in recent years the regime has come to realize that it will have to break out of its shell in order to make economic progress. Foreign-language instruction has become popular, both in the context of regular school studies and as a college major. Despite the regime's insistence that capitalism is doomed to be replaced by socialism, students are increasingly exposed to capitalist ideas to prepare them to do business with foreigners (and, incidentally, to participate in the growing domestic capitalist market). As early as 1996 Kim Il-sung University offered a few lectures on capitalism, taught by professors visiting from North Korea–affiliated universities in Japan.[3]

A few North Korean students have been sent abroad in small groups to study science, technology, and market economies, especially to Chinese universities. Students have also been sent to Western countries, including several hundred to the United States, usually for a period of a few weeks or months, for example, at Syracuse University in New York. Another approach to exposing North Korean students to foreign knowledge is to bring foreign classes into the country. After almost ten years of negotiations, the Pyongyang University of Science and Technology (PUST) opened in 2010. Funded primarily by foreign evangelical organizations and staffed by foreign faculty, it had an uneasy relationship with the North Korean authorities who authorized it. Since the imposition of increasingly severe UN sanctions and the 2017 US prohibition against travel to North Korea by American citizens (who comprised the largest number of faculty members), the university has been struggling.

As a direct result of the country's economic problems beginning in the 1980s and peaking in the 1990s, the educational infrastructure crumbled. In the mid-1990s, the economy was in such bad shape that many students and even some teachers were skipping school in order to search for food. Meanwhile, school buildings fell into disrepair, and fuel was so scarce that classrooms were often unheated in the middle of winter. Although conditions have improved somewhat since then, North Korean school facilities lag far behind those found in South Korea. It has become the responsibility of students, their families, and teachers to provide school equipment, repair school buildings, and bring wood or coal to heat classrooms. These days most school supplies for students must be purchased by parents. Middle- and upper-class parents living in cities purchase these supplies at department stores. Everyone else shops in the local markets, where quality and price are lower. The government requires that schools contribute quotas of recycled goods such as metal and rubber and locally sourced goods such as mushrooms and seafood. Raising rabbits for their fur and meat is also a required task for many students; those who cannot bring to school, say, their quota of rabbit skins, are supposed to bring money instead, and students who do not fill their quotas are publicly criticized.

The life of North Korean teachers is not easy. As government employees, they do not receive enough money to live on. Hence, they must depend on students and their parents to make up the difference. Students who want special attention or recommendations to college are expected to provide gifts to teachers and administrators in the form of money, food, cigarettes, or items of clothing. Many teachers take second jobs in the unofficial market economy, including hiring themselves out as tutors. Given the important role they play in indoctrinating students, university professors work under the watchful eye of the government and the party. A German professor who taught for a year at the prestigious Kim Il-sung University said she was required to obtain official approval for every lecture she delivered.[4]

It should come as no surprise that graduates of major universities and professional schools can expect to be given better jobs, have more promising marriage prospects, and enjoy a better life in general than common laborers. A good education can sometimes even compensate for poor political class status. While science and technology are important subjects for obtaining professional jobs in the government-controlled economy, the dramatic growth of the private economy has made business training a better path to wealth.

The trend in North Korean education is for more time and resources to be devoted to science and technology, with special emphasis on information technology. Both Kim Jong-il and Kim Jong-un have strongly promoted education. In 2019, on the occasion of the Fourteenth National Conference of Teachers, a speech previously made by Kim Jong-un was delivered under the title "Teachers Should Fulfill Their Duty as Career Revolutionaries in Implementing the Party's Policy on Bringing about a Radical Turn in Education."

In the speech, Kim Jong-un complained that "education has not kept up with the party's intention and it is left far behind the worldwide trend in the development of education."[5] The government says it is trying to promote independent thought and initiative in students, although it is hard to see how these goals fit in with the continued importance placed on political ideology. The imposition in recent years of international economic sanctions on North Korea provides a serious challenge to its educational system. Whether the Kim regime can have both nuclear weapons and a better education system is a serious question for the future.

FOOD: LIVING ON THE EDGE

Putting food on the table is the first concern of most North Koreans. The effective end of the Public Distribution System (PDS) in the mid-1990s dramatically changed the lives of the people, who had depended on the system since Kim Il-sung abolished private enterprise in the late 1950s. Every two weeks workers received ration coupons that they took to their designated PDS center to purchase food and staples for a nominal fee—as long as the items were in stock.

The amount of food authorized by the ration coupons depended on occupation, age, and political status. Workers in nationally strategic and difficult occupations such as heavy industries were supposed to receive the most generous rations—as much as 900 grams a day. High-ranking military officers received 850 grams and party members 700 grams. At the other end of the scale, women over fifty-five and men over sixty-one received coupons worth 400 grams of food, and children 200 to 300 grams, which is the same amount that prisoners received, if they were lucky. Party members and military officers received most of their grain ration in white rice, whereas ordinary workers received only 30 percent rice, and the least fortunate 10 to 20 percent rice, with the remainder usually being corn. By comparison, a typical American consumes about 1,800 grams of food a day, most of it loaded with calories.

Beginning in the early 1970s, two days of rations were deducted from every fifteen-day ration period as a contribution to "wartime reserves," and other deductions were often made for one campaign or another. Farmworkers were paid in crops produced on their collective farms. In the 1980s, PDS distribution centers began running out of food. By the mid-1990s, distribution centers could provide only a few days' rations each month. Although the food supply recovered somewhat after the turn of the century, in 2016 the UN's Food and Agriculture Organization (FAO) estimated that the average daily distribution was only 360 grams of food, less than the FAO's recommended minimum of 600 grams.[6]

North Koreans vividly remember the 1990s famine, when even some members of the political elite class died of starvation. In those days it was common, outside of Pyongyang, to come across dead people lying in the streets. A video smuggled out of the country showed shoeless children in the marketplace picking single grains of rice out of the mud. During the famine, city residents asked relatives who lived on farms to send them food, for which they traded household possessions. They also went on the street to beg, and some turned to burglary, robbery, swindling, and prostitution. In the last stages of hunger, people went into the woods and fields to pull up grass and peel bark off trees, then ground this material up and mixed it with a little grain. These alternative foods wreaked havoc on the digestive system while supplying little nourishment. The three million residents of Pyongyang received the best food rations. At the same time, it is estimated that Kim Jong-il spent over $100 million renovating his father's mausoleum. All three Kims have been exceptionally well fed; the Chinese refer to them as "the three fats."

The Economic Management Improvement Measures of July 2002 largely ended the ration system except as it continued to supply the top one or two million cadres. People now purchase most of their food at the markets. In a 2015 survey, defectors reported that 23 percent of their food in North Korea had been sourced from the PDS, 61 percent from markets, and 15 percent homegrown.[7] According to defectors, poor people have to spend as much as 90 percent of their income on food, compared to next to nothing when the rationing system was in place.[8]

Market prices fluctuate according to how much food is available, rising in early spring after most of the fall harvest has been consumed and peaking in early summer before the barley harvest. Prices also reflect how much food aid North Korea is receiving, because even though much of the aid is siphoned off by the upper political class and the military, the donated food takes pressure off the food system and lowers prices in the market for everyone else. Because of transportation difficulties, prices differ among provinces, with the lowest prices in farming areas and along the Chinese border, where food can be smuggled in.

In addition to food imported from abroad, North Koreans have increasingly depended on food grown in private garden plots and on secretly appropriated public land. In these gardens farmers conscientiously grow vegetables such as beans, cabbage, radishes, peppers, garlic, potatoes, corn, and pumpkins. Houses in the countryside are covered with vegetable vines and surrounded by edible plants, while crops in the fields of collective farms are thin. To prevent thieves from raiding garden plots, farmers sleep outdoors next to their crops. As harvest season approaches, collective farms post guards in the fields.

The reasons for North Korea's chronic food shortages are not hard to find. Agricultural productivity is sapped by lack of incentives for farmers working on collective farms, and by the severe limitations that centralized socialist economic management imposes on agriculture. The land and climate also limit how much food North Koreans can grow. Much of the northern half of the Korean Peninsula is hilly and mountainous—unsuitable terrain for farming, especially rice farming. The temperatures in the North are lower than is ideal for growing rice, and the North gets less annual rainfall than the South. In short, considering topography and climate alone, North Korea's attempt at self-sufficiency in food production is a losing battle.

With little foreign exchange available to import fertilizer, and with domestic fertilizer factories idled, farm productivity has declined. Electricity is often unavailable in rural districts, limiting the use of pumps to irrigate fields. Due to lack of fuel and spare parts, functioning farm machinery is in short supply. Much farmland continues to be tilled by hand or plowed by oxen. Farmers also face a shortage of insecticides and plastic sheeting to cover seedbeds in the springtime. Shortages of trucks and fuel make it difficult to get crops to market before they spoil.

The high point of North Korea's domestic grain harvests was apparently reached in the late 1980s and early 1990s, with annual production in the range of five to six million tons.[9] Current annual production (in the second decade of the century) has averaged between four and five million tons—similar to what it was in 1970. In the mid-1990s, grain production slipped to three million tons, which was about three million tons short of the minimum domestic demand.[10] Early in the 1990s the government launched a "Let's Eat Two Meals a Day" campaign, which was overtaken by the famine of 1995–1998, when two meals were only a dream for many people. The best estimates are that between half a million and one million people died of starvation during the famine, constituting 3 to 5 percent of the population.[11]

The consequences of the ongoing food shortages are easy to see simply by looking at the people. As one visitor observed, "nobody is apple-shaped or pear-shaped. Everyone is banana-shaped."[12] Those who are most immediately affected by food shortages are the young and the old. In late 1998, near the end of the famine period, a World Food Programme (WFP) survey of children from age six months to seven years estimated that 16 percent of the children were wasting and 62 percent were stunted.[13] A WFP survey in early 2005 found 7 percent wasting, 37 percent stunted, and 23 percent underweight.[14] Conditions have gradually improved, even though some years are leaner than others. In 2019 the WFP estimated that 43 percent of North Koreans were still undernourished.[15] By their size, North Korean children look several years younger than their South Korean counterparts, and throughout their lives these undernourished children are likely to suffer from a mental and physical "disease burden."[16]

When food production fails to meet demand, as is the case almost every year, the Kim regime can either purchase food from other countries or request food donations. The second option is preferred because it saves hard currency to fund the country's weapons programs. Donation requests put the international community in a bind because UN and unilateral economic sanctions have been imposed to reduce the Kim regime's ability to use its economy to produce weapons of mass destruction. On the other hand, humanitarian concerns prevent the foreign community from denying food to hungry North Koreans, who are essentially being held hostage by their regime. Since the imposition of international economic sanctions beginning in 2006, food aid has continued, although at a reduced level. The Kim regime has also placed further restrictions on foreign-aid workers sent to the country to estimate food needs and monitor food distribution.

Most food aid is delivered through the UN's WFP and donated by individual nations, with one of the largest donors being the United States. American food aid began in 1996 and peaked in 1999 at 695,000 tons. By 2007, the total American contribution was just over two million tons, at a cost of about $700 million.[17] Plans to resume food aid in 2012 were abandoned when North Korea reneged on a missile agreement. The first South Korean delivery of aid, 150,000 tons of rice, was made in 1995, after which about 100,000 tons of grain and 300,000 tons of fertilizer were sent to the North every year until 2008, when the Kim regime froze relations with South Korea to protest the election of a conservative president. Even under recent left-leaning governments, the donation process has been fraught with difficulties. The Kim regime is unhappy that South Korea has participated in UN sanctions. As recently as 2019 the regime rejected South Korea's offer of food aid by arguing that it was "not a fundamental solution to the stalemate in inter-Korean relations."[18]

As the North Korean economy has improved, food has become more plentiful. Since the demise of government rations, the market has taken over food supply, providing a larger amount and variety of foods than were available with ration tickets. The kinds of food eaten depend in part on one's economic class. The upper class of top officials, along with the new upper class of successful entrepreneurs, live almost as well as middle-class foreigners. In Pyongyang they patronize foreign-currency restaurants, where they might spend more on a meal than most North Koreans earn in an entire month.

For the upper class, polished sticky white rice remains the ideal food and the center of most meals. The rice is eaten with fresh vegetables and pieces of fish or meat. As a side dish, kimchi, made with fermented cabbage, radishes, and various other ingredients and stored underground in large earthenware pots, is served with most meals. The dish that North Koreans are most proud of is *naengmyeon*, an unappetizing-looking cold dish made of black buckwheat noodles and vegetables. It is a summertime specialty originating in the North and popular with Koreans everywhere. Dog meat (called "sweet meat") is eaten a few times a year and is thought to be good for one's health. In recent years a variety of easy-to-prepare canned and packaged foods have become available in the cities. Ready-to-eat food can also be found in the many government-sponsored but privately run sidewalk kiosks. Except in season, fresh fruit is hard to find due to problems with transportation and refrigeration.

Wealthy families are developing a taste for Western foods. As far back as 2004, the party newspaper *Nodong Sinmun* boasted that hamburgers were being provided to university students in Pyongyang, "filled with the ardent benevolence of the great general [Kim Jong-il]."[19] Pyongyangites can now consume hamburgers (under the Korean label of "minced beef and bread") at many Pyongyang restaurants. Pizza, which is also available at many restaurants, apparently arrived in 2001 when Kim Jong-il brought an Italian chef to North Korea to teach Koreans how to prepare Italian food to be served at one of the hotels frequented by foreigners.[20] Many other Western foods are also available to those who can afford them, including all kinds of snacks, sweets, and beverages, some domestically manufactured and some imported from China.

Members of what might be called the ordinary city-dwelling class live better than they did a couple of decades ago. To supplement their meager PDS rations, they shop in the markets with money they make at side jobs. While they can afford some rice, they rely more heavily on corn- and potato-based dishes. Their diet includes vegetables in season, homemade kimchi, and once or twice a week some fish or meat such as pork, chicken, lamb, or even beef. Over the years the regime has sponsored campaigns to raise rabbits and goats as additional sources of meat. Army posts, collective farms, and schools are often assigned quotas of rabbits, goats, and chickens to raise. Duck and ostrich farms have also been mentioned in the press, as have turtle farms and catfish breeding ponds. For those who cannot afford to purchase meat, the strange *injogogi* (artificial meat made from the processed dregs of soybean oil) is widely available.

Many rural North Koreans do not yet have enough to eat and live largely on corn-based foods supplemented with locally grown vegetables. Barley and potatoes are also eaten as substitutes for white rice. On special occasions, fish or small pieces of chicken or pork may be added to the meal, although many North Koreans only get the chance to eat meat and eggs a few times a year. Those who live in the hilly and mountainous regions do not have access to as much locally sourced produce as those who live in the plains, and they also find it more difficult to obtain seafood.

As for beverages, Koreans have always liked tea—mostly barley or corn tea rather than the teas that Westerners are familiar with. The upper class can purchase all kinds of bottled beverages. Popular alcoholic drinks include beer, rice wine, *soju* (a potent beverage distilled from vegetables such as rice, barley, or potatoes), and the lowly *makolli*, a homemade milky-white rice wine popular with farmers.

North Korean food shortages continue, and until the state relinquishes its control over food production and devotes substantial funds to upgrading the country's physical infrastructure, what the government calls the "food problem" will remain unsolved. Isolated as it is and under international economic sanctions, North Korean food production is at the mercy of the weather, which often deals a severe blow to farmers in the form of droughts and floods. It is not the government but rather the emerging private sector that has saved the North Korean people. According to South Korea's Ministry of Environment, the average South Korean throws out almost four hundred grams of food a day. In 2016 South Korea produced 14,388 tons of food waste every day, amounting to over five million tons a year—more than North Korea's typical annual food production.[21] Unfortunately, the political and practical problems of getting that uneaten food to North Korea have been insurmountable.

HOUSING: SUBSTANDARD AND IN SHORT SUPPLY

Housing in North Korea is characterized by a strange combination of public and private ownership. Almost all dwellings and land are owned by the government, and yet in the last twenty years it has become common to trade and build homes on the unauthorized market economy. Homes are also private in the sense that they are strictly off-limits to foreigners except for a few model apartments in Pyongyang that serve as propaganda properties. Those spacious Pyongyang apartments that one sees on the Internet are not the homes of ordinary North Koreans. The only way to discover what real housing looks like in North Korea is to ask defectors who used to live there.

Three-quarters of the capital city of Pyongyang was destroyed during the Korean War, giving the regime the opportunity to design a new city. During the Kim Il-sung era, Pyongyang followed the Soviet style of city planning and architecture: wide streets, drab concrete buildings, and plenty of monuments and parks. Kim Jong-il added color and some variety to building styles, and Kim Jong-un has continued in this fashion. At first glance Pyongyang appears to be a modern city with towering apartment buildings in pleasing pastel shades. Compared to most large cities, Pyongyang is serene and orderly. Visitors often find the city not so much quiet as disquieting, like an enormous Potemkin village.

Apartment buildings in Pyongyang were built in waves. Other North Korean cities did not share in this high-rise building boom because foreign visitors were rarely allowed to visit them, so it didn't matter what they looked like. An early wave of construction, while Kim Il-sung was still alive, was completed in preparation for the 1988 socialist World Festival of Youth and Students, which hosted thousands of foreign guests. For this event, the North Koreans built the May First Stadium, which remains the world's largest-capacity sports stadium, and the 105-story concrete Ryugyong Hotel, which never opened because of structural problems. High-rise buildings were later built along Kwangbok, Munsu, and Tongil Streets. More recently, Changjon Street, Mirae Scientists' Street, and Ryomyong New Town added

their towering buildings to the city's profile. Most buildings are still constructed of poured concrete, of which North Korea has a large domestic
supply. Construction is often done by soldiers drafted for the job, and much
of it appears to be shoddy by first-world standards.

The top cadres in Pyongyang live in spacious apartments or in detached
garden homes located in exclusive neighborhoods surrounded by guarded
walls. They may also enjoy the use of a modest dacha in the countryside.
Officials of somewhat lower rank live in high-rise apartments of three or four
rooms, while mid-level officials get an apartment with two rooms. On the
back streets of Pyongyang and other cities can be found single-story and
duplex homes. These simple dwellings are also found in the countryside,
along with single-story multiplex "accordion houses" and a few older tile-
roofed houses.

Either the state or a government-run collective owns virtually all dwellings in North Korea. Until the promulgation of the "July 1 [2002] Economic
Management Improvement Measures," housing was granted free by the
government; under the new measures the government began charging rent on
homes and fees for utilities. In the absence of electric meters, electricity

Older and newer apartment buildings in Pyongyang, 2011. *Wikimedia Commons,*
by Joseph Ferris III, CC-BY-2.0.

usage fees are based on what lights and electronic devices residents own. Inspectors come by and make a list of how many lights are installed and what appliances are in use. In a game of cat and mouse, residents try to hide some items, or they simply bribe the inspectors to make an incomplete list.

Housing, along with consumer goods, has always been in short supply. In 2018 a South Korean government organization estimated that North Korea could supply adequate housing for only 60 to 80 percent of its residents.[22] Extended families often live in two-room apartments, newlyweds typically wait several years before they can move into their own apartment, and as a temporary measure two families sometimes share one apartment.

Power outages and power surges are a common occurrence. Residents of smaller cities and towns live without electricity for days or even weeks at a time. In Pyongyang, power is supplied to apartment buildings primarily in the morning, evening, and around lunchtime. At night, people use kerosene lanterns and candles for lighting, even in new apartment buildings. Streets and public spaces are not lit, except for monuments to the Kim family, which are brightly illuminated. Without power, there is no running water or elevator service, hence the preference (and higher rents) for apartments at lower levels. The newest apartment buildings rise thirty to even eighty stories high. Carrying water up and garbage down from upper-level apartments is an unpleasant daily task.

Residents try to be creative to alleviate the electricity shortage. Some people purchase batteries that can store electricity while the power is on. Chinese-made solar panels are becoming popular. It is sometimes possible to bribe an electricity official to hook up a line to a nearby factory power source. And people who have the money may buy homes near lighted monuments or elite housing in order to benefit from better power supplies.

Only the homes and apartments of the elites boast central heating. Otherwise, people warm themselves with small stoves, huddle under blankets, and insulate their windows with vinyl sheeting. Houses generally have *ondol* heating, in which coal briquettes about the size and shape of a gallon can are placed in a stove under the sealed floor to provide heat. Many apartment buildings are constructed to provide space for *ondol* heating as well. Another alternative is to wire the floor under one room to warm it (this kind of heating would be too expensive for an entire apartment). In summer, homes are cooled with fans, never air-conditioners. Because water cannot be pumped into apartments when the power is out, residents keep a filled water tank in reserve. In the absence of hot water for bathing, people go to a neighborhood public bath or use a workplace bathhouse.

The regime keeps watch over residents in the city and countryside by recruiting a representative from each *inminban* (neighborhood or people's group consisting of twenty to forty households), usually a housewife or retired worker. The *inminban* leader is responsible for managing neighborhood security, cleaning, maintenance, recycling, and road repair. The group leader also checks to see that households participate in required communal activities, including composting and farming assistance. In apartment buildings, residents take turns acting as security guards, recording the comings and goings of visitors. Walls are often constructed around a house or group of houses to provide a measure of security. Burglary is a common crime, and families try to keep at least one member home at all times.

Apartments in newly constructed buildings generally come unfinished and unfurnished. Residents put wallpaper on the walls and live on the smooth, clean floor in the traditional Asian style. A refrigerator may be purchased, but it is impractical for storing food because of the intermittent supply of electricity. A small washing machine might be purchased as well. Every home must put up pictures of Kim Il-sung (on the left) and Kim Jong-il (on the right), displayed on a prominent wall.

According to one South Korean reporter, a North Korean "dream home" might look like this: It would be built in an area (almost certainly in Pyongyang) that has a reasonably good flow of electricity. It would have multiple rooms to house multiple family members. It would be small enough to be easily heated. If it is an apartment, it would be situated on one of the lower floors and have a place to store the family bicycles. It would have a veranda for storage, garden use, and perhaps even to raise animals such as rabbits, chickens, or a pig for food. If it is a house, it would have a small yard for a vegetable garden. The building would have modern metal window frames to keep out the cold. It would be close to transportation; if it is near a train or bus station, rooms could be (illegally) rented out to travelers or prostitutes. If it is located close to a public market, it could serve as an illegal salesroom, or at least a convenient storeroom. A house in good repair would be preferable to an apartment, but far too expensive for most people living in the city. [23]

Changes in the economy and relaxed government controls have transformed the housing market. Legally, all property is still owned by the state or by state-related organizations. People reside in their homes by virtue of a state-issued residence permit. As long as the state doesn't object, they may live in their homes until they die, and the homes can then be passed on to their heirs. Of course the government can step in at any time to evict the tenants or tear down their homes for new developments. The quasi-privatization of real estate seems to have begun during the 1990s famine, when starving people, with no job and nothing left to sell, "sold" their residence permits (but not the actual property) and moved in with others—or, in extreme destitution, lived out on the streets. As this procedure became more common and as the government failed to halt it, people discovered that they could trade homes by bribing the local housing authorities to change the names on residency permits. Thus, a thriving real estate market developed, with real estate brokers, buyers and sellers, and government officials all benefiting. The obvious difference between the North Korean real estate market and a capitalist market is that what is bought and sold is permission to reside in a home, not title to the home itself.

The government is well aware of the enduring housing shortage but simply doesn't have the money to put up enough buildings while supporting a million people in the army and developing weapons of mass destruction. So private initiative has started to fill the gap. What typically happens is that a state organization authorizes a consortium of wealthy individuals, which may include Chinese investors, to acquire land for a building. This may be done by paying residents in existing dwellings to move out and then developing the now vacant land. In the countryside, managers of an agricultural collective may be bribed to declare some of their land unsuitable for cultivation and then turn the land over to developers. As long as the right people are bribed and as long as the entire process is pursued under the guise of a government organization, no one seems to object. A building gets built, and the government doesn't have to pay for it. As soon as construction begins on a building, apartments are sold to provide further construction funding. Investors consequently get their money back quickly, with significant interest. Local housing officials may receive "ownership" of some of the new apartments. Because this entire construction process is technically illegal, it is impossible to know how many of the new high-rise apartment buildings in Pyongyang were constructed with private funds and are essentially controlled by private investors.

The North Korean real estate market has experienced booms and busts, but mostly booms. Residence permits for apartments in Pyongyang's new high-rise buildings are said to sell for as much as $100,000, with deluxe apartments going for two to three times as much. All payments of this magnitude are made in US dollars. The people who have this kind of money, the so-called *donju*, have obviously earned it in the illegal market economy, because people working only at their state-assigned jobs make just a few hundred dollars a year.

Barring a change in the Kim regime's attitude toward the quasi-private real estate market, the main thing investors must be concerned with, given the continuing severe housing shortage, is that people will not want to live in certain kinds of dwellings. This is what seems to be happening in regard to the upper floors of high-rise apartment buildings as people discover that it is impractical to live there without a reliable power supply. And after the spectacular 2014 collapse of a brand new twenty-three-story Pyongyang apartment building, which killed several hundred people, prospective buyers have begun to examine buildings carefully for signs of structural defects.

Like the rest of the economy, the housing market has undergone dramatic, if unofficial, changes. One's dwelling place need no longer be assigned by the government. If it is deemed unsuitable, it can be traded. A South Korean survey of North Korean defectors found that by 2017 only 18 percent of them had lived in a home assigned to them by the government, 14 percent had inherited their home, 59 percent had purchased their home, 6 percent had actually built their home, and 2 percent lived with friends or relatives.[24] Private real estate transactions have become firmly established in the culture despite being technically illegal, although they do require the payment of bribes, as does almost everything else in North Korea. In 2020, reports surfaced that the government was cracking down (again) on illegal real estate transactions, classifying them as "anti-socialist practices that deserve strong legal punishment."[25] It is likely, however, that the privatization of real estate has gone too far for the government to stop it.

HEALTH AND HEALTH CARE: VICTIMS OF THE BAD ECONOMY

North Korea is not a healthy place to live, physically or psychologically. Decades of military-first priorities have shortchanged the social welfare system. As North Korea is a relatively closed society under the control of a highly secretive government, it has been difficult to get any information about people's health and health care. This situation started to change in the late 1990s when North Koreans began to defect, and now that over thirty thousand defectors, including former doctors, live in South Korea, descriptions of the North's health-care situation are more complete. The underlying causes of poor health are easy to find, even if they can't be statistically quantified. Malnutrition is arguably the most basic cause. The constitutions of those who grew up in the 1990s were weakened, and today, two decades later, nutritious food is still in short supply for many North Koreans, especially in the countryside and in the northeast provinces, where most defectors lived.

And then there is the water quality problem. Countrywide electricity shortages hamper the operation of water filtration plants and pumping stations, affecting even people living in the larger cities. Without electricity, pumps cannot provide water to homes and apartment buildings. A UN Children's Fund (UNICEF) survey in 2012 found that only about 3 percent of North Koreans had access to piped water.[26] Many North Koreans must travel to the nearest river to obtain water for cooking and drinking. Without a steady supply of electricity, sewage plants operate intermittently, dumping raw sewage into the same waterways that people use for bathing and drinking. A 2004 survey jointly sponsored by UNICEF and the WFP estimated that only about half of households had flush toilets.[27] Human waste is often used as fertilizer, contaminating water runoff as well as the crops grown in the fields. Coal-burning power plants pollute the air, and dust from China blows east onto the Korean Peninsula.

Workplace accidents are common. Construction work that would be performed with machinery in developed economies is done by hand. Mines are death traps. Speed battles force workers to work too fast. In the provinces, doctors sometimes find it necessary to amputate the limbs of injured workers for lack of proper instruments and medicines for surgical treatment.[28] Smoking continues to be popular, especially among men, despite the fact that the government has been sponsoring antismoking campaigns for years. Fortunately, it appears that smoking rates are gradually declining. A recent World Health Organization report estimates that 44 percent of North Korean men smoke, down from 52 percent in 2012.[29] Most women disapprove of smoking, nor is it popular among young adults. Male smokers can choose from several dozen brands of cigarettes sold in the country, and they prefer brands with stronger tobacco. Supreme Leader Kim Jong-un is the country's most prominent smoker.

Heart disease is believed to be the country's leading cause of death.[30] Other serious illnesses include cancers, AIDS (although the government officially denies this), hepatitis B, syphilis, and a wide range of infections, including parasitic infections. Tuberculosis is estimated to kill sixteen thousand North Koreans every year.[31] Most of these diseases could be controlled or cured with proper medical interventions. Since the 1990s, starvation has not been a primary cause of death, although few North Koreans are overweight, with the exception of Kim Jong-un.

At this writing, the impact of the COVID-19 pandemic in North Korea is difficult to gauge, thanks to the Kim regime's traditional secrecy. It does not appear that the government has admitted to even one case, although some islands of infection almost certainly exist, even in the face of the government's relatively good control over the movement of people and the shutdown of the border in January 2020. In August, an official hint that the pandemic might not be completely under control was provided by a KCNA report on a recent meeting of the Politburo, presided over by Kim Jong-un: "The meeting seriously assessed some defects in the state emergency anti-epidemic work for checking the inroads of the malignant virus, and studied measures to overcome the defects urgently."[32]

Little is known about the mental health of North Koreans, but given the life stresses they face, mental illness must be a problem. A large proportion of defectors who arrive in South Korea suffer from a variety of mental illnesses, some of which they may have had in North Korea and some resulting from their difficult defection journey, separation from the families they left behind, and the problems of adapting to a new social environment.

According to foreign estimates, infant mortality in North Korea is low by global standards: 20 per 1,000 live births, compared to 3.0 in South Korea and 5.3 in the United States.[33] Maternal mortality is 89 per 100,000 live births, compared to 11 in South Korea and 19 in the United States.[34] Contraception is widely practiced, abortions are privately available, and the fertility rate is below 2.0. Since the famine days of the 1990s, more women have been reluctant to marry and bear children. Far too many North Koreans must struggle with poor heath throughout their lives. The cumulative effect of this poor health translates into an estimated life expectancy for women of seventy-six years, and for men sixty-eight years (in 2016). The comparable rates in South Korea are eighty-six years for women and eighty years for men.[35]

North Korea's health-care system has crumbled in the face of economic pressures. Yet, despite overwhelming evidence to the contrary, every year the North Korean government insists that it has the best health-care system in the world, with a 2014 KCNA article boasting that "hospitals and other public health establishments can be seen everywhere to let the people enjoy free medical service."[36] Closer to the truth is a travel warning from the government of the United Kingdom:

> Health facilities in North Korea are poor. Standards of clinical hygiene in hospitals are low. Anesthetics are sometimes unavailable. Evacuation is likely to be necessary for serious illness or injury. Avoid surgery if at all possible. Facilities for dental treatment are also poor. Make sure you take sufficient supplies of any medication that you may need. Most foreign-manufactured medicines aren't available. Even when they are, they're sometimes out of date and inappropriately prescribed. Local medical supplies, including oriental medicines exist, but can also be limited.[37]

Since the founding of North Korea, its health-care policy has been based on three principles: universal free medical care, preventive medicine, and a "section doctor" or "doctor-in-charge" system whereby a primary-care physician is assigned to a geographical area or to a workplace or housing compound comprising the equivalent of 50 to 150 households. Patients are first seen by the doctor at a local clinic. More serious cases are supposed to be referred to a local hospital, then up to a county hospital, then to a hospital in the provincial capital, and finally to a hospital in Pyongyang. None of these medical facilities has adequate medicine or equipment to treat serious cases, except for a few of the showcase Pyongyang hospitals.

The most famous of the elite hospitals is the Pyongyang Maternity Hospital, a favorite spot for North Korean officials to take foreign visitors to demonstrate the alleged superiority of their health-care system. Gaining admission to the better-equipped hospitals like the Pyongyang Maternity Hospital, the Pyongyang Medical University Hospital, the Red Cross Hospital, the Kim Manyu Hospital, or the elite Bonghwa Clinic is only a dream for most people. Even if those hospitals admitted ordinary people, which they rarely do, getting timely transportation to them would be extremely difficult. Travel from one city to another often takes days and requires the payment of bribes to get on trains, buses, or open-bed trucks. Most patients are treated locally with whatever medicines are available. Patients in need of complicated operations or modern medicines such as antibiotics must pull through by themselves.

Since the 1990s the government has been unable to adequately fund its medical facilities, which are supposed to provide free medical care to the people. In the health-care field, as everywhere else in North Korea, private enterprise has taken over what the government can no longer provide. Patients who have sufficient money can bribe their way into better hospitals and appointments with top doctors. For virtually everyone, at any medical facility, it is necessary to pay for services. Doctors generally expect payment in money or goods or reciprocal favors. Medicines must be purchased from private vendors. Even meals must be brought into the hospital. North Korea's doctors perform as well as they can under the circumstances. As employees of the state, they receive only subsistence wages, although they benefit from gifts of food and homemade consumer goods donated to them by grateful patients. They have learned to practice medicine with what is available to them. What must be most difficult for medical professionals is the frustration of watching patients suffer and die from diseases that could easily be cured if the proper medicines and equipment were available.

North Korea has no shortage of doctors. It has been estimated that the country has about 150,000 doctors—about the same number as South Korea, which has twice the population.[38] The regime even sends thousands of doctors and nurses to other countries, where they earn foreign currency to remit back home to their families and to the regime.[39]

The country relies on imports for its modern medical devices and for much of its prescription and nonprescription drugs. The intermittent nature of electricity means that medical equipment is frequently inoperable and medicines that require refrigeration can go bad. China is the source of most imported medicines, but South Korean, Japanese, and American medicines command higher prices. With the closure of the border in 2020 to combat the COVID-19 pandemic, fewer medicines became available from China. According to a South Korean report, the North Korean Ministry of Public Health issued an order for local hospitals to manufacture their own medicines, although such a task would seemingly be impossible.

Physicians write prescriptions and expect their patients to find the medicine in the local markets. Purchasing one's own medicine creates special problems. Patients cannot be assured of the quality of their medicines, and they may not follow recommended procedures when they self-medicate.[40] Because modern (or at least modern Western) medicine is in short supply, doctors frequently resort to traditional Asian herbal remedies, which in North Korea is called *Koryo* (Korean) medicine. The doctors may go into the countryside to search for the herbs and then mix the medicine themselves.

Numerous foreign organizations have provided funds and medicine to help North Korea. Sometimes the government welcomes or at least accepts this foreign assistance, and sometimes it is rejected, especially if the medical aid comes from South Korea. The North Korean government has been so unhelpful to visiting health-care workers that some of the foreign health-care organizations, including Doctors without Borders, Oxfam, and CARE, have temporarily withdrawn from the country.[41] Recently, the Global Fund to Fight AIDS, Tuberculosis and Malaria, which has supported TB treatment for almost two hundred thousand North Korean patients, ended its North Korean intervention due to "unique operating conditions" in the country.[42]

In contrast to this dismal state of health care, an entire mini-industry is devoted to the health of the Kim family, who, along with top cadres, have access to the Bonghwa Clinic, which provides medical care comparable to that found in hospitals in developed countries. A handful of top cadres have also been sent abroad to receive medical treatment in Beijing, Moscow, and Paris, and top foreign medical specialists are sometimes flown into Pyongyang to advise North Korean doctors on special procedures to treat the leader.

It is hard to be optimistic about the future of North Korea's health-care system. Substantial assistance from the international community seems unlikely as long as the Kim regime continues to develop weapons of mass destruction. The good news is that the unofficial privatized health-care system is replacing the struggling socialist system. The bad news is that, like the privatization of the rest of the economy, "private" health care will benefit only the minority who have connections, assets, and skills that enable them to profitably participate in the new economy. For most North Koreans, privatization will mean struggling to find self-help remedies for their health problems.

RELIGION: TOTALLY BANNED

Every year since 2001 the United States has designated North Korea as a "country of particular concern" under the 1998 International Religious Freedom Act, which requires the government to release an annual report on such countries. As of December 2019, the listed countries were Myanmar, China, Eritrea, Iran, Pakistan, Saudi Arabia, Tajikistan, Turkmenistan, and of course North Korea. The report concluded that there was "an almost complete denial by the [North Korean] government of the rights to freedom of thought, conscience, and religion, and in many instances, violations of human rights committed by the government constituted crimes against humanity."[43]

And just as regularly, the North Korean government vigorously objects to such criticism. For example, in January 2018, responding to the previous year's designation, the North Korean foreign ministry complained that "the 'religious freedom' much chanted like [a] monk's prayers by the U.S. is nothing more than a means to seek internal disintegration and overthrow the systems in countries that are not in its favor. . . . To us who have accomplished the great historic cause of perfecting the national nuclear forces with confidence in final victory in the showdown with imperialism and the U.S., the stereotyped talk of 'religious freedom' by the U.S. is nothing more than a scream of a loser."[44]

Before the communists came to power, Confucianism was the most popular belief system in Korea, although unlike most Western religions, Confucianism is an elaboration of principles about the conduct of human affairs rather than the worship of a supreme being. Buddhism was introduced into Korea in the fourth century and Christianity in the nineteenth century, around the same time that Chondoism (Chondokyo, or "religion of the heavenly way") emerged as an indigenous variant of Confucianism. Shamanism and belief in fortune-tellers were and still are popular.[45] The North Korean penal code provides for a maximum sentence of three years in prison for such practices as fortune-telling, but defectors say that even government officials have their fortunes told, and when the law is enforced the usual prison sentence is just a few months. However, as is the case for many crimes in North Korea, when the regime decides to launch a campaign, anyone caught can pay a high price as a lesson to others. In early 2019 reports coming out of North Korea claimed that one person convicted of fortune-telling had been executed in public late the previous year, and another had received a life sentence in prison.[46]

When Korea was liberated from the Japanese, a survey conducted in the northern half of the country counted 1.5 million practicing Chondoists, 370,000 Buddhists, 200,000 Protestants, and 57,000 Roman Catholics.[47] Except for some of the Chondoists, most of these religious believers fled to the South between liberation and the beginning of the Korean War. Only 60 of 400 Buddhist temples stayed open (mostly as cultural relics), and the 1,500 Christian churches have disappeared. Although the first North Korean constitution, drafted in 1948, declared that "citizens have the freedom to engage in religious activities," Kim Il-sung had other ideas. In a 1962 speech, he explained:

[We] cannot carry such religiously active people along [on] our march toward a communist society. Therefore, we have tried and executed all religious leaders higher than a deacon in the Protestant and Catholic churches. Among other religiously active people, those deemed malignant were all put to trial. Among ordinary religious believers, those who recanted were given jobs while those who did not were held in prison camps. [48]

Indeed, in the late 1960s, with the completion of a nationwide political classification of the people, Protestants, Buddhists, Catholics, and Confucians were assigned to their own subgroups in the "hostile" class. The South Korean government estimates that virtually all North Koreans who openly practiced religion were killed or imprisoned between the end of the Korean War and 1970, effectively wiping out the public practice of religion. [49]

The 1972 DPRK constitution guaranteed freedom of religion, along with the freedom to engage in "antireligious propaganda activities." Article 68 of the 2016 edition of the constitution takes a seemingly more favorable position on religion, stipulating that "citizens shall have freedom of religion. This right shall be guaranteed by permitting the construction of religious buildings and the holding of religious ceremonies." But then it adds, "Religion shall not be used in bringing in outside forces or in harming the state and social order," a provision that effectively bans the practice of religion.

One indication of the Kim regime's view of religion is the arrest and conviction of foreign visitors who try to spread the Christian faith. The most severe punishment in recent years was meted out to an American who was convicted in 2013 by the North Korean Supreme Court of bringing in "anti-DPRK literature" and attempting "state subversion." Although he could have been sentenced to death, the sentence was reduced to fifteen years' hard labor in consideration of his alleged confession. [50] Fortunately, he and another American were released the following year after the US director of national intelligence traveled to Pyongyang with a personal letter to Kim Jong-un from President Barack Obama.

The only religion that is allowed in North Korea is the worship of the Kim family, which during Kim Il-sung's reign very closely resembled a formal religion. Apart from any philosophical objection to religion, the regime has very practical reasons to ban its practice. No civic organizations have ever been tolerated in North Korea, because they would compete with the Workers' Party of Korea. The regime must be well aware of the important role that churches played in the downfall of communism in Eastern Europe. Consequently, churches in North Korea must not only be controlled by the party; they must actually be party organizations.

In 1972, at a time when the two Koreas enjoyed a very brief period of rapprochement, the Kim regime revived several defunct religious organizations so they could participate in the united-front campaign against South Korea, whose religious organizations opposed the authoritarian government then ruling in the South. The Korean Buddhist League appeared in 1972, the Korean Christian Federation in 1974, and the Central Guidance Committee for Korean Chondoists also in 1974. The Korean Catholics Association was established as a separate organization in 1988. The WPK Central Committee's United Front Department runs all these organizations. Representatives of North Korean religious groups travel to international meetings where they promote their government's political positions, and foreign religionists are invited to North Korea as official visitors. The Reverend Billy Graham twice visited North Korea, and his son has made a separate visit as well. An invitation has been extended to the pope, who has so far declined. In short, religion in North Korea is a government public relations project. The sponsorship of religious organizations and toleration of churches also serve to parry international criticism of the Kim regime's antireligious policies.

In the late 1980s and early 1990s, a Catholic church (not associated with the Roman Catholic Church) and three Protestant churches were constructed in Pyongyang, although it does not appear that they regularly function as churches. Their congregations seem to consist of a few security agents and a small number of religious believers who have somehow been permitted to practice their faith, at least on Sundays. Interestingly, one of the Protestant churches, the Chilgol Church, is said to be built on the same spot as the church that the young Kim Il-sung and his parents attended in the days when Pyongyang was a center of Western religion in Korea. On his 2003 trip to Russia, Kim Jong-il approved the idea of building a Greek Orthodox church in Pyongyang, which opened in August 2006.

In addition to serving a public relations role, state-controlled religion has brought in hard currency. Most of the Pyongyang churches seem to have been built with foreign donations, and foreign (mostly South Korean) religious organizations have been generous humanitarian donors to North Korea. For example, between 1995 and 2006, the South Korean Catholic community sent $38 million in aid—certainly enough money to warrant the Kim regime's toleration of one small Catholic church in Pyongyang.[51]

Because the open practice of religion is a sure ticket to prison, it is difficult to tell how many North Koreans practice religion secretly. Estimates range from ten to fifty thousand, with perhaps an additional thirty thousand already imprisoned.[52] An unknown number of "house churches"—perhaps as many as several hundred throughout the country—hold services, sometimes with the knowledge of local officials. Worshippers meet in groups of half a dozen or fewer, usually in someone's home. In a 2008 survey of 755 North Korean defectors, only ten said they had participated (secretly) in church services while in the North, forty-three said they had known of others who participated in church services, and thirty-three said they had seen a Bible.[53] People caught worshipping or having in their possession religious literature can receive prison sentences of ten years or more for "antisocialist activities." Korean citizens captured in China and returned to North Korea are vigorously interrogated, and if they confess to having been in contact with South Korean or other foreign religious organizations, they are immediately sent to prison.

After undergoing more than half a century of religious repression, most North Koreans seem no more interested in religion than in politics, and it is difficult to know what place religion would play in their lives if the authorities permitted it. Religions, especially of the more emotional kind, sometimes proliferate when times are difficult. On the other hand, mainstream religions are on the decline in most parts of the world, including South Korea, with the younger generations especially likely to adopt secular views of the world.

SPORTS AND AMUSEMENTS: SIMPLE PLEASURES FOR THE PEOPLE

The lives of the North Korean people may be dogged by hunger and filled with state-mandated work, yet the people do find time to enjoy themselves. Like almost everything else in North Korea, amusements are sponsored or at least must be sanctioned by the government. The regime has decided what sports to promote and what amusements to allow based on at least three considerations. First, they should involve group activity in practice and performance so the regime can keep track of people. Second, the pursuits should not require the expenditure of great amounts of money, which the country does not have. And third, amusements should be engaged in outdoors whenever possible, to avoid the costs of constructing expensive indoor facilities.

The regime's goals for amusements are likewise three in number. First, to teach people to be loyal supporters of the regime and help them become healthy "guns and bombs to protect the leader." In this sense, sports can be considered a form of socialist education and military training. Second, to keep people busy in their spare time: a contemplative citizen is, for the regime, a dangerous citizen. And third, to promote North Korea to the outside world as a nation of happy people who are competitive in international sports.

Kim Il-sung was not known to be a sportsman. Kim Jong-il was keen on a number of sports, especially shooting and horseback riding, and at his various private estates he had race courses, shooting ranges, and gymnasiums. Kim Jong-un is a basketball fan, although after reaching adulthood and gaining considerable weight, he presumably no longer plays the game. He has, however, been pictured riding a large white horse on the slopes of the "sacred" Mount Paektu.

The sports that ordinary North Koreans play are somewhat limited by the availability of facilities. Few public gymnasiums exist, so most sports are played outdoors. The most popular field sport is soccer. In winter, ice-skating on a few rinks and on rivers and ponds is popular. Table tennis is played at parks and indoors. Bicycling is also popular as a method of transportation in both country and city. As part of the daily warm-up for students and workers, morning calisthenics under the direction of a leader are mandatory. North Korea is justly famous for its mass gymnastic displays, especially the world-famous displays staged at the Arirang Festival in Pyongyang. These programs can hardly be classified as a sport or amusement because children are required to perform them, and the training and performance are truly arduous. Held in August (in most years) as a way of attracting foreign tourists, the festival features thirty thousand school students creating gigantic card displays as a background to tens of thousands of perfectly choreographed youth dancing in the Rungrado May First Stadium.

For its national sports teams, the government recruits promising athletes at an early age. North Korea has competed in most of the Summer Olympic Games since 1964 and about half of the Winter Games, winning a respectable number of medals in weightlifting, wrestling, boxing, and gymnastics. Athletes have also competed in judo, shooting, volleyball, and table tennis, and in the winter, speed skating. Since 1974, North Korean athletes have competed in the Asian Games in archery, basketball, canoeing, swimming, and diving, along with its Olympic sports. North Korea's appearance in

Arirang mass games, 2007. The card section is spelling out "Forever Prosperity of Kim Il-sung's Korea." *Wikimedia Commons, by stephan, CC-BY-SA-2.0.*

World Cup soccer has been limited: it competed in 1966 and 2010 but did not qualify or enter in other years. North Korea hosts its own international sporting event in the form of the Pyongyang Marathon held every April since 1981, except in 2020. It advertises through an attractive website, and in recent years it has been open to foreign runners and draws several hundred foreigners a year, in addition to about a thousand North Koreans.

Kim Jong-un has been especially keen to attract foreigners to his hermit kingdom, not only to obtain hard currency but also to give North Korea the appearance of a normal country. The Pyongyang Golf Club, situated seventeen miles from the city, opened in 1987, complete with a North Korean sports myth. The course pro boasted to a foreigner that Kim Jong-il played the par seventy-two course that year in thirty-four strokes, getting a birdie on every hole and making five holes-in-one (another story says it was eleven holes-in-one). Pyongyang has at least two bowling alleys, the more famous being the Golden Lane Bowling Alley.

Kim Jong-un has been particularly interested in North Korea's potential as a skiing destination. In 2013 the Masikryong Ski Resort opened in the mountains near the eastern coastal city of Wonsan. North Korea claimed it cost over $35 million to build, although cost is hard to estimate because all of the construction was done by the military (in only ten months, it was claimed). In 2018 another ski facility debuted near the border city of Kang-gye, two hundred miles north of Pyongyang, and that one was supposed to have been built in only a month. And in 2019 North Korea's third set of slopes was opened as part of a large hot springs spa at Yongdok, about halfway between Pyongyang and Wonsan. Needless to say, only visiting foreigners or the wealthiest 1 percent of the North Korean people can afford to ski or play golf.

For the entertainment of ordinary citizens, the regime has built a few amusement parks in the bigger cities, the most famous one being in Pyong-yang. Each county is supposed to have a "children's palace" with indoor and outdoor recreational facilities, but they don't look like Pyongyang's show-place children's palace at Mangyongdae. Movies used to be a popular form of entertainment before the arrival of personal video players and smart phones. Virtually the only movies shown were quasi-propaganda films (especially promoted by Kim Jong-il, who fancied himself a movie expert). Most North Koreans have access to television, which only carries uninteresting government channels. In any case, intermittent electricity supply reduces the value of television. Likewise, only government stations are available on the radio. What is new is that, beginning in the early years of the century, various media smuggled in from outside the country became accessible: first video-tapes, then DVDs and CDs, then flash drives, and now SD cards. North Koreans, especially young ones, now have clandestine access to South Kore-an video games, music, movies, and TV shows.

More traditional entertainments can be engaged in at little or no cost. *Eumjugamu* (Korean for three Chinese characters meaning "drinking, music, dancing") remains a popular entertainment. It is easy to find someone who can play a guitar accompaniment, and wealthier North Koreans have their own *noraebang* or karaoke rooms. At a completely different level, Kim Jong-il was famous for his drinking parties, complete with dancing girls, whereas Kim Jong-un has been more discreet in his amusements. For ordinary Koreans, dance parties in public halls or outdoor venues are popular and provide a great place for young people to meet. Card playing and gambling are traditional pursuits. On pleasant days, a walk in the park with friends or fishing in a river or lake are quiet diversions. Occasionally, companies will host vacation retreats.

Children play the kinds of games children everywhere play: hide-and-seek, fighting with wooden swords for the boys, a game called *ttakji* that resembles marbles but is played with folded pieces of paper thrown at each other, and card games. For a bit of local traveling, school trips are provided for children. All in all, entertainment options for North Koreans are poor compared to what South Koreans can enjoy, but since the North Koreans have never had anything better, they are satisfied with what they have.

LIFE EVENTS: THE SAME THE WORLD OVER

Tracing the lives of North Koreans from birth to death is an undertaking far beyond the limitations of even an entire book. Here, the focus is on a few milestones in a North Korean's life, and even this goal is difficult to achieve because, despite the regimentation imposed by the Kim regime, people are still people, and each life has its unique aspects. This is especially so since the regime's adoption of a de facto laissez-faire economic policy in the 1990s. Today, in addition to the influences of the regime on people's lives,

A quiet day fishing, 2011. The political poster in the background reads, "We go 10,000 *li* [680 miles] following the general [Kim Jong-il]." *Wikimedia Commons, by Mark Fahey, CC-BY-2.0.*

there is now growing influence from foreign cultures. The widening gap between the lives of the newly wealthy and the rest of the country also complicates the task of description. Although North Koreans remain more regimented than most peoples, they are beginning to adopt an individualistic lifestyle closer to what is found in the West. [54]

To begin at the very beginning, North Korean women who become pregnant can visit local clinics or a local hospital for prenatal checkups, and then gain admission to a local hospital for childbirth. Abortions are illegal but possible, and contraception is widely practiced. When a baby is born, it is registered with the local authorities and with the police. Virtually all children receive basic vaccinations, but many do not get a good start on a healthy life because of poor nutrition. Since most parents work long hours, children are usually sent to day nurseries as early as the age of one. Children of all ages spend relatively little time with their parents: an hour or two at breakfast time, a couple of hours late in the evening, a few more hours on Saturday, and all day on Sunday. The state assumes responsibility for the remainder of their lives. At age five children enter kindergarten, then move on to elementary school, middle school, and high school.

Sometime between the ages of nine and eleven, children join the first level of what might be called the Kim national family. If they are in good standing with their teachers and local party officials, they are admitted to the Korean Children's Union (*Sonyondan*), often referred to by foreigners as the Young Pioneers, taking the name from the old Soviet youth organization. Formal admission to the Young Pioneers occurs on a national holiday such as Kim Il-sung's birthday, National Foundation Day, or the Korean People's Army Foundation Day. At home, a little celebration will be held, comparable to a birthday party, perhaps with rice cakes and boiled eggs. Admission to the Young Pioneers brings further responsibilities in the way of social and labor participation, adding to the school responsibilities the children already have. As a sign of membership, they can now proudly wear a distinctive revolutionary red neckerchief, which becomes part of their school uniform.

At around the age of fifteen, students become eligible for membership in the next level of political participation, the Kimilsungist-Kimjongilist Youth League (the name has changed several times over the years). Membership means more adult responsibilities, including youthful military training, and is the final step before membership in the Workers' Party of Korea, for which they will become candidates in their late twenties after honorably completing military service. Party membership is not as important as it was a few decades ago, but anyone who aspires to a position in the bureaucracy must join.

Children legally become adults at the age of seventeen, which means they are entitled to vote—not merely a privilege but a requirement. On Election Day, which is a national holiday, Koreans go to their polling place and insert a ballot imprinted with the names of the party's chosen candidates into the ballot box, under the watchful eyes of party officials. Elections in North Korea always achieve participation rates of above 99 percent, with 100 percent of the ballots cast for the party's candidate. Also at the age of seventeen, students are drafted into the military. Since 2015, males have been required to serve for ten years, while females serve until the age of twenty-three. Students who have been accepted into a college or university, those who do not meet the minimum mental or physical standards (which are notoriously low), and those who can gain an exemption through bribery or personal connections do not have to serve, or may serve a shorter period of time.

In Kim's North Korea, romance does not have a place in youth culture. Young people are supposed to be totally focused on their work. Marriage or romantic connections are not permitted in college or for enlisted soldiers. Public displays of affection such as walking hand in hand are frowned upon. North Korea has no overt sex culture of the sort that young people in most societies are familiar with, including music, films, videos, novels, advertisements, and pornography. In reality, it is difficult to deny the impact of hormones, and young people find clandestine ways to enjoy romance, if not sex. Secret dating takes the form of after-dark meetings in parks, or stolen moments in workplace corners or at home when parents are away. Spending time together among crowds at the markets and at movie theaters, amusement parks, and social events is another way that romantic couples can be together without drawing attention to themselves.

As soon as a man, now in his late twenties, is discharged from the army, he is on the lookout for a wife. Women may be available for marriage several years earlier, but an increasing number are taking their time before committing to marriage, and some even forego the institution entirely. It is unusual but not impossible to form a common-law marriage and live together without reporting to the authorities. Most couples look for prospective marriage partners at parties and dances or in the workplace or their neighborhood, or they go on blind dates arranged by friends or parents. In recent years matchmaking programs have even begun to be available on smart phones and comput-

Political poster in Pyongyang for an upcoming election of delegates to the Supreme People's Assembly, encouraging everybody to cast a yes vote. *Wikimedia Commons, by jensowagner, CC-BY-2.0.*

ers. For the most part, potential mates will be found locally, because long-distance romances are impractical.

What men and women look for in a potential mate has changed over the years. Until the 1990s, party membership and government employment were desirable qualifications. Good *songbun* (political status) was always important. Today, economic potential and mutual feelings of attraction play greater roles. Pyongyang residency remains a desirable qualification. Anyone who has access to foreign currency (the only currency that's worth anything) is a desirable mate: diplomats, trading company employees, taxi and truck drivers, blue-water sailors, and even fishermen. For women, the important thing is to avoid marrying a man who is trapped in a job that pays him only a government salary. Men are on the lookout for similar qualifications in a potential wife. A woman should have experience in business, perhaps because her mother works in the market. Whereas divorced women and widows were previously shunned as marriage partners, now older women of the emerging *donju* (moneymaking) class can be considered a desirable catch. Of course, the reality is that most marriages occur between two ordinary people with no special skills who happen to live close to each other.

How elaborate a North Korean wedding is depends largely on the economic class of the marriage partners. The vast majority of North Koreans keep it a simple family affair. Ideally, the wedding is preceded by an engagement ceremony at which the bridegroom's family gives the future bride wedding clothes and cosmetics and the bride's family provides household goods. More valuable gifts, such as mobile phones or television sets, are exchanged by families of some wealth. Most weddings are held in the autumn, after the harvest has been gathered, or in the spring, after the planting is done. The wedding is most likely to be held on a Sunday, the only free day most people have. If many guests have been invited, the ceremony and reception may be held in a community or company hall. If only a few family members and friends are coming, the wedding party will first visit the family home of the bride and then continue the wedding celebration at the home of the groom's parents.

On the wedding day, the bride wears the traditional Korean dress (called a *hanbok* in South Korea, *Choson-ot* in North Korea), and the groom wears a Western-style suit. Food and drink, including alcohol, are served, and it is traditional for a hen and rooster to be presented in the room, either alive or cooked or in the form of a replica. The wedding is presided over by a good friend or a workplace supervisor. The ruling Kim is always thanked for making the wedding possible, and the newly married couple will soon make a visit to the closest Kim family shrine to present flowers of thanks and respect. At the wedding, guests offer the new couple presents of a small amount of cash or useful gifts such as food. For couples who want to put on a bigger show than they can afford, it is now possible in cities to rent clothes, table settings, and even food to put on display. Few couples have the time to go on any kind of honeymoon; besides, personal travel is not a part of North Korean culture.

As soon as possible, the new couple will move into their own home. In the meantime, which may extend for months or even years given the chronic housing shortage, they are likely to live with the groom's family. And thus they start their married life. Despite the vaunted gender equality of communism (Mao famously said that women hold up half the sky), the family roles of North Korean women and men are still influenced by Confucian tradition, even though Confucianism has long since disappeared. The man is the formal head of the household, while the woman takes care of the house and the children. Both husband and wife are likely to be employed, the man working at a state-assigned job and the woman either at a similar job or in the capitalist market. Women are generally assigned to lower-paying jobs than men, and those who are employed in the government bureaucracy rarely attain positions of much responsibility. Women who want to run a large private business must gain the protection or sponsorship of male party members and government officials.

Since the 1990s famine and the emergence of a capitalist market economy, the roles of husbands and wives have begun to change. Because men generally find it more difficult than women to leave their state-assigned jobs, which pay next to nothing, it is the women who are free to go into the marketplace and make money. To the extent that money means power in the home, the new role for women as breadwinners has destabilized the North Korean family. Many men are unhappy and even angry that they have to depend on their wives for most of the household income, and frustration is presumably an important cause of domestic violence, drinking, and drug abuse. Men are also much more likely to be unfaithful to their spouses than women are.

The new role of women is also the reason that some women are choosing not to marry at all. They can now support themselves without a husband, and in fact have more money to spend on themselves without the burden of supporting a husband and children. Women's freedom from state-assigned work also seems to be an explanation for why women are more likely to defect to South Korea than men. Married women have become reluctant to bear children amid the country's continued economic problems. Whereas North Korea's estimated fertility rate in 1995, just before the onset of the famine, was 2.12 (that is, just above the replacement rate), by 2020 it had sunk to 1.92, a figure well above South Korea's (at 1.29 estimated for 2020) but close to that of the United States (1.84, estimated for 2020).[55]

Spouses who find themselves dissatisfied with their marriage now have the option of seeking a divorce, something that was almost unheard of a few decades ago. Grounds for divorce include adultery, criminal conviction, unwillingness or inability to have children, domestic conflict between daughter-in-law and mother-in-law (a traditional problem in Asian societies), and irreconcilable personal differences. Divorces are granted by a judge who carefully examines the marital situation—and who is often willing to accept a bribe of a few hundred dollars to grant the divorce if one of the spouses opposes separation. After a divorce, the mother usually receives custody of any children and is entitled to 10 to 15 percent of the husband's (usually negligible) income.

As the family ages, life stays about the same, with occasional challenges presented by North Korea's economic problems. Reaching the age of sixty, traditionally a milestone of Korean life, is a cause for celebration. When life does finally end, typically in the late sixties for men and the late seventies for women, the funeral is usually held at home, with the deceased buried in a coffin supplied by the workplace or by the family. Funerals have traditionally lasted three days. Given the problems of long-distance travel in North Korea, some family members may find it difficult to arrive at a funeral in a timely fashion. On the other hand, family members usually live in the same county, so travel is often not a problem. Since North Korea does not seem to have professional undertakers, a local person with experience in funerals is likely to take charge. Friends and family come to the house to offer condolences and a small gift of cash. Incense is burned in front of a picture of the deceased. Unlike in South Korea, where many families have a countryside burial site for extended family members, in North Korea bodies are buried in a local public cemetery. There are no hearses; instead, the body is carried in a bus or truck. Cremation is becoming more common. And in North Korea, as in any country, even though life is valued cheaply by the regime, the death of a loved one is truly mourned by family and friends.

Chapter Ten

Conclusion

North Korea's trajectory can be followed both chronologically and topically. Chronologically, from 1945 until the end of the 1950s, the main events were North Korea's economic recovery under communism, its devastation as a result of the Korean War, and its second economic recovery effort. In the 1960s the rebuilding continued, with particular emphasis on the country's militarization. The 1970s were North Korea's economic high point, whereas in the 1980s the economy plateaued and then began to falter. In the 1990s the country encountered three shocks that had far-reaching effects. First, in the aftermath of the downfall of communism in the Soviet bloc in the late 1980s, North Korea's economy collapsed. Then a series of floods and droughts, beginning in 1995, devastated the domestic food supply. As starvation set in, people turned to their own resources to find food, sowing the seeds of capitalism. At almost the same time, the country's founder, Kim Il-sung, died of a heart attack and was succeeded by his eldest son, Kim Jong-il, who proved unable or unwilling to address the calamitous economic situation—despite the fact that he had been running the country from behind the scenes for at least a decade. During the three years following his father's death, the new Kim lived in virtual seclusion, forcing his people to try to save themselves. As many as a million died of starvation.

The disasters of the 1990s were a hard lesson for North Koreans. In the following decade they continued to develop a people's economy, which Kim Jong-il opposed but was unable to stop. Kim, who styled himself a military-first leader, launched the country's first long-range ballistic missile in 1998 and conducted the country's first nuclear test in 2006. When he died in 2011, his youngest son, Kim Jong-un, then only twenty-eight years old, took power and tacitly accepted the new capitalist economy, while remaining firmly in control of politics and vigorously promoting the country's nuclear and missile programs. This pattern of economic liberalization, political control, and military modernization has continued through the second decade of the century, and as long as Kim Jong-un remains healthy, there is little reason to expect any dramatic change in North Korea's direction.

Topically, the news for North Korea is mostly bad. In terms of geography, North Korea's mountainous terrain is a challenge to farming, construction, and engineering. Geopolitically, North Korea is a relatively small country in the neighborhood of larger countries, including South Korea. Historically, North Korea is a wounded, even traumatized nation. Its government is saddled with an archaic family dynasty more suited to the Middle Ages than the contemporary era. In the absence of even a hint of democracy, the country lacks a self-correcting mechanism. Its second- and third-generation rulers are feared but neither liked nor respected.

North Korea has a robust if outmoded military force that is charged with deterring and defending against foreign attacks and keeping its people under control. Thanks to the Kim regime, the country has a growing arsenal of weapons of mass destruction—weapons that could be used only in a suicidal conflict. Its foreign policy rests heavily on implicit and explicit military threats, and it is designed to maintain independence and isolation from the rest of the world. The country's primary foreign policy goal, unification with South Korea, can only be accomplished with the demise of the Kim regime.

Arguably the worst news for North Korea is that its economy is struggling and disconnected from the global marketplace. Even before international sanctions were imposed, the country was impoverished and isolated. The Kim regime still wants to follow the principles of central-command socialism, which never worked well for other countries and entirely ceased working for North Korea twenty years ago. Lack of technology and scientific progress in virtually all fields except munitions is a further drag on the economy.

North Koreans enjoy few human rights. All North Koreans, from the highest party cadres to the youngest children living in prison camps, are essentially servants of the leader. Only when North Koreans escape from their country, as thousands have already done, do they gain access to the human rights that most citizens in democratic societies are accustomed to. Except for a few often mentally disturbed individuals, no one in the last several decades has ever considered immigrating to North Korea. Yet even with the lack of human rights and the depressed economy, North Koreans live their lives as normally as possible, trying to avoid trouble while seeking the sort of pleasures that people all over the world desire.

So with all this bad news, what does the future hold for Kim's North Korea? The ruling Kim is the cornerstone and linchpin of North Korea. The country is built to support him as one great Kim estate. However, no estate or kingdom lasts forever. Contradictions and cracks are already appearing in the edifice. The North Korean elites follow Kim out of fear and self-interest, not admiration and respect. The gap is widening between these elite supporters, numbering a million or so, and the rest of the country. The gap between younger and older generations is also widening, thanks in part to information coming from outside the country. The economic and technological gap between South Korea and North Korea is widening as well. If Kim is to extend his reign, he has plenty of problems to solve.

Over the last several years, Kim Jong-un has tried to address these issues by giving citizens greater economic independence so that at least some of them they can fend for themselves and begin to taste the pleasures of a middle-class life. This approach has worked for the leaders in China, where people can gain wealth even though they lack political freedom. The strategy requires that the regime always be on guard to prevent citizens from getting too much too fast, and from stepping too far outside the regime's political boundaries. Wealth will pacify most, but a strong police presence is necessary to keep others under control.

There are, however, two important differences between China and North Korea. First, in North Korea one man, from one family, must remain in control. In China, it is sufficient if the Chinese Communist Party remains in power. People are more fragile than parties. If anything should happen to Kim Jong-un before a successor becomes available, the prevailing political structure is in great danger of collapsing. Second, China as a country controls almost all the Chinese people in the region. Kim's North Korea controls only a third of the Korean people on the peninsula, and the poorest third at that. South Korea, with its economic success and alluring culture, is always looming over North Korea, providing the North Korean people, if they can free themselves from the domination of the Kim regime, a viable and attractive alternative just across the border.

Given the certainty that the Kim regime will eventually disappear from the scene, how might that happen? The future is certainly cloudy, and for the most part the clouds are dark. Many foreign analysts, including ourselves, have suggested scenarios.[1] It is unlikely that the North Korean people will be able to mobilize themselves and attack the regime and its soldiers. But cracks within the ruling elites, perhaps beginning with the incapacitation or demise of the leader, will open the door for citizens to take practical action. Foreign assistance or intervention might also play a role. The process is likely to be messy, and quite possibly lengthy. As Mao said, "revolution is not a dinner party." Of course, once the North Korean political structure has cracked and people are free to choose the life that South Koreans now enjoy (with all its flaws), some accommodation will have to be made with those South Koreans. The two peoples are unlikely to rush into each other's arms after being separated for over three-quarters of a century.

All Koreans in the North and the South know the song "Our Hope Is Unification." The song, originally under the title "Our Hope Is Independence," was popular during the Japanese colonial occupation, and the words were changed after Korea became divided. This song, along with the well-known "Arirang," brings tears to Korean eyes even today. Standing by her father's deathbed in 1991, Dr. Oh promised that she would work for Korean unification and that she would one day visit the family's hometown in North Korea. Nearly three decades later, unification looks to be as far off as ever. On the one hand, for South Koreans of the younger generation, North Korea seems like a distant country that has nothing to do with them. On the other hand, North Korean defectors yearn to see their hometowns again and eagerly wish for unification.

What prevents that unification? The previous chapters provide many answers. The South Korean people would never agree to give up their democracy, and the Kim family would never willingly relinquish its hold on the North Korean people. Autocracy is firmly embedded in the structure of North Korean society. Moreover, the very human predisposition to resist change and cling to the status quo preserves the division of the Korean Peninsula. In the years ahead, changes will continue to appear in North Korea, but the essential nature of the country is likely to remain static as long as the Kim family holds on to power. Without risking war or internal violence, the best hope people have for a better future is to learn all they can about foreign life and culture so they can make informed choices as Kim's grip on power gradually loosens and, ultimately, as the opportunity to live in a unified Korea approaches. Toward this end, those of us who live outside the boundaries set by the Kim regime can support the North Korean people by working to supply them with the kind of information that people throughout the rest of the world have access to in their daily lives.

Notes

1. GEOGRAPHY AND HISTORY

1. Duck K. Choi, *Hanbando Hyongsongsa* [Geology and tectonic evolution of the Korean Peninsula] (Seoul: Seoul National University Press, 2014), 3, in Korean.

2. "Pyongyang Residence Permits Sell for 1,500 USD in North Korea," *Daily NK*, June 26, 2018, in English.

3. Quoted in Korean Central News Agency (KCNA), August 13, 1994, in English.

4. Quoted in KCNA, August 6, 1994, in English.

5. Baik Bong, *Kim Il Sung: Biography (I)* (Beirut, Lebanon: Dar Al-talia, 1973), 527–28.

6. Baik Bong, *Kim Il Sung*, 529–32.

7. Baik Bong, *Kim Il Sung*, 533.

8. The Research Institute of History, Academy of Sciences of the Democratic People's Republic of Korea, *History of the Just Fatherland Liberation War of the Korean People* (Pyongyang: Foreign Languages Publishing House, 1981), foreword, https://archive.org/stream/HistoryOfTheJustFatherlandLiberationWarOfHteKoreanPeople/KoreanWar_djvu.txt.

9. "Respected and Beloved Comrade Kim Jong-un Gave On-the-Spot Guidance at the Newly Built Sinchon Museum," *Nodong Sinmun Online*, July 23, 2015, in Korean.

10. "Service Personnel, People of DPRK Pledge to Take Revenge on U.S. Imperialists, Class Enemies," KCNA, July 26, 2015, in English.

11. "69 Pct of High School Students Believe South Invaded North in Korean War," *Dong-A Ilbo Online*, June 18, 2013, in English.

2. LEADERSHIP

1. Soon Ok Lee, *Eyes of the Tailless Animals: Prison Memoirs of a North Korean Woman* (Bartlesville, OK: Living Sacrifice Book Company, 1999).

2. "Kim Jong-il's Only Public Speech" can be found under that title on YouTube, thanks to Curtis Melvin, a vigilant observer of North Korea, https://www.youtube.com/watch?v=v02nlU_ZATk.

3. Chil-nam Choe and Chol Pak, "Sacred Three Years," *Nodong Sinmun*, July 2, 1997, 3–4, in Korean.

4. Kenji Fujimoto, *Kim Jong-il-ui yorisa* [Kim Jong-il's chef], *Monthly Chosun* (Seoul), 2003, originally in Japanese and translated into Korean. Also, Kenji Fujimoto, *Kin Seinichi no Shiseikatsu* [Kim Jong-il's private life], 2004, in Japanese.

5. Kim Hong-kun, "The Respected and Beloved Supreme Commander," *Nodong Sinmun*, April 23, 1998, 2, in Korean.

6. "Notice to All Party Members, Servicepersons and People," KCNA, December 19, 2011, in English.

7. "Kim Jong-il Will Always Be with Us," KCNA, December 21, 2011, in English.

8. Kim Hyun, "N. Korean Leader Names Third Son as Successor: Sources," Yonhap News Agency, January 15, 2009, in English. Some reports suggest that the introduction might even have been in 2008.

9. Included in a documentary program titled *Great Dedication—Year 2009, Year of Transformation*, Korean Central Television (KCTV) via satellite, February 13, 2010, in Korean.

10. "Prospects for Kim Jong-un Leadership Succession," *Vantage Point* 35, no. 1 (January 2012): 7.

11. "'On-the-Spot Guidance Tours' by DPRK's Kim Jong-il Explained," *Chosun Ilbo*, Internet version, February 19, 2001, in English.

12. Yi Kyo-tok, *Kim Jong-il Hyongjijido-ui Tuksong* [Characteristics of Kim Jong-il's on-the-spot guidance], Korea Institute for National Unification, September 1, 2002, 1–23, in Korean.

13. "Number One Events," *Chosun Ilbo*, Internet version, May 20, 2001, in English.

14. "DPRK Leader Inspects KPA Unit No. 802," Korean Central Broadcasting Station (KCBS), November 10, 2005, in Korean.

15. To take one example: "DPRK Leader Inspects KPA Unit 1337," KCBS, November 11, 2005, in Korean.

16. "DPRK Leader Inspects KPA Unit No. 802."

17. "Legend of Love That Blossomed on the Path of On-the-Spot Guidance," KCTV, February 13, 2004, in Korean.

18. Fujimoto, *Kim Jong-il-ui yorisa* [Kim Jong-il's chef], 2003, in Korean (translated from the Japanese edition titled *Kin Seinichi no Ryoryinin*); Fujimoto, *Kin Seinichi no Shiseikatsu* [Kim Jong-il's private life], 2004, in Japanese; and Kenji Fujimoto, *Kaku to Onna o Aishita Shogun-Sama* [The general who loved nukes and women], 2006, in Japanese. At this time it appears that none of Kenji Fujimoto's books is available in English.

19. Fujimoto, *Kin Seinichi no Ryoryinin*, 8–9.

20. Ermanno Furlanis, "I Made Pizza for Kim Jong-il," in 3 parts, *Asia Times Online*, August 4–18, 2001, in English.

21. Kim Mi-yong, "President's Cattle Ranch—Ranch for 'Nobility,' Including Kim Jong-il," *Chosun Ilbo*, Internet version, March 12, 2002, in Korean.

22. Han Young Jin, "The Dear Leader's Apples and the No. 8 Farm," *Daily NK*, May 30, 2005, in English.

23. Yi Tae-nam, "The Future of a Prosperous and Rich State Lies in Upholding the General," *Nodong Sinmun*, June 28, 2001, 2, in Korean.

24. Fujimoto, *Kin Seinichi no Shiseikatsu*, 18–27, 32–42; Fujimoto, *Kin Seinichi no Ryoryi-nin*, 74–80. Yi Yong-kuk, *Nanun Kim Jong-il Kyonghowoniotta* [I was Kim Jong-il's body-guard].

25. Konstantin Pulikovskiy, *The Oriental Express: Through Russia with Kim Chong-il* (Vladivostok: Gorodets, 2002), electronic version, in Russian.

26. Chon Song-ho, "Heart of 10 Million Soldiers and People," *Nodong Sinmun*, via the Uriminjokkiri website, March 2, 2004, in Korean.

3. THE GOVERNMENT

1. "Kim Jong-un Hosts Dinner for South Korean 'Special Envoy' Delegation 5 March," KCBS, March 5, 2018, in Korean.

2. 2019 Version of the Constitution from North Korea's Naenara website, http://naenara. com.kp/main/index/en/politics?arg_val=leader3, in English.

3. Nicholas Wadhams, writing for SentinalSource.com on May 15, 2016, https://www. sentinelsource.com/news/national_world/what-not-to-call-kim-jong-un-and-other-advice/ article_03a4f3da-c826-5023-8f9e-69d90bec5b87.html.

4. *Understanding Workers' Party of Korea* (Pyongyang: Foreign Languages Publishing House, 2016), 1–2, in English, https://www.kfausa.org/wp-content/uploads/2020/04/ Understanding-Workers_-Party-of-Korea.pdf.

5. Andrei Lankov, "North Koreans Care Less about KWP Membership than Ever," NK News, April 21, 2015, https://www.nknews.org/2015/04/north-koreans-care-less-about-kwp-membership-than-ever.

6. Seol Song Ah, "Inside North Korea's Supreme People's Assembly," *Daily NK* for *The Guardian*, April 22, 2014, https://www.theguardian.com/world/2014/apr/22/inside-north-koreas-supreme-peoples-assembly.

7. James C. Scott, *Weapons of the Weak: Everyday Forms of Peasant Resistance* (New Haven, CT: Yale University Press, 1985).

8. "DPRK Adopts 'Law on Consolidating Position of Nuclear Weapons State' on 1 Apr," KCNA, April 1, 2013, in English.

9. Marion P. Spina Jr., "Brushes with the Law: North Korea and the Rule of Law," *Korea Economic Institute: Academic Paper Series* 2, no. 6 (June 2007).

10. Kim Il-sung, "For the Implementation of the Judicial Policy of Our Party," April 29, 1958, in *Kim Il-sung, Works*, vol. 12 (Pyongyang: Foreign Languages Publishing House, 1983), 182, in English.

11. Cindy Hurst, *North Korea: A Government-Sponsored Drug Trafficking Network* (Fort Leavenworth, KS: Army Foreign Military Studies Office, Joint Reserve Intelligence Center, 2006).

12. Andrei Lankov and Seok-hyang Kim, "A New Face of North Korean Drug Use: Up-surge in Methamphetamine Abuse across the Northern Areas of North Korea," *North Korean Review* 9, no. 1 (Spring 2013): 45–60.

13. A list and comparison of the original and revised principles may be found in Fyodor Tertitskiy, "The Party's 10 Principles, Then and Now," NK News, December 11, 2014, https:// www.nknews.org/2014/12/the-partys-10-principles-then-and-now.

14. Cho Jung-hyun et al., *White Paper on Human Rights in North Korea, 2013*, Korea Institute for National Unification, 2013, 73.

15. "Traitor Jang Song Taek Executed," KCNA, December 13, 2013, in English.

16. "Report on Enlarged Meeting of Political Bureau of Central Committee of WPK," KCNA, December 8, 2013, in English.

17. "Public Trials Carried Out Nationwide," *Asia Press International*, August 28, 2018, in English.

18. All criminal code citations come from David Hawk with Amanda Mortwedt Oh, *The Parallel Gulag* (Washington, DC: Committee for Human Rights in North Korea, 2017), appendix 2.

19. Lee Chul-mu, "Making Money from Crime in North Korea," *New Focus*, July 16, 2015, in English.

20. A series of reports on human rights is available in PDF form online from the Committee for Human Rights in North Korea. The most relevant to the prison situation are reports by David Hawk, among them, *The Hidden Gulag*, 2nd ed. (2013) and *The Parallel Gulag* (2017). The Korean Institute for National Unification publishes an annual report on the North Korean human rights situation titled *White Paper on Human Rights in North Korea*. The reports are available in English on the institute's website: https://www.kinu.or.kr/main/eng.

21. "Fatality Rate at N. Korean Prisons Estimated at 25 Pct: Report," Yonhap News Agency, March 7, 2017, in English. Citing a report by Go Myong-hyun of the Asan Institute for Policy Studies.

22. Pyongyang Broadcasting Station, January 18, 2002, in Korean.

23. Soon Ok Lee, *Eyes of the Tailless Animals: Prison Memoirs of a North Korean Woman* (Bartlesville, OK: Living Sacrifice Book Company, 1999).

24. David W. Lovell, "Corruption as a Transitional Phenomenon: Understanding Endemic Corruption in Postcommunist States," in *Corruption: Anthropological Perspectives*, ed. Dieter Haller and Cris Shore (London and Ann Arbor: Pluto Press, 2005), 69.

25. Andrei Lankov, "Why North Korea Is So Corrupt, and Why That May Be Good," NK News, October 16, 2015, https://www.nknews.org/2015/10/why-north-korea-is-so-corrupt-and-why-that-may-be-good.

26. "N. Korea Declares War on Corruption," Yonhap News Agency, December 10, 2018, in English.

27. "Kim Jong-un's 2019 New Year Address," KCNA, January 1, 2019, in English.

28. "North Korean State Security Agents Extort Borderland Cash Brokers," *Daily NK*, February 26, 2018, in English.

29. Ambassador Robert King, "North Korea Is a Corrupt Mafia State: Bribes, Corruption, and Crime Are Key to Understanding the Kim Regime, Now with Its Third Generation Family 'Godfather,'" quoted in "Ex U.S. Envoy Slams N. Korea as 'Corrupt Mafia State,'" Yonhap News Agency, April 30, 2019, in English.

30. Sissela Bok, *Lying: Moral Choice in Public and Private Life* (New York: Vintage, 1989).

31. Bok, *Lying*, 26.

4. HUMAN RIGHTS

1. "*Nodong Sinmun* Calls for Observing Revolutionary Principle," KCNA, December 10, 2006, in English.

2. *Resident Registration Project Reference Manual*, published by the Social Safety Department Publishing House (now the Ministry of People's Security), 1993, marked "Absolute Secret." Copy published by *Monthly Chosun Online*, November 1, 2007, in Korean, and written by Pak Sung-min and Pae Chin-yong. The same classification and an extended discussion can be found in the *White Paper on Human Rights in North Korea, 2015* (Seoul: Korea Institute for National Unification, 2015), chap. 3, sec. 4.

3. A good discussion of *songbun* may be found in Robert Collins, *Marked for Life: Songbun, North Korea's Social Classification System* (Washington, DC: Committee for Human Rights in North Korea, 2012).

4. Cho Jung-hyun et al., *White Paper on Human Rights in North Korea, 2013*, Korea Institute for National Unification, 2013, 208.

5. "60 Percent of Female N. Korean Defectors in China Trafficked into Sex Trade," Yonhap News Agency, May 21, 2019, in English.

6. Keum-Soon Lee, "Policy Implications of North Korean Escapees: Protection and Resettlement Assistance," *KINU Insight* (Korea Institute for National Unification), June 2007, 6, in English.

7. *White Paper on Human Rights in North Korea*, published by the Korea Institute for National Unification, available in English on the KINU website under "Publications," https://www.kinu.or.kr/main/eng.

8. *Report of the Commission of Inquiry on Human Rights in the Democratic People's Republic of Korea*, Human Rights Council of the Twenty-Fifth Session of the General Assembly, February 7, 2014; *Report of the Detailed Findings of the Commission of Inquiry on Human Rights in the Democratic People's Republic of Korea*, same source and date; https://www.ohchr.org/en/hrbodies/hrc/coidprk/pages/reportofthecommissionofinquirydprk.aspx.

9. "U.N. Human Rights Chief Calls for Urgent Action on N. Korea," Kyodo World Service, February 18, 2014, in English.

10. "China Rejects Sending N. Korea to World Rights Court," AFP World Service, February 17, 2014, in English.

11. "ROK President: Too Early to Press DPRK on Human Rights," *Korea Herald*, Internet version, October 25, 2000, in English.

12. Doug Struck, "A Survivor Recounts Horrors of N. Korea's Prison Camps," *Washington Post*, May 3, 2003, A20.

13. Obama interview with three defectors at the White House, January 23, 2015, cited by *JoongAng Daily Online*, January 24, 2015, in English.

14. Mike Theiler, Reuters, quoted on the *Daily Beast* website, September 30, 2018, https://www.thedailybeast.com/trump-kim-jong-un-and-i-fell-in-love.

15. "Trump on North Korea Talks: Kim Jong-un Is a 'Real Leader,'" *Daily Beast*, March 1, 2019, https://www.thedailybeast.com/trump-on-north-korea-talks-kim-jong-un-is-a-real-leader.

16. Mona Charen, "Trump's Infatuation with Kim Jong-un Excuses North Korea's Grievous Abuses of Its People," *Tyler Morning Telegraph*, December 15, 2019, https://tylerpaper.com/opinion/columnists/mona-charen-trump-s-infatuation-with-kim-jong-un-excuses/article_bee86f84-1f59-11ea-bb03-1b3e49d31222.html.

17. Meghan Keneally, "Trump Calls Kim a 'Tough Guy' When Asked about North Korean Dictator's Human Rights Abuses," ABC News, June 14, 2018, https://abcnews.go.com/International/trump-calls-kim-tough-guy-asked-north-korean/story?id=55891550.

18. A spokesperson for the DPRK foreign ministry, KCBS, March 1, 2001, in Korean.

19. Quoting a spokesperson for the Ministry of Foreign Affairs, KCNA, December 21, 2019, in English.

5. THE MILITARY

1. Pak Nam-chin, "Immortal Course during Which the Military Assurance for the Consummation of the Chuch'e Cause Has Been Provided," *Nodong Sinmun*, June 26, 1997, 3, in Korean.

2. "Paper on Comrade Kim Chong-il's Military Feats," KCNA, November 4, 1997, in English.

3. "Army Mainstay of Revolution," KCNA, March 9, 1998, in English.

4. "All Citizens in This Land Are Soldiers," KCNA, April 25, 2003, in Korean.

5. "Love Gun-Barrel Families," a KCBS report on a *Nodong Sinmun* article, January 29, 2004, in Korean.

6. "N. Korean Soldiers Given 70 Grams of Food per Meal: Report," Yonhap News Agency, August 8, 2016, in English.

7. "Let Us Thoroughly Stamp Out the Current Problems of People Damaging Farm Produce and Violating Traffic Rules," KPA Publishing House, August 2002. Referred to in an article titled "Information Shows Even Cannibalism Is Practiced in North Korea; a Document Shows How Bad North Korea's Food Situation Is," *Yomiuri Weekly*, December 21, 2003, 24–25, in Japanese.

8. Chu Song-ha, "Content of the Lecture Material of the North Korean Army's General Political Department," *Dong-A Ilbo*, Internet version, June 3, 2004, in Korean.

9. "Haesol Tamhwa Charyo" [Explanatory statement collection], issued in January 2002, smuggled out of North Korea and published in Japan's *Shukan Bunshun* under the title "We Have Obtained Secret Documents of North Korea That Show Morale of Troops in the Korean People's Army Is Plummeting; Soldiers Are Becoming Rowdy, Selling Military Supplies, Watching Porno Videos," February 6, 2003, 33–35, in Japanese.

10. O Su-kyong, "Our-Style Socialism Trail-Blazing, Consolidating and Developing under the Banner of the Military-First Principle," *Nodong Sinmun*, May 28, 2004, in Korean.

11. "Q&A: 'We Don't Need Nuclear Weapons,'" *Washington Times*, April 15, 1992.

12. "We Should Not Fall Prey to the Big Powers," *Nodong Sinmun*, commentary, February 21, 1993.

13. "Pyongyang Succeeds in Launching First Artificial Satellite," *The People's Korea*, no. 1825 (September 19, 1998): 8, in English.

14. Madeleine Albright, *Madam Secretary* (New York: Hyperion, 2003), 590.

15. "DPRK Vice Foreign Minister for U.S. Affairs Issues Statement," KCNA, December 3, 2019, http://www.mfa.gov.kp/en/dprk-vice-foreign-minister-for-u-s-affairs-issues-statement.

16. "U.S. Urges End to Destabilizing Rhetoric after N.K. Diplomat Warned U.S. Crossed 'Red Line,'" Yonhap News Agency, July 28, 2016, in English.

17. Citing a KCBS news story titled "U.S. Imperialists and Their Stooges Escalate Nuclear Threat and Blackmail against DPRK," March 15, 2017, in English.

18. KCBS broadcast titled "We Will Mercilessly Punish Those Who Are Trying to Daringly Eclipse the Splendid Sun of Our Destiny," February 23, 2016, in Korean.

19. "U.S. Is Not Safe Haven for Aggressors, Provocateurs," *Nodong Sinmun* article carried by KCNA, March 20, 2016, in English.

20. "Korean People's Army General Staff Spokesperson's Statement," KCBS, August 8, 2017, in Korean.

21. "U.S. Urges End to Destabilizing Rhetoric."

22. "Kim Jong-un Makes New Year Address," KCNA, January 1, 2018, in English.

23. Quoted by Kyodo World Service, January 3, 2018, in English.

24. "DPRK Newspaper Threatens to Blow Up U.S. Base," Hong Kong AFP, March 12, 2001, in English.

25. "Ultimatum by the Long-Range Artillery Force of the People's Army Large Combined Unit on the Front," KCBS, March 26, 2016, in Korean.

26. Yi Hyon-to, "The United States 'Most Important Stronghold' for Military Strategy against the DPRK and Asia," originally published in *Nodong Sinmun* and carried by North Korea's Uriminjokkiri web page, September 23, 2004, in Korean.

27. KCBS, June 27, 1999, in Korean.

28. "Communique Issued by KPA Supreme Command," KCNA, November 23, 2010, in English.

29. "DPRK Military Warns ROK to Cancel Plan for Firing Drill on Yonpyong Island," KCNA, December 17, 2010, in Korean.

30. "N. Korea Says Ready to Launch 'Sacred War' against S. Korea," Kyodo World Service, December 23, 2010, in English.

6. FOREIGN RELATIONS

1. Kim Il-sung, "On Eliminating Dogmatism and Formalism and Establishing Juche in Ideological Work," speech to party propaganda and agitation workers, December 28, 1955, in *Kim Il Sung Works*, 9:395–417 (Pyongyang: Foreign Languages Publishing House, 1982), quote from 395–96, in English.

2. *Nodong Sinmun*, commentary, October 5, 1990, cited in "Pyongyang Raps Moscow on Diplomatic Ties with Seoul," *The People's Korea*, no. 1491 (October 13, 1990): 8, in English.

3. "North-South Joint Liaison Office Completely Ruined," KCNA, June 16, 2020, in English.

4. "Important Communique by the Committee for the Peaceful Reunification of the Fatherland," KCBS, March 22, 2016, in Korean.

5. Sim Chol-yong, "Stern, Hard Blow at Traitorous Maneuver," *Nodong Sinmun*, Internet version, June 5, 2011, in Korean.

6. Survey by the Institute for Peace and Unification Studies, Seoul National University, reported by Yonhap News Agency, "Nine in 10 Defectors Wished for Unification While Living in N. Korea: Poll," October 30, 2018, in English.

7. A Seoul National University poll published in *Chosun Ilbo Online*, "Most Young S. Koreans Don't Believe in Reunification," January 27, 2018, in English.

8. "US Spurs Pyongyang's Risky Nuclear Moves," *Global Times*, February 20, 2016, in English.

9. "Cao Shigong: Denuclearization Is the Premise and Guarantee of Peace and Stability on the Peninsula," *Huanqiu Shibao Online*, February 27, 2017, in Chinese.

10. Kim Chol, "[China] Must Not Continue Its Reckless Behavior of Chopping Down the Pillar of [North] Korea-China Relations Any Longer," KCNA, May 3, 2017, in Korean.

11. Pak Tu-sik, "Report by Washington-Based Correspondent," *Choson Ilbo*, April 17, 1997, in Korean.

12. Hu Xijin, editor in chief of *Huanqiu Shibao*, quoted on the Chinese blog *Sina Weibo*, September 8, 2017, in Chinese.

13. "KAPPC Spokesman on DPRK Stand toward UNSC 'Sanctions Resolution,'" originally broadcast on KCBS and relayed on KCNA, September 13, 2017, in English.

14. An excellent book-length discussion of these emigrants is Tessa Morris-Suzuki's *Exodus to North Korea: Shadows from Japan's Cold War* (Lanham, MD: Rowman & Littlefield, 2007).

15. Kim Su-hye, "Japan Changed a Lot after North Korea's Bomb Testing: For the First Time in 46 Years, Japan Revealed 'Chosun Registration' Population," *Chosun Daily*, March 12, 2016, in Korean.

16. Hataru Nomura, "Saddled with Huge Debts, Membership Cut to One-Tenth, Forsaken by North Korea," *Sapio*, March 22, 2006, in Japanese.

17. Sam Kim, "N. Korea Demands Massive Compensation from U.S. for 60 Years of Enmity," Yonhap News Agency, June 24, 2010, in English.

18. "Tremendous Damage Caused by U.S. Imperialists to S. Korea Estimated," KCNA, November 29, 2003, in English.

19. Quote from a *Nodong Sinmun* article cited by KCNA, December 3, 1998, in English.

20. Lonely Planet website, https://www.lonelyplanet.com/north-korea (accessed November 6, 2018).

7. THE ECONOMY

1. A good source on the Korean economy during the colonial period is Lee Young-hun, *Hanguk Kyongjesa II* [The history of the Korean economy, II] (Seoul: Ilchogak, 2016), in Korean.

2. For a well-structured review of North Korea's economic history, see Doowon Lee, "North Korean Economic Reform: Past Efforts and Future Prospects," in *Reforming Asian Socialism: The Growth of Market Institutions*, ed. John McMillan and Barry Naughton, 317–36 (Ann Arbor: University of Michigan Press, 1996).

3. "Full Text of Kim Jong-un's 2019 New Year Address," KCNA, January 1, 2019, in English.

4. For example, see Yonho Kim, *North Korea's Mobile Telecommunications and Private Transport Services in the Kim Jong-un Era*, US-Korea Institute, SAIS, Johns Hopkins University, 2018.

5. "Kim Jong-il's 'Monologues': Top Secret Instructions Given to Association Leaders," *Gendai*, January 1, 2003, 122–34, in Japanese.

6. "On Correctly Understanding the State Measure That Has Readjusted Overall Prices and Living Expenses," lecture material from the Korean People's Army Publishing House, July 2002, in Korean.

7. Charles K. Armstrong, "The Destruction and Reconstruction of North Korea, 1950–1960," *Asia-Pacific Journal* 7 (March 16, 2009).

8. Armstrong, "The Destruction and Reconstruction of North Korea."

9. News conference by Yong-hwan Ko, KBS-1 Television Network, September 13, 1991, in Korean.

10. Joseph S. Chung, "The Economy," in *North Korea: A Country Study*, ed. Andrea Matles Savada (Washington, DC: Federal Research Division of the Library of Congress, 1994), 126.

11. "Let Us Thoroughly Fulfill the Tasks Set Forth in the New Year's Joint Editorial," *Minju Choson*, January 15, 2000, in Korean.

12. A good history and update of the agricultural situation is provided by W. Randall Ireson, "North Korean Agriculture: Recent Changes and Prospects after Unification," *International Journal of Korean Studies* 20, no. 2 (Fall/Winter 2016): 18–41.

13. Editorial by Lee Jong-seok, "Sanctions on North Korea Haven't Led to Serious Food Shortages as Many Predicted," *Hankyoreh Online*, January 7, 2019, in English.

14. Chong Son-chol, "Being Strong-Willed with the Principle of Independence Is a Fundamental Requirement in Our Times' Politics," *Nodong Sinmun*, March 23, 2001, in Korean.

15. "National Exhibition of August 3 Consumer Goods Opened," ExploreDPRK.com, August 3, 2016, https://exploredprk.com/life/national-exhibition-of-august-3-consumer-goods-opened.

16. "Let Us Achieve the Country's Overall Full-Scale Development through the Hot Wind of Competition between Provinces," *Nodong Sinmun*, Internet version, March 18, 2019, in Korean.

17. Latest CIA trade figures according to Wikipedia, https://en.wikipedia.org/wiki/List_of_countries_by_imports, https://en.wikipedia.org/wiki/List_of_countries_by_exports (accessed May 30, 2020).

18. Eui-Gak Hwang, *The Korean Economies* (Oxford: Clarendon Press, 1993), 196.

19. Trade statistics from various publications of the [South] Korea Trade Association and the Korean Trade-Investment Promotion Agency, in Korean.

20. Kim Chol-chun, "The Great Leader Kim Jong-il's Economic Ideology of Expanding and Developing Trade in Our Own Way," *Kyongje Yongu*, February 10, 2008, in Korean.

21. "Meet the North Korean Firm Which Reinvents Itself to Beat Sanctions," provided by Agence France-Presse, December 1, 2017, published in the *South China Morning Post*, Internet version, April 15, 2019, in English, https://www.scmp.com/news/china/diplomacy-defence/article/2122438/meet-north-korean-firm-which-reinvents-itself-beat.

22. "Let Us Adhere to the Line on Building a Self-Reliant National Economy to the End," *Nodong Sinmun*, September 17, 1998, in Korean.

23. Akihiko Kaise, "Pyongyang Puts Out Call for Foreign Investors in 'International Tourism Zone,'" *Asahi Shimbun*, April 20, 2015, in English.

24. *Report on Exploitation of Overseas Korean Workers' Wage by the North Korean State* (Seoul: North Korea Reform Radio, May 2018), in English and Korean.

25. Kim Se-chin, "Exclusive: North Korea Operating Illegal Gambling Sites Overseas—Raising Slush Funds for Kim Jong-un?," MBC TV online, July 2, 2014, in Korean.

26. Myungchul Lee, "North Koreans Increasingly Look for Work Abroad to Earn Higher Pay," Radio Free Asia, Internet version, https://www.rfa.org/english/news/korea/north-koreans-increasingly-look-for-work-abroad-to-earn-higher-pay-11142018150950.html.

27. *Report on Exploitation of Overseas North Korean Workers' Wage*.

28. *Report on Exploitation of Overseas North Korean Workers' Wage*.

29. See, for example, Dianne E. Rennack, *North Korea: Economic Sanctions*, CRS Report for Congress, October 17, 2006.

30. "DPRK Ambassador to the UN Warns UN Sanctions Would be 'Declaration of War,'" Agence France-Presse, January 10, 2003, in English.

31. For example, Marcus Noland, *The (Non) Impact of UN Sanctions on North Korea*, East-West Center Working Papers, Economics Series No. 98 (February 2009).

32. See, for example, Matthias Maass, "Beyond Economic Sanctions: Rethinking the North Korean Sanctions Regime," *North Korean Review* 7, no. 2 (Fall 2011): 45–56.

8. TRANSPORTATION AND COMMUNICATION

1. "Step up Propaganda by the Press and Publications Dynamically to Spur the Building of a Powerful State," *Nodong Sinmun* editorial carried by KCNA, February 12, 2004, in Korean.

2. "DPRK Estimated to Have 1 Million Telephones," *Choson Ilbo*, Internet version, May 8, 1999, in English.

3. "Six North Koreans Executed for Trying to Sell Phonebook Abroad," *Daily NK*, April 23, 2018, in English.

4. Nam Mun-hui, "Acquire Contracts for North Korean Cellular Phone Project," *Sisa Journal*, July 4, 2002, in Korean.

5. Kang Chol-hwan, "Rumors of Suspension of Mobile Phone Service in DPRK but Not for Foreigners," *Choson Ilbo*, June 3, 2004, in Korean.

6. Chad O'Carroll, "Inside North Korea's Cell Network," NK News, August 20, 2015, in English.

7. Ri Chol-hyok, "Noteworthy Measure of Banning Use of Mobile Phones in School," *Nodong Sinmun*, Internet version, December 18, 2018, in Korean.

9. CULTURE AND LIFESTYLE

1. W. Courtland Robinson, *Lost Generation: The Health and Human Rights of North Korean Children, 1990–2018* (Washington, DC: Committee for Human Rights in North Korea, 2019). Chapter 4 is devoted to education, including the topics of food shortages, compulsory labor, and required school donations.

2. "*Nodong Sinmun* Calls for Intensifying Socialist Education," KCNA, March 21, 2017, in English.

3. Yi Pong-hyon, "Kim Il-sung University Gives Capitalism Lectures," *Hangyore Sinmun*, January 17, 1996, 1, in Korean.

4. Jeannette Goddar, "Attentive Care by the 'Great Leader,'" *Spiegel Online*, November 21, 2007, in German.

5. KCNA report (in English) of September 4, 2019, on Kim Jong-un's speech to "leading officials of the Central Committee of the Workers' Party of Korea" on August 22, 2019; conveyed to the participants of the Fourteenth National Conference of Teachers.

6. "N. Korea's Food Rations Remain at 60 Pct of U.N. Recommendation: Report," Yonhap News Agency, June 16, 2016, in English.

7. James Pearson and Seung-Woo Yeom, "Fake Meat and Free Markets: Here's How North Korea Feeds Itself," Reuters, November 13, 2017, https://www.businessinsider.com/r-fake-meat-free-markets-ease-north-koreans-hunger-2017-11.

8. Yi Ki-chun and Na Chong-yon, "A Study of North Korean Household Economy and Consumer Behaviors Following the 1 July Economic Management Improvement Measures" (paper presented at the Korean Society of Consumer Studies 2007 Spring Seminar, Seoul, May 12, 2007), in Korean.

9. "N. Korea's Annual Grain Production Remains at 1970s Levels," Yonhap News Agency, November 4, 2012, in English. For a broader view, see Stephan Haggard and Marcus Noland, *Famine in North Korea: Markets, Aid, and Reform* (New York: Columbia University Press, 2007), 35.

10. Estimates of supply and demand are more complicated. See Haggard and Noland, *Famine in North Korea*, especially 41ff.

11. Stephan Haggard and Marcus Noland, *Hunger and Human Rights: The Politics of Famine in North Korea* (Washington, DC: US Committee for Human Rights in North Korea, 2005), 18. See also chapter 3 in Suk Lee, *The DPRK Famine of 1994–2000: Existence and Impact*, Korea Institute for National Unification, Studies Series 05–06, 2005, in English.

12. Cited in Nicholas D. Kristof, "Hunger and Other North Korean Hardships Are Said to Deepen Discontent," *New York Times*, February 18, 1992, A6.

13. *Nutrition Survey of the Democratic People's Republic of Korea*, report by the EU, UNICEF, and WFP, November 1998, available on the North Korea page of the WFP website, https://www.wfp.org/countries/democratic-peoples-republic-korea. See also W. Courtland Robinson et al., "Mortality in North Korean Migrant Households: A Retrospective Study," *Lancet* 354, no. 9175 (July 24, 1999): 291–95.

14. *DPRK 2004 Nutrition Assessment, Report of Survey Results*, February 2005, on the North Korea page of the WFP website.

15. "North Korea Slashes Food Rations by Almost 50%: UN," *JoongAng Daily Online*, March 13, 2019, in English.

16. Robert E. Black et al., "Maternal and Child Undernutrition: Global and Regional Exposures and Health Consequences," *Lancet* 371, no. 9608 (January 19, 2008), Internet version.

17. Mark E. Manyin, *U.S. Assistance to North Korea: Fact Sheet*, CRS Report for Congress, updated October 11, 2006, 2.

18. "N. Korea Turns Up Nose at S. Korean Food Aid Offer," *Chosun Ilbo Online*, May 28, 2019, in English.

19. Cho Myong-yong, "Noble Benevolence for Coming Generations," *Nodong Sinmun*, December 6, 2003, in Korean.

20. Ermanno Furlanis, "I Made Pizza for Kim Jong-il," in 3 parts, *Asia Times Online*, August 4–18, 2001, in English.

21. Ben Jackson, "Don't Waste That Banchan: Where South Korea's Food Waste Goes," *Korea Exposé*, May 23, 2018, https://www.koreaexpose.com/banchan-south-korea-food-waste.

22. "North Korea Suffers from Housing Shortage: Report," Yonhap News Agency, April 28, 2018, in English.

23. Shin Jun-shik, "A North Korean Dream Home," *New Focus*, October 13, 2014, translated into English by Sinae Hong.

24. Chung Kunsik et al., *Pukhan Sahoe Byundong 2017: Sijanghwa Jungbohwa, Sahoe Munhwa, Sahoe Bojang* [Social changes in North Korea, 2017: Marketization, information, social culture, social welfare] (Seoul: Seoul National University Institute for Peace and Unification Studies, 2018), 43, in Korean.

25. Jong So Yong, "N. Korea Cracks Down on Illegal Housing Transactions," *Daily NK*, July 8, 2020, https://www.dailynk.com/english/north-korea-cracks-down-illegal-housing-transactions.

26. "N. Koreans Lack Access to Clean Water: Report," Yonhap News Agency, November 5, 2012, in English.

27. Central Bureau of Statistics, Institute of Child Nutrition, DPRK, "DPRK 2004 Nutrition Assessment: Report of Survey Results," dated 2005 and available as a PDF document on the Nautilus Institute website, https://nautilus.org.

28. Mike Bratzke, "Last Tango in Pyongyang," *Wolgan Chosun*, November 1, 2004, in Korean.

29. "Smoking Rates Decline in North Korea," *Daily NK*, May 20, 2019, in English.

30. Sara Talpos, "In Defectors from the North, Doctors in South Korea Find Hope—and Data," UNDARK, June 20, 2017, https://undark.org/2017/06/20/north-korea-health-care-norns.

31. Avram Agov, "Facing the Tuberculosis Crisis in North Korea: The Humanitarian Work of the Eugene Bell Foundation," 38 North, July 31, 2019, https://www.38north.org/2019/07/aagov073119.

32. "17th Enlarged Meeting of Political Bureau and 5th Meeting of Executive Policy Council of 7th Central Committee of WPK Held," KCNA, August 26, 2020, in English.

33. CIA World Factbook, "Country Comparison: Infant Mortality Rate," 2017 estimates, https://www.cia.gov/library/publications/the-world-factbook/fields/354rank.html.

34. CIA World Factbook, "Country Comparison: Maternal Mortality Rate," 2017 estimates, https://www.cia.gov/library/publications/the-world-factbook/fields/353rank.html.

35. World Health Organization Country Statistics, https://www.who.int/countries/en.

36. "Popular Healthcare System in DPRK," KCNA, January 14, 2014, in English.

37. Government of the United Kingdom, "Foreign Travel Advice: North Korea," April 6, 2020, https://www.gov.uk/foreign-travel-advice/north-korea/health.

38. Marian Chu, "What Is Healthcare Like Up North?," *Korea Biomedical Review*, December 12, 2017, http://www.koreabiomed.com/news/articleView.html?idxno=2103.

39. "Pyongyang's Flying Doctors Pull in $15M a Year: NIS," *JoongAng Daily Online*, November 24, 2015, in English. Also, Kang Soo Jeong, "N. Korean Doctors in Libya Caught Smuggling Gold and Medical Supplies," *Daily NK*, June 15, 2015, in English.

40. Mun Dong Hui, "N. Korea Orders Hospitals to Manufacture Their Own Medicines," *Daily NK*, July 7, 2020, https://www.dailynk.com/english/north-korea-orders-hospitals-manufacture-their-own-medicines.

41. Haggard and Noland, *Hunger and Human Rights*, 87–88.

42. Eric Talmadge, "U.S. 'Maximum Pressure' Sanctions on North Korea Keep Medical Care from Thousands of Patients," Global News, July 14, 2018, https://globalnews.ca/news/4331849/us-sanctions-north-korea-medical-care.

43. US Department of State, "Democratic People's Republic of Korea (DPRK) 2018 International Religious Freedom Report," executive summary, published 2019, https://www.state.gov/reports/2018-report-on-international-religious-freedom/democratic-peoples-republic-of-korea.

44. "FM Spokesman Flays U.S. Trumpeting about 'Religious Freedom,'" KCNA, January 11, 2018, in English.

45. A good English-language survey of religion in North Korea is David Hawk's *Thank You Father Kim Il Sung: Eyewitness Accounts of Severe Violations of Freedom of Thought, Conscience, and Religion in North Korea* (Washington, DC: US Commission on International Religious Freedom, November 2005). Updates on the state of religious freedom in North Korea can be found in the commission's annual reports.

46. "Crackdown on Superstitious Behavior Leads to Life Sentence for Unlucky Fortune Teller in North Korea," *Daily NK*, April 30, 2019, in English.

47. Statistics from the South Korean government's annual *White Paper on Human Rights in North Korea, 2015*, citing a 1950 North Korean government estimate (Seoul: Korea Institute for National Unification, 2015), 217.

48. Quoted from the 2015 white paper, which cites Tae-woo Koh, *North Korea's Policy on Religion* (Seoul: Minjok Cultural Publishing Company, 1989), 79.

49. Kang In Duk, "North Korea's Policy on Religion," *East Asia Review* 7, no. 3 (Autumn 1995): 91.

50. "DPRK Supreme Court Spokesman Exposes Crimes of American," KCNA, May 9, 2013, in English.

51. "Religious Bodies Get Greater Role in N. Korea with Aid from South," Yonhap News Agency, June 22, 2006, in English.

52. Mok Yong Jae, "Scale of Christianity in North Korea," *Daily NK*, May 22, 2011, in English.

53. "Religious Believers Do Exist in N. Korea: Survey," Yonhap News Agency, February 26, 2008, in English.

54. Culture is changing rapidly in North Korea. The following English-language sources provide interesting insights into this culture, but in many respects the information is a decade behind the times. Helen-Louise Hunter, *Kim Il-song's North Korea* (Westport, CT: Praeger, 1999); Andrei Lankov, *North of the DMZ* (Jefferson, NC: McFarland, 2007); Barbara Demick, *Nothing to Envy: Ordinary Lives in North Korea* (New York: Spiegel and Grau, 2010); John Everard, *Only Beautiful, Please* (Stanford, CA: Stanford University Press, 2012); Robinson, *Lost Generation*.

55. CIA World Factbook, "Country Comparison: Total Fertility Rate," 2020 estimates, https://www.cia.gov/library/publications/the-world-factbook/fields/356.html.

10. CONCLUSION

1. We have briefly discussed unification prospects and future scenarios in papers written some years ago, for example, Kongdan Oh, "Prospects for Korean Unification," *Education about Asia* 8, no. 2 (Fall 2003): 19–23. Brief discussions of unification scenarios may be found in Kongdan Oh and Ralph Hassig, "North Korea: The Hardest Nut," *Foreign Policy*, no. 139 (November/December 2003): 44–46, and "Golden Eggs," *The World Today*, May 2007, 4–6. A far more thorough and recent discussion can be found in Andrei Lankov's *The Real North Korea* (Oxford: Oxford University Press, 2013), 187–202.

Index

About the Authors

Kongdan (Katy) Oh was born in South Korea, although her parents originally came from the northern half of Korea. She attended Sogang University, a Jesuit institution, in Seoul and graduated with a BA in Korean literature and Oriental history before going on to Seoul National University, where she earned an MA in Korean literature. For several years she taught for the University of Maryland's college program in Korea before coming to the United States to attend the University of California at Berkeley, where she earned an MA and a PhD in Asian studies. She then worked for over thirty years as a researcher on Asian affairs, first at the RAND Corporation in Santa Monica, California, and then at the Institute for Defense Analyses in Alexandria, Virginia. She is a widely cited expert on Korean affairs.

Ralph Hassig is a retired adjunct professor of psychology at the former University of Maryland University College. He was born in Fort Wayne, Indiana; educated in Michigan at Albion College (BA in psychology); and then attended the University of California, Los Angeles, where he earned an MA and PhD in social psychology. He later attended the University of San Francisco, where he received an MBA in marketing. He has taught at several universities in California and Virginia, and for five years he was on the faculty of the University of Maryland University College in Asia, where most of his assignments were in Japan and Korea. He is the author, coauthor, and coeditor (with his wife, Kongdan Oh) of several books and numerous articles on North Korea.